I0528144

Apocalypses

of Ezra

SCRIPTURAL RESEARCH INSTITUTE
Published by Digital Ink Productions, 2024

Copyright

Apocalypses of Ezra

Second edition. March 17, 2024

Copyright © 2024 Scriptural Research Institute.

ISBN: 978-1-998288-68-7

These English translation were created by the Scriptural Research Institute in 2020 through 2023.

The image used for the cover is an artistic reinterpretation of 'Last Judgement' by Jan van Eyck, painted between 1430 and 1440. The original painting is in the Metropolitan Museum of Art, in New York.

Table of Contents

TABLE OF CONTENTS

TABLE OF CONTENTS

TABLE OF CONTENTS

Forward to the Judahite Apocalypse of Ezra

In the early centuries of the Christian era, a number of texts called the Apocalypse of Ezra were in circulation among Jews, Christians, Gnostics, and related religious groups. The original is believed to have been written in Judahite or Aramaic, and is commonly known as the Jewish Apocalypse of Ezra, as Ezra is believed to have been an ancient Judahite. This translation is referred to as the Judahite Apocalypse of Ezra, as the book has nothing to do with modern Judaism. This version of the Apocalypse was translated into Greek sometime before 200 AD and circulated widely within the early Christian churches.

In the book, it is claimed that the prophet Ezra wrote 904 books, and its popularity seems to have inspired many Christian-era Apocalypses of Ezra, presumably beginning with the 'Latin' Apocalypse of Ezra which claimed to be the 'second book of the prophet Ezra.' This prophet Ezra is not the scribe Ezra from the books of Ezra, but a prophet named Shealtiel who lived a couple of centuries earlier. In the apocalypse, he is called Ezra by the angel Uriel, which translates as 'helper' or 'assistant.'

The Judahite Apocalypse of Ezra was adopted under a variety of names into the Bibles of most older churches before the Protestant Reformation. In the 4th century, it was called 3rd Ezra by Archbishop Ambrose (Aurelius Ambrosius) of Milan, who numbered it in sequence after the 1st and 2nd Ezras from the Septuagint. This name continues to be used in Slavic, Armenian, and Georgian Eastern Orthodox Bibles, however, Jerome (Eusebius Sophronius Hieronymus) rejected the majority of books attributed to Ezra when he translated the original Latin Vulgate Bible.

At the time, there were a large number of Apocalypses of Ezra in circulation, most of which had been written recently, and as a result of this confusion, Jerome rejected everything other than the Septuagint's 2nd Ezra, for which there was a Hebrew translation that could be used for comparison. This book was subsequently split into two books of Ezra and Nehemiah, based on the internal division of the text.

In 1592, Pope Clement VIII's creation of a Catholic Bible added both 1st and 3rd Ezra into the Catholic Bible under the names 3rd and 4th Esdras. Esdras was the direct Latin transliteration of the Greek version of Ezra's name: Ἐσδρας. During the Protestant Reformation, the books of 3rd and 4th Esdras were renamed 1st and 2nd Esdras, as they continue to be listed in Protestant Bibles that include them.

Unfortunately, the Latin translation of the Apocalypse of Ezra that Clement added to the Catholic Vulgate included the shorter Latin Apocalypse of Ezra, resulting in the Catholic and Protestant Bibles having longer, and self-contradicting versions of the apocalypse in comparison to Orthodox Bibles. The Latin translation of the Judahite Apocalypse of Ezra did circulate for centuries without the addition of the shorter Latin Apocalypse of Ezra, as evidenced by the Slavonic translation, which is believed to have been translated from Latin and not Greek.

The oldest complete copy of the Judahite Apocalypse is a Syriac manuscript dated to the 6th or 7th centuries, known as Manuscript B.21 Inf. (fols. 267a-276b) at the Biblioteca Ambrosiana in Milan, Italy. The manuscript contains multiple deviations from the majority of the manuscripts. It is composed in a mixture of two Syriac scripts, the introduction is written in the Estrangēlā script, which entered into use in the 1st century AD, while the majority of the main body of the text is composed in the Serṭā script which developed in the 6th century.

There are also somewhat random words in the main body written in the older Estrangēlā script, which, when coupled with the significant differences in the text, are generally accepted as signs of a major redaction when the Serṭā version was prepared. Serṭā was the main script used by the Jacobite Syrian Church of India, suggesting Manuscript B.21 was a Jacobite Syriac version of the Apocalypse. The older Thomas churches in India had entered into communion with the Church of the East by 500 AD, and remained in communion with the Syrian churches until the schism of 1653. Therefore, the Serṭā edits in the Apocalypse are also sometimes called the Jacobite edits.

The Jacobite lectionaries from the 12th through 15th centuries also include a few quotes from the Apocalypse, indicating it was an accepted Christian text in India at the time. Unfortunately, there are a number of deviations in some of the more disputed terms found in the other manuscripts, for example, not referring to Enoch and Leviathan. This limits the value of comparative analysis between the manuscripts, however, there are also places where it sheds light on how some of the strange terms in the Apocalypse originated.

The Ethiopian version uses another name for the Apocalypse: Ôɨzɨra Sutuåelɨ (ዐዝራ ሱቱኤል), which is derived from the fact that the text claims to have been written by 'Sutuåelɨ, who is also called Ôɨzɨra.' Sutuåelɨ is the Ethiopian translation of She'alti'el (שְׁאַלְתִּיאֵל), the name of one of King Jehoiachin's sons. Jehoiachin was the second last King of Judah before it was conquered by

4

the Babylonians, and was considered the first 'King of the Exiles' (ראש גלות) in Babylon. His son Shealtiel was the second 'King of the Exiles,' and this does correlate with the setting of the Judahite Apocalypse of Ezra. This reference to 'Shealtiel, who is also called Ezra,' is found in most translations of the apocalypse, other than the longer Catholic version, where it is both redundant and conflicting, as the author is identified at the beginning of the longer text. The introduction of the Catholic version is the introduction of the shorter Latin Apocalypse of Ezra, which identifies the author as Ezra the Scribe and provides his genealogy. Ezra the Scribe was a Levite, and so his genealogy has nothing to do with the line of David, a Judahite king.

Shealtiel is widely accepted as being the second exilarch of Judah, after his father Jehoiachin, who was taken captive by the Babylonians. Jehoiachin was listed as being on the king's ration list in Babylon circa 592 BC as Iaáúkinu (𒀀𒅖𒊏𒀀𒁺𒆠𒉡), along with his five sons, although they were not named. In the Masoretic text, Jehoiachin's seven sons were listed as Shealtiel, Malkiram, Pedaiah, Shenazzar, Jekamiah, Hoshama, and Nedabiah.

According to the Septuagint's 4th Kingdoms and Masoretic Kings, Jehoiachin was released from prison in 562 BC, when Amel-Marduk became the king of

Babylon, and subsequently became a high-ranking official in the Babylonian court. Amel-Marduk was the son of Nebuchadnezzar II, the king who had destroyed Jerusalem, however, based on Babylonian records, the two were estranged over accusations of destroying religious sanctuaries. It is generally accepted that Amel-Marduk was originally named Nabu-shum-ukin, Nebuchadnezzar's eldest son, whom Nebuchadnezzar imprisoned, and that he changed his name after being released from prison to praise Marduk, the dominant god of Babylonia. The two names, Nabu-shum-ukin and Amel-Marduk are never found together, with Nabu-shum-ukin being found mainly in earlier texts, and Amel-Marduk appearing in later texts, however, Nabu-shum-ukin was found as late as 563 BC, the year before Amel-Marduk assumed the throne.

The Leviticus Rabbah, a rabbinical text from the 6th through 8th centuries AD, claims that Amel-Marduk was imprisoned by his father Nebuchadnezzar alongside the exilarch Jehoiachin, because some Babylonian officials had proclaimed him king while Nebuchadnezzar was still alive, suggesting a failed coup had taken place. According to the Targum Sheni, a rabbinical text from sometime between the 4th and 10th century AD, Amel-Marduk also freed the Judahites that were captive in Babylon, however, the books of Ezra claimed it was King

Cyrus who freed them when he captured Babylon a few decades later. The Travels of Benjamin, originally published around 1170 AD, reports that the Tomb of Ezekiel in Al Kifl, Iraq, was reported to have been built by King Jehoiachin. The tomb was unrecorded before the Islamic era, however, may have been there.

The rabbinical text Pirkei De-Rabbi Eliezer, from the 8th century AD, reported that Ezekiel had been buried in Babylonia. This was less than a century after the time of Muhammed, and as Ezekiel was not mentioned in the Quran, it is very unlikely that the tomb of Ezekiel would have been built by Muslims, and accepted by Jews in that century. It is also unlikely that anyone would have known where Ezekiel was buried if there wasn't a large enough grave marker to survive for over the 1200 years between his death and the time of Rabbi Eliezer, suggesting that someone had built a tomb for him in ancient Babylon. Ezekiel is believed to have died circa 570 BC, while Jehoiachin was still imprisoned in Babylon, suggesting the tomb was built shortly after he was released in 562 BC. If so, the theory that some historians have, about Amel-Marduk being unpopular in Babylonia due to reversing Nebuchadnezzar's religious policies, seems likely.

Amel-Marduk ruled for less than two years before Neriglissar's coup. He was reported to be weak and incompetent in the surviving records from Neriglissar's reign, and from all accounts other than the Judahite, was despised by the Babylonians. Neriglissar was recorded as being a wealthy businessman during the reign of Nebuchadnezzar, and it is theorized that much of his wealth originated in the destruction of Jerusalem. This theory is based on the report in the Book of Jeremiah, who was present at the plunder of Jerusalem, that a government official named Nrgl Shr-tzr (נרגל שר־אצר) was present when the temple and palace were sacked. If this was the same Neriglissar, then he would have had a large number of Judahite slaves, which Amel-Marduk reportedly released. This suggests his successful coup less than two years into Amel-Marduk's reign and Amel-Marduk's vilification in Babylonia, was economically motivated, and Neriglissar likely reversed the policies of Amel-Marduk, re-enslaving the Judahites and others, who would then not be freed again until Cyrus conquered Babylon, as reported in Ezra. The Judahite exilarch Jehoiachin disappears from all records around this time, suggesting he was killed, and based on the Judahite Apocalypse of Ezra, Shealtiel appears to have been the exilarch by 557 BC, which he identifies as 30 years after the destruction of Jerusalem.

In the Septuagint's 2nd Ezra (Masoretic Ezra-Nehemiah), and 1st Paralipomenon, after Cyrus II of

Persia conquered Babylon, he released the Judahites that had been held there, and they were led back to Jerusalem by Zerubbabel the son of Shealtiel. Zerubbabel is also confirmed as the son of Shealtiel, in the writings of Haggai, both in the Hebrew and Greek translations. However, the Masoretic Divrei-hayyamim deviates here, and refers to Zerubbabel as the son of Pedaiah, suggesting that the Zerubbabel in question may not have been viewed as the same Zerubbabel by the author. This is likely due to a dispute over the legitimacy of Zerubbabel's claim to the throne of Judah, as the Edomites had occupied Judah, and Divrei-hayyamim appears to have originated in Edomite, likely by one of the Israelite priesthoods that were later evicted from the temple by Ezra the scribe.

Both Shealtiel and Zerubbabel continued to be viewed as part of the legitimate dynasty of Judah well into the Second Temple era, as the lineage of Jesus in the Gospel of Mathew, traced Jesus' descent from Solomon through Jehoiachin, Shealtiel, and Zerubbabel. The Gospel of Matthew is the only gospel accepted by the Byzantine Orthodox church that is also accepted by modern scholars as having originated in Judea before the destruction of the Second Temple, and according to church documents, was originally written in Aramaic, supporting the view that at least some Judeans viewed Solomon's linage as continuing after Zerubbabel returned from Babylon.

The shorter Latin Apocalypse of Ezra has become fused with the Judahite Apocalypse of Ezra in most Catholic and Protestant translations, however, scholars divide the Catholic versions of 4th Esdras (Protestant 2nd Esdras) into three sections, with only the core twelve chapters that correspond to the Orthodox and Ethiopian versions of the book labeled as 4th Ezra. The opening two chapters, which are only found in the Catholic version, are labeled as 5th Ezra, while the last 2 chapters found in the Catholic version, as well as fragments surviving of an ancient Greek translation, are labeled 6th Ezra. One of the Greek fragments, Oxyrhynchus Papyri 1010, is the oldest surviving fragment of the various Apocalypses of Ezra, dated to the 4th century AD, unfortunately, only two paragraphs survive. 5th Ezra and 6th Ezra appear to have originally been one document, which is commonly called the Latin Apocalypse of Ezra, although it was almost certainly not written in Latin.

There is no consensus of when the Judahite apocalypse was written, and traditional dating for it, based on the Catholic apocalypse, places its origin in the 1st or 2nd centuries of the Christian era, as the Latin apocalypse is very pro-Christian, and anti-Jewish. However, this dating is invalidated by the fact that the Latin apocalypse was not originally part of the Judahite apocalypse. When viewed separate from the influence of the Latin Apocalypse of Ezra, the Judahite Apocalypse of Ezra appears to have been written by someone either following an archaic Israelite religion, or someone who was very ignorant of what later became Judaism and Christianity. It contradicts the Torah in significant and obvious ways, meaning the author could not have had access to the Torah when he wrote the Apocalypse.

The apocalypse repeats and references some of the stories found in the Torah and the other books set before the fall of Judah, so the author must have been familiar with the content but was working from memory. This is similar to the story in the Talmud of Ezra rewriting the Torah from memory after it was lost during the destruction of Jerusalem. If this story was true, then it could not have been the Ezra from the late-Persian era, as that Ezra would have never seen the pre-Babylonian era Torah. This would have had to have been an earlier Ezra, one old enough to have been in Jerusalem before it fell to the Babylonians, which at least supports the idea that there was someone called Ezra in the early Babylonian captivity era.

The translations of the Judahite Apocalypse of Ezra all have specific errors that indicate the work originated in a Semitic language and one that strongly suggests that the language was Judahite. One of the most well-established errors is the apocalypse referring to Enoch being made at the same time as Leviathan, before God made Adam, the ancestor of everyone known as Enoch in the Torah. This is considered such an obvious error, that some translations, like the Revised Standard Version of the Christian Bible, substitute the name Behemoth for Enoch.

Based on the context and phonetics, it is likely that the word mistransliterated as Enoch (Ενωχ) was ånq (𐤐𐤉𐤟), meaning 'lizard' or 'reptile' in ancient Canaanite and Aramaic dialects. This appears to be an interpretation or alternate reading of the term remes (רֶמֶשׂ), meaning 'insects,' found in the first creation narrative of Bereshit. The Greek translation in Cosmic Genesis used the term herpetà (ἑρπετὰ), which translates as 'reptiles,' suggesting the Aramaic version of Bereshit the Greeks translated referred to 'reptiles' and not 'insects.' This mistranslation in the apocalypse could not have happened later than the Greek translation, as the Latin translator could not have misread the Greek word herpetà (ἑρπετὰ) as Enôch (Ενωχ). It most likely took place when the Greek translation was made, as the word is found in both Canaanite and Aramaic dialects, and therefore a Semitic translator is unlikely to have made the error.

The oldest Ge'ez manuscript, Manuscript Add. 1570, at Cambridge University in England uses the alternate name Åimišidiliti (አምሽድሊት) instead of Enoch, which indirectly supports the original Apocalypse as reading 'reptile.' Åimišidiliti does not have an inherent meaning in Geʿez, however, could be the result of a scribal error that switched a ni (ን) with a mi (ም) and a la (ለ) with a di (ድ), meaning the earlier Ethiopic word was åinišilaliti (እንሽላሊት), meaning 'lizard.'

Another obvious error is the reference to the Sea of Sodom having fish. The term Sea of Sodom is unique, however, could be read as a reference to the Dead Sea, which is where Sodom supposedly once stood. This location is not firm, as the sea was never described as covering the ruins of the city, but, is still the most likely sea to be identified as the Sea of Sodom.

The Dead Sea was referred to as either the Sea of Salt, or the Sea of Arabah in the Torah and Tanakh, and never as the Sea of Sodom. This error almost certainly originated from a scribe misreading the Sea of Edom as the Sea of Sodom. The term was the older name of the Gulf of Aqaba, recorded in Egyptian as ym jdwmô (𓏭𓈖𓇋𓂧𓅱𓅓𓊪𓈗) during the early Iron Age. Written in Judahite, this would have been ym hådm (𐤉𐤌 𐤀𐤃𐤌), meaning the Sea of Edom, which was later reinterpreted as the Red Sea after the Edomites were pushed north by the Nabatean Arabs. The Edomites were pushed north out of their homeland during the early Persian era, indicating that the scribal error probably took place after that, and also that the original text dates to the Neo-Babylonian era. If the name originated in a scribal error, it was likely a Judahite text that was being copied, as the Canaanite script's H (𐤀) looked similar to its S (𐤎), while the Aramaic H (𐡄) did not resemble the S (𐡎).

Both the Syriac and Geʻez translations support this interpretation, although only indirectly. The Syriac manuscript uses the translation of ymmå wSbṭå (ܝܡܐ ܘܣܒܛܐ), meaning Sea of Sabaites. The Sabaites (Σαβαῖται) were recorded in Greek records as living in southern Arabia, and in the context of the Apocalypse, appears to be a reference to the modern Yemeni coast. Based on Greek records from the 1st century BC, the capital of the kingdom of Adramitae (Αδραμιταε), the country that controlled the southern coast of Arabia, was known as Sabbatha (Σαββαθα). Adramitae is known to be the kingdom of Ḥadramawt (𐩢𐩳𐩧𐩣𐩩), and Sabbatha is now the ruins of Shabwa (𐩦𐩨𐩥𐩩). This name appears to be a reinterpretation of what would have already been the Sea of Sodom in the Hebrew translation of the Apocalypse, however, the Geʻez translation also supports there having been another name used in some Syriac copies, likely earlier than the Jacobite edits.

The Ethiopic manuscripts use the name hayɨmanoɨ (ሃይማኖት), which is not proper Geʻez, but a transliteration of the Syriac hymyná (ܝܡܝܢܐ), generally meaning 'the right,' but also meaning 'the south' if written by a Judahite. The Ge'ez term for 'right' was yäman (የማን), which shares the same root, but is not the same word, derived independently from the Old South Arabic ymn (𐩺𐩣𐩬). The definition of 'south' is unique to Judahites, as the original god of Jerusalem was the sun god Shalim, and left and right also referred to the north and south based on the rising of the sun. This usage is commonly found in the Masoretic texts, even after the Judahites had stopped worshiping the sun. The term 'Sea of the South' appears to be an alternate, and later reference to the Gulf of Aqaba and Red Sea, which does support the interpretation of 'Sodom' being a mistranslation of 'Edom.'

The name of god is also a curiosity in this Apocalypse, as it is not consistent with Second Temple references to Yahw or Lord Sabaoth, instead referring to Domine Dominator, a Latin translation of the Greek Κύριε Κύριε found in other ancient Israelite texts, such as Ezekiel. The Hebrew or Aramaic original is unclear, however is likely based on the term Ba'al Ba'al, meaning Lord Ba'al, which Jews were still calling their god during the time of the prophet Hosea, around a century before Judah fell to Babylon. This further supports the early origin of the Apocalypse of Ezra, or at least parts of it. Only Christian copies of the Judahite Apocalypse of Ezra survive, and therefore it is unclear how much the text was changed in the early Christian centuries.

There are references to either the angel Uriel's 'son Jesus,' the 'Christ,' or Shealtiel's 'descendant Joshua,' 'the messiah' depending on how the verse is interpreted. While this is often assumed to be a prophecy of Jesus ben Joseph, 'God' is not identified as speaking in the verse, and the prophecy is significantly different from the life of Jesus recorded in the gospel. This messiah was to rule for four hundred years, before dying for seven days, and then returning with the dead at the beginning of the immortal age. None of this correlates with the life of Jesus in the gospels.

While is possible that the specific reference to the name 'Jesus' was a Christian addition to the text, it is also worth noting that when Zerubbabel led the Judahites back to Jerusalem after Cyrus freed them, he was accompanied by a High Priest named Jesus or Joshua, depending on the source. Yeshu (יֵשׁוּעַ) and Yehoshua (יְהוֹשֻׁעַ) are two variants of the same name, one Aramaic, and the other Judahite in origin, however, both were translated as Jesus (Ἰησοῦς) in Greek. The Masoretic Ezra-Nehemiah records his name as Yeshua (יֵשׁוּעַ), indicating the text was written in Aramaic, while the Book of Zechariah reports his name was Yehoshua (יְהוֹשֻׁעַ),

and Zechariah was a Judahite who lived in Jerusalem when the events took place.

The prophecy about Jesus living for four hundred years before he dies, seems like an odd thing for a Christian to write after he was dead. The author appears to know as little about Christianity, as he did about Judaism. Much like the prophecy of the messiah in the book of Isaiah, the prophecy itself, regardless of later attempts to Christianize it, does appear to have existed in the pre-Christian version, and indicates a strong connection to the Messianic Judaism of the Babylonian, Persian, and Greek eras.

Based on the depressed attitude of the author Shealtiel, and his ongoing demand from God for answers, most scholars believe that he must have witnessed the destruction of the Second Temple, which would place his life circa 70 AD. However, this dating is based on the false late dating of the Catholic version of 4th Esdras, which cannot be applied to the core text of the Judahite apocalypse itself. Shealtiel's state of mind would be equally despondent if he had survived the original fall of Jerusalem to the Babylonians, as he would if he had witnessed the much later Roman destruction of Jerusalem.

The text itself has never been used by Rabbinical Jews, and there is no evidence of the Masorites having any interest in it, which raises the question of why the early Christians would have been interested in a text that had just been written and had inaccurate prophecies about Jesus. The early churches clearly saw this text as very ancient, and several major denominations continue to view it as an authentic document from the Babylonian captivity, such as the Ethiopian Orthodox Church, which teaches that it was written by the exiled king Shealtiel in Babylon, circa 557 BC.

Shealtiel's demands for answers to the question 'Why do bad things happen to good people?' seems to have resonated within the early Christian church, who, like Shealtiel, seem to have been unwilling to accept 'I'm God, and I don't have to answer your questions.' This cavalier attitude was one of the reasons why many early Christians stopped worshiping the old gods, and sought a more reasonable God that would actually help people. The motif of Ezra demanding answers from God was repeated in the other Apocalypses of Ezra, some of which seem antitheist, which was likely the reason the Byzantine Orthodox Church ultimately did not include the Judahite Apocalypse of Ezra in the Orthodox Greek or Latin Bibles.

Judahite Apocalypse of Ezra: Chapter 1

In the thirtieth year after the destruction of the city,[1] I, Shealtiel,[2] (who is also called Ezra,)[3] was in Babylon lying troubled on my bed, and my thoughts came up over my heart as I saw the desolation of Zion and the wealth of those who dwelt in Babylon. My spirit was greatly troubled, and I began to speak words full of fear before the Highest,[4] and said, "Dominating Lord,[5] you spoke at the beginning when you planted the earth, and yourself alone commanded the people, and gave a body to Adam without mind, which was the creation of your hands, and breathed into him the breath of life, and he was made living before you."

"You led him into paradise, which your right hand had planted before the earth ever came forward. To him, you gave the commandment to love your way, which he transgressed, and immediately you appointed death in him and his generations, from whom came nations, tribes, people, and families, beyond counting. Every people followed after their own will, did terrible things before you, and despised your commandments. Again in the process of time, you brought the flood on those who lived in the world and destroyed them. It happened to all of them, that as death was for Adam, so was the flood to these."

"Nevertheless, one of them you left, namely, Noah with his family, of whom came all righteous men. It happened that as they who lived on the earth and began to multiply, and had gotten many children, and were a great people, they began again to be more ungodly than the first. Now when they lived so wickedly before you, you chose a man from among them, whose name was Abraham."

"You loved him and to him only you showed your will, and made an everlasting covenant with him, promising him that you would never forsake his descendants. To him you gave Isaac, and to Isaac, you gave Jacob and Esau. As for Jacob, you chose him and put Esau aside, and so Jacob became a great multitude."

"It happened, that when you led his descendants out of Egypt, you brought them up to Mount Sinai. Lowering the sky, you grabbed hold of the Earth, moved the whole world, and made the depths tremble, and troubled the men of that age. Your glory went through the four gates of fire, earthquake, wind, and cold,[6] that you might give the law to the descendants of Jacob, and diligence to the generation of Israel. Yet you did not take away from them a wicked heart, that your law might bring out fruit in them."

"For the first man,[7] bearing a wicked heart sinned, and was overcome, and so are all those who are born from him. Thus infirmity was made permanent, and the law in the heart of the people with the malignity of the root, so that the good died away, and the evil still lived. So the times passed, and the years were brought to an end. Then you raised a servant called David, whom you commanded to build a city in your name and to offer incense and oblations to you there."

"When this was done, after many years, those who inhabited the city forgot you, and did all things that Adam and all his generations had done, for they also had wicked hearts. So you gave your city over into the hands of your enemies. Are their deeds then any better, those who inhabit Babylon, that they should have dominion instead of Zion? When I went there and saw impieties without number, then my mind saw many evildoers in this thirtieth year, so that my heart failed me. I have seen how you allow them sinning, and have spared wicked doers, and have destroyed your people, and have preserved your enemies, and have not signified it."

"I do not understand how this may be allowed to continue. Are those of Babylon then better than those of Zion? Are there any other people that know you besides Israel? What generation has so believed your covenants as Jacob? Yet their reward does not appear, and their labor has no fruit, for I have gone here and there through the heathens, and I see that they flow in wealth, and do not think on your commandments. Therefore, weigh our wickedness in the balance, and also theirs who live in the world. Will your name be found nowhere but in Israel? When was it that they who live on the Earth have not sinned in your sight? What people have so kept your commandments? You will find that Israel has kept your commands, but not the heathens."

Judahite Apocalypse of Ezra: Chapter 1 Notes

1 The city of Jerusalem was destroyed by the Neo-Babylonian Empire in 587 BC, which would place the origin of the text in 557 BC. At the time, Neriglissar was the king of Babylon, who was not a member of the royal family, but a noble who usurped the throne in 560 BC. In 557 BC, Neriglissar led a campaign into Anatolia in an attempt to conquer parts of Lydia. He died the year after the story is set, following which his son Labashi-Marduk was killed, and another noble named Nabonidus seized the throne.

2 Codex Sangermanensis: Salathihel

- Manuscript B.21: Šltåyl (ܫܠܬܐܝܠ)

- Manuscript Add. 1570: Sutuåeli̇ (ܣܘܬܘܐܠܝ)

The Latin name Salathiel is a direct transliteration of the name Salathiêl (Σαλαθιηλ), found in the Septuagint's 1st Paralipomenon as the name of one of King Jehoiachin's sons. The spelling of the Latin name proves the Latin translation was made from a Greek translation, and not directly from a Semitic text. The Hebrew translation of the name in the Masoretic text is She'alti'el (שְׁאַלְתִּיאֵל), which is also listed as the name of a son of King Jehoiachin in Divrei-hayyamim. Shealtiel is widely accepted as being the second exilarch of Judah, after his father Jehoiachin, who was taken captive by the Babylonians. Jehoiachin was listed as being on the king's ration list in Babylon circa 592 BC as Iaåúkinu (𒅀𒀪𒌑𒆠𒉡), along with his five sons, although they were not named. In the Septuagint and Masoretic text, Jehoiachin's seven sons were listed as Shealtiel, Malkiram, Pedaiah, Shenazzar, Jekamiah, Hoshama, and Nedabiah.

According to the Septuagint's 4th Kingdoms and Masoretic Kings, Jehoiachin was released from prison in 562 BC, when Amel-Marduk became the king of Babylon, and subsequently became a high-ranking official in the Babylonian court. Amel-Marduk was the son of Nebuchadnezzar II, the king who had destroyed Jerusalem, however, based on Babylonian records, the two were estranged over accusations of destroying religious sanctuaries. It is generally accepted that Amel-Marduk was originally named Nabu-shum-ukin, Nebuchadnezzar's eldest son, whom Nebuchadnezzar imprisoned, and that he changed his name after being released from prison to praise Marduk, the dominant god of Babylonia. The two names, Nabu-shum-ukin and Amel-Marduk are never found together, with Nabu-shum-ukin being found mainly in earlier texts, and Amel-Marduk appearing in later texts, however, Nabu-shum-ukin was found as late as 563 BC, the year before Amel-Marduk assumed the throne.

The Leviticus Rabbah, a rabbinical text from the 6th through 8th centuries AD, claims that Amel-Marduk was imprisoned by his father Nebuchadnezzar alongside the King Jehoiachin, because some Babylonian officials had proclaimed him king while Nebuchadnezzar was still alive, suggesting a failed coup had taken place. According to the Targum Sheni, a rabbinical text from sometime between the 4th and 10th century AD, Amel-Marduk also freed the Judahites that were captive in Babylon, however, the book of Ezra, claimed it was King Cyrus when he captured Babylon a few decades later.

The *Travels of Benjamin*, originally published around 1170 AD, reports that the Tomb of Ezekiel in Al Kifl, Iraq, was reported to have been built by King Jehoiachin. The tomb was unrecorded before the Islamic era, however, may have been there. The rabbinical text *Pirkei De-Rabbi Eliezer*, from the 8th century AD, reported that Ezekiel had been buried in Babylonia. This was less than a century after the time of Mohammed, and as Ezekiel was not mentioned in the Quran, it is very unlikely that the tomb of Ezekiel would have been built by Muslims, and accepted by Jews in that century. It is also unlikely that anyone would have known where Ezekiel was buried if there wasn't a large enough grave marker to survive for over the 1200 years between his death and the time of Rabbi Eliezer, suggesting that someone had built a tomb for him in ancient Babylon. Ezekiel is believed to have died circa 570 BC, while Jehoiachin was still imprisoned in Babylon, suggesting the tomb was built shortly after he was released in 562 BC. If so, the theory that some historians have, about Amel-Marduk being unpopular in Babylonia due to reversing Nebuchadnezzar's religious policies, seems likely.

Amel-Marduk ruled for less than two years before Neriglissar's coup. He was reported to be weak and incompetent in the surviving records from Neriglissar's reign, and from all accounts other than the Judahite, was despised by the Babylonians.

Neriglissar was recorded as being a wealthy businessman during the reign of Nebuchadnezzar, and it is theorized that much of his wealth originated in the sack of Jerusalem. This theory is based on the report in the book of Jeremiah, who was present at the sack of Jerusalem, that a government official named Nrgl Shr-tzr (נרגל שר־אצר) was present when the temple and palace were sacked. If this was the same Neriglissar, then he would have had a large number of Judahite slaves, which Amel-Marduk reportedly released. This suggests his successful coup less than two years into Amel-Marduk's reign, and Amel-Marduk's vilification in Babylonia, was economically motivated, and Neriglissar likely reversed the policies of Amel-Marduk, re-enslaving the Judahites and others, who would then not be freed again until Cyrus conquered Babylon, as reported in Ezra.

In the Septuagint's 2nd Ezra (Masoretic Ezra-Nehemiah), and 1st Paralipomenon, after Cyrus II of Persia conquered Babylon, he released the Judahites that had been held there, and they were led back to Jerusalem by Zerubbabel the son of Shealtiel. Zerubbabel is also confirmed as the son of Shealtiel, in the writings of Haggai, both in the Hebrew and Greek translations. However, the Masoretic Divrei-hayyamim deviates here and refers to Zerubbabel as Shealtiel's nephew. This is likely due to a dispute over the legitimacy of Zerubbabel's claim to the throne of Judah, as the Edomites had occupied Judah, and Divrei-hayyamim appears to have originated in Edomite, likely by one of the Israelite priesthoods that were later evicted from the temple by Ezra the scribe.

Both Shealtiel and Zerubbabel continued to be viewed as part of the legitimate dynasty of Judah well into the Second Temple era, as the lineage of Jesus in the Gospel of Mathew, traced Jesus' descent from Solomon through Jehoiachin, Shealtiel, and Zerubbabel. The Gospel of Matthew is the only gospel accepted by the Byzantine Orthodox church that is accepted as having originated in Judea prior to the destruction of the Second Temple, and according to church documents, was originally written in Aramaic, supporting that at least some Judeans viewed Solomon's linage as continuing on after Zerubbabel returned from Babylon.

3 Codex Sangermanensis: Ezras

- Manuscript B.21: Ôzra (ܐܘܙܪ)

- Manuscript Add. 1570: Ôizira (ዐዝራ)

The Latin name Ezras and Old Armenian name Ezras (Եզրաս) are not direct transliterations of the Greek name Esdras (Εσδρας) found in the Septuagint's books of Ezra but are transliterations of the Greek Ezras (Εζρας). This indicates the Greek translation of the apocalypse was not dependent on the Septuagint, and was translated by someone who did not believe Ezra the scribe and Shealtiel (this Ezra) were the same person. The Ge'ez Ôizira (ዐዝራ) and Old Georgian Ezra (ეზრა) both appear to be based on the Syriac Ôzra (ܐܘܙܪ), suggesting they may have been translated directly from a Syriac manuscript. The Greek translation also appears to have been based on a Syriac manuscript, however, most academics believe the apocalypse was written in Hebrew, not Syriac.

The linguistic evidence of the origin in Hebrew over Syriac would be equally valid if the original apocalypse was written in Judahite before the development of Hebrew.

In the Arabic Apocalypse of Daniel, which is a separate apocalypse set in the same era, the name is transliterated as Ôzrh (عزره) instead of the usual Arabic Ôzrā (عزرا), suggesting the word translated into Arabic was the Judahite word ôzrh (𐤀𐤆𐤋𐤏) or Aramaic ôzrh (𐡀𐡆𐡓𐡇), not the Hebrew name Erza (עֶזְרָא).

There are several theories about the origin of the name, the simplest being that the messenger Uriel was calling Shealtiel his assistant. The later reference to Phalthihel (or Felekatyal), which is generally accepted as a transcription error of Shealtiel, specifically in the Ge'ez translation, suggests it may have been a political title, essentially a precursor to the concept of the exilarch. The third common interpretation is that the original name was Azariah, one of Daniel's students from some versions of the Book of Daniel. This interpretation requires the original apocalypses mentioning Azariah to have been written in Neo-Babylonian, as Eziraia (𒀹𒂍𒈨), however, this would include the name of the god Ia (𒈨), the name of the 'terrible god' of floods, whose name was not generally mentioned in public. All three youths were given alternative names in the Book of Daniel, none of which appear to be Babylonian. The logical substitute for Ia (𒈨) would have been Ilu (𒀭), meaning 'god,' rendering the Neo-Babylonian spelling as Ezirailu (𒀹𒂍𒀭). The simplification of the name in the Judahite or Hebrew translation is likely because the scribe recognized it could not have originally been Azrael (עֲזַרְאֵל) or Ôzryål (עׇזְרִיאֵל), the name of the Classical Judahite psychopomp, whose name was also avoided. Azrael continues to be the angel of death in several religions, including Islam, as Ôzrāåīl (عزرائيل), and Sikhism as Ajaraila (ਅਜਰਾਈਲ). Azrael, in the form of Ezrael (Εζραελ), was an angel who punished the dead in the early Christian Apocalypse of Peter, however, was replaced by Thanatos (Θάνατος) as the angel of death in later Greek Christian texts.

The section of text translated as 'Shealtiel, who is also called Ezra' is not found in all translations of the apocalypse, and generally missing from later Latin manuscripts. Within the longer Latin version of the apocalypse, which combines the shorter Latin apocalypse with the Judahite apocalypse, it is a redundant line, as the author is introduced earlier in the text.

There was probably someone identified in the original version of the apocalypse, however, it cannot be known at this point if Shealtiel, Ezra, or both were originally identified. There is a conflict in chapter 3, when Phalthihel (or Felekatyal) visits the author, as those names are accepted as scribal errors of Shealtiel. Even in an apocalypse where the author was given visions by an extraterrestrial whose name keeps changing, his visiting himself seems unlikely. This conflict is likely why the Catholic version was created, which changed Shealtiel to Ezra the scribe so that when Shealtiel visited Ezra it wasn't so confusing. However, the interpretation of Phalthihel as a scribal error of Shealtiel is not necessarily correct, and this could have simply been a different person. If Phalthihel was Shealtiel, then it suggests the original author of the apocalypse was someone else who lived during the era of Shealtiel, such as Azariah.

4 Codex Sangermanensis: Altissimum. Translation: Highest

- Manuscript B.21: mrymå (محزيما)
- Manuscript Add. 1570: Girumä (ገሩም). Translation: Wonderful

The Syriac word mrymå (محزيما) appears to be an alternate spelling of mrômå (محزوما), meaning 'heights,' which would explain the Latin translation. The origin of the strange Syriac spelling is most likely a mistransliteration of the Hebrew word mrwm (מרום), meaning 'height,' by misreading the w (ו) as a y (י). This misreading could not have happened in Judahite, Imperial Aramaic, Syriac, or Greek, as those scripts did not have a similar looking W and Y. This almost certainly means that the Apocalypse was either written in Hebrew, or translated into Hebrew before being translated into Syriac.

The Highest is a reference to God, or a god, found in many ancient religions in the region. According to the Torah, the ancient people of Jerusalem worshiped El elyovn (אֵל עֶלְיוֹן), which the Greeks translated as theô tô ypsistô (Θεω τω υψιστω), both of which translate as 'Highest God,' when Abraham passed through the region. The Greek translation of Sanchuniathon's Bronze Age writing that has survived to the present referred to the primordial creator god of the Canaanites as Elioun (Ελιουν), which appears to be the same god. According to Sanchuniathon, Elioun was the 'highest' (υψιστος) god, who made the sky and the land, and they made the rest of the gods.

The Greek term 'god the highest' (θεω τω υψιστω) shows up in several Second Temple Era Judean texts, including 1st Ezra, Judith, 3rd Maccabees, Psalms, and the Wisdom of Joshua ben Sira. Most of these texts were not redacted during the Hasmonean period and were not copied by the Masorites, however, Psalms does appear to have been redacted, as the Masoretic version has the term Yehvah Elyom which strongly supports the Hasmonean redactors as having replaced El with Yehvah. The term El Elyon is known to have been a major god of the Canaanites called ål wålyn ($\mathcal{Y}^\wedge \mathcal{L}\mathcal{N}\mathcal{1}\ \mathcal{L}\mathcal{N}$) in the Sefire Treaty from circa 750 BC.

5 Codex Sangermanensis: Domine Dominator. Translation: Sir Lord (or Mr. Lord, lord Lord, Dominating Lord)

• Manuscript B.21: mryå mrx (مريا مرخ). Translation: lord to finish (or to smooth)

• Manuscript Add. 1570: Åibïlï Åigïziåä (ኣብል:ኣጊዚኣ). Translation: jackel (or lion) lord

This is a Latin translation of the Greek Cyrie Cyrie (Κύριε Κύριε) found in other translations of ancient Judean texts. The Hebrew or Aramaic original is unclear, and the term is likely based on the term Ba'al Ba'al ($\mathcal{LOS}\ \mathcal{LOS}$), as the prophet Hosea claimed the Jews were calling their god Ba'al in his time about a century earlier. Ba'al meant both the words 'the lord,' and was the title of the god: 'The Lord.' This does not conclusively prove the text is that old, a similar term appears in the prayer of the high priest Simon in 3rd Maccabees, however, any prayer of a high priest would likely quote the name or title of God found in the scriptures they had available at the time, which may have included the Apocalypse of Ezra. The translation Dominating Lord is used here, as it is the closest to the surviving Latin text.

6 The gates that unleashed the elements were also described in the Astronomical Book (3rd Enoch), which likely dates to around the same era. They were believed to be physical gates in the metal sky that the elements were pushed through into the world by the power of God.

The context of the elements is distinctly different than the context of the elements found in the hymn of the three youths in some versions of the Book of Daniel, in which the youths treated the elements as lesser deities, similar to the ancient Canaanite religion. Daniel and the three youths were supposedly in Babylon at the same time as Shealtiel, however, there are 14 different versions of the book of Daniel, and all are believed to have been heavily reworked in the Persian and Greek eras, as Daniel was viewed as an astrologer and not a prophet by the Judeans. The author of 4th Maccabees places the three youths in Assyria instead of Babylon, suggesting they were added to the Daniel narrative at some point. The story of Daniel and the three youths does directly contradict the alternate beginning to the book of

Daniel, found in the chapter generally labeled Susanna, which supports the story of the three youths being a later addition to Daniel, and the original youths being Samaritans that were taken prisoner to Assyria.

The metal sky above the flat Earth, is consistent with Neo-Assyrian and Neo-Babylonian cosmology, supporting the origin of this apocalypse and the Astronomical Book in that era. At the time, the Egyptians had apparently switched to the round Earth model according to the Greek philosophers, meaning these books could not have been written by the Israelites in southern Egypt. Southern Egypt had a large Judahite and Samaritan population at the time, as refugees from the Assyrian and Babylonian wars had been settled there by the Egyptians. Jeremiah and the other survivors who escaped the Babylonians settled there after the destruction of Jerusalem, and it is believed to be where the Lamentations were written.

7 Codex Sangermanensis: adam

Based on context, this was a mistranslation of the Hebrew word adam (אָדָם), Aramaic word ădm (ܐܕܡ), or Judahite word ădm (𐤀𐤃𐤌), all of which also translates as 'man,' or 'human.' The word indicates the original text was written in Judahite or Aramaic, as adamu (𒀀𒁕𒈬𒌋) did not mean 'man' in Neo-Babylonian, but 'red,' 'blood,' or 'noble.' The mistranslation of 'Adam' likely occurred in the Greek translation, as all the Central Semitic languages, including

Aramaic, Arabic, and Canaanite dialects, use the word ådm the same way.

Judahite Apocalypse of Ezra: Chapter 2

The messenger[1] that was sent to me, whose name was Uriel,[2] gave me an answer, saying, "Your heart has gone too far in this world, and you think you can comprehend the way of the Highest."

I replied, "Yes, my lord."

He responded, "I am sent to show you three ways and to set out three riddles before you. If you can explain one to me, I will also show you what you want to see, and I will show you where the wicked heart comes from."

I stated, "Continue, my lord."

Then he said to me, "Go on your way, and weigh me the weight of a fire, or measure for me the blast of the wind, or call me back to a day that has past."

Then I replied, "What man can do this, that you should ask such things of me?"

He answered me, "If I should ask you how great dwellings are under the sea, or how many fountains are in the depths, or how many fountains are above the sky, or which are flowing out of paradise, would you say to me, I never went down into the deep? Nor as yet into the depths of the Earth? Nor have I ever climbed up into the sky?[3] Nevertheless, now I have asked you only about the fire, wind, and of the days which you have passed through, and of things from which you can not be separated, and yet you cannot give me an answer regarding them."

He also said to me, "Your own things, and those who have grown up with you, you can not know, so how could your body then be able to comprehend the way of the Highest, and, the world now being outwardly corrupted, to understand the corruption that is evident in my sight?"

Then I replied to him, "It was better if we did not exist at all, than that we should still live in wickedness, and to allow it, and to not know why."

He answered me, "I went into a forest on a plain, and the trees debated and said 'Come, let us go and make war against the sea that it may retreat from before us, and that we may make more forests.' The waters of the sea also debated, and said, 'Come, let us go up and conquer the forests on the plain, that we may make another country for ourselves there.' The thoughts of the forest were in vain, for the fire came and consumed it. The thought of the waters of the sea came likewise to nothing, for the sand stood up and stopped them. If you were to judge now between these two, who would you side with? Who would you condemn?"

I answered, "Obviously it is a foolish thought that they both have devised, for the ground is given to the forest, and the sea also has his place to carry his waters."

Then he answered me, "You have given a correct judgment, but why not judge yourself also? For like as the ground is given to the forest, and the sea to his water, even so, those who live on the Earth may understand nothing but that which is on the Earth, and he who dwells above the sky may only understand the things that are above the height of the sky."

Then I answered, "I beg you, Lord, explain this to me. It was not my intent to inquire about the high things, but of those who have passed by us daily, namely, Israel is given up as an insult to the heathens. What is the reason that the people who you have loved are given over to ungodly nations, and why is the law of our fore-fathers treated as nothing, and the written covenants have no effect? We pass away out of the world like grasshoppers, and our life is astonishment and fear, and we are not worthy of mercy. What will he then do, when his name is what we are called by?" This is what I asked.

Then he answered me, "The more you search, the more you will marvel, for the world will soon pass away, and cannot comprehend the things that are promised to the righteous in the time to come, as this world is full of unrighteousness and imperfections. But in regards to the things of which you ask me, I will tell you, that while the evil has been sown, its destruction has not yet come. If therefore, that which is sown is not overturned, and if the place where the evil is sown has not passed away, then that which is sown with good cannot come. For the grain of the evil seed has been sown in the heart of Adam from the beginning, and how much ungodliness has it brought up until this time? How much will it still bring out until the threshing time comes? Consider now yourself, how great fruit of wickedness the grain of the evil seed has brought out. When the grain will be cut down, which is beyond counting, how great of a floor will they cover?"

Then I replied, "How, and when will these things happen? Why are our years few and evil?"

He answered, "Don't rush the Highest, for your haste is in vain, and cannot speed him up, as you are getting ahead of yourself. Didn't the minds of the righteous also question these things in their rooms, saying, 'How long will I hope in this way? When does the beginning of the fruit of our reward come?'"

To these questions, Jeremiel the great messenger (and commander of watchers)[4] answered, "When the number of seeds has been filled among you, for he has weighed the world in the balance. By measure, he has measured the time, and by number has he counted the time, and he does not move or change them until the said measure is fulfilled."

Then I answered, "Dominating Lord, even we are all full of impiety. For our sake, assume that the floors of the righteous are not filled, because of the sins of those who live on the Earth."

He answered me, "Go to a woman with a child, and ask her when she has fulfilled her nine months, if her womb may keep the birth within her any longer."

Then I said, "No, lord, she cannot do that."

He said to me, "In the grave, the chambers of the minds are like the womb of a woman. Like a woman who is in labor rushes to escape the necessity of the labor, even so, these places rush to deliver those things that are committed to them. From the start, search for what you desire to see, and it will be shown to you."

Then I answered, "If I have found favor in your sight, and if it is possible, and if I may know, show me whether there is more to come than is past, or more past than is to come. What is past I know, but what is still to come I don't know."

He said to me, "Stand up on the right side, and I will explain the riddle to you."

So I stood and saw, and, look, a hot burning oven passed by before me, and it happened that when the flame was gone by I looked, and, saw only the smoke still remained. After this, there passed by before me a watery cloud which sent down a great deal of rain with a storm, and when the stormy rain had passed, the drops still remained. Then he said to me, "Consider. The rain is more than the drops, as the fire is greater than the smoke, but the drops and the smoke remain behind. So the time which has passed was much longer."

Then I prayed, and said, "Will I live, do you think, until that time? What will happen in those days?"

He answered me, "As for the signs of which you ask me, I may tell you some part of them. But regarding your life, I am not sent to tell you, as I do not know it."

Judahite Apocalypse of Ezra: Chapter 2 Notes

1 Codex Sangermanensis: angelus. Translation: angel

• Manuscript B.21: mlåkå (ܠܐܠܟܐ). Translation: messenger

• Manuscript Add. 1570: mäliåäki (መልአክ). Translation: ruler

The Latin angelus, Old Slavonic angɛlu (ᚼᛈᛈᛞᚼᚭᚭ), and Old Georgian angelozi (ანგელოზი) words are derived from the Greek word angelos (ἄγγελος), meaning 'messenger.' This term is used in the Septuagint in parallel to the Masoretic text's mal'ach (מַלְאָךְ), also meaning 'messenger.' The Latin transliteration of 'angelus' in the Orthodox vulgate did not refer to 'messengers' in the human sense, where the term was translated as 'nuntius' or 'legatus,' but extraterrestrial messengers. This was later incorporated into Latin Christianity as a species of supernatural undergods, which became the angels of modern Catholic and Protestant Christianity. The Old Armenian word hreštak (հրեշտակ), meaning 'envoy,' appears to be a direct translation of the Syriac word mlåkå (ܡܠܐܟܐ) or Greek word angelos (ἄγγελος), both meaning 'messenger,' while the Ge'ez term appears to be a transliteration of the same term.

2 Codex Sangermanensis: Urihel

• Manuscript B.21: Åuråyl (ܐܘܪܐܝܠ)

• Manuscript Add. 1570: Ôuraåel (ዑራኤል)

Uriel was the Latin transliteration of the Greek Oyriêl (Οὐριήλ) and Hebrew Uri'el (אוּרִיאֵל), meaning 'light god.'

41

Uriel is generally found in literature that was later deemed heretical within Judaism, including the Book of the Watchers (1st Enoch), both versions of the Book of Tobit, the Testament of Solomon, and the Life of Adam and Eve. Most of these books were accepted by early Christians and Gnostics, along with other books that include Uriel, such as the Apocalypse of Peter and the Secret Book of John, he continues to be viewed as a messenger by most Christian denominations. In his earliest textual representations, he was one of the four angels that represented the four winds, while by the Greek era, he was viewed as the governing messenger (planet) of one of the seven skies (crystal spheres) above the flat Earth.

3 Codex Sangermanensis: caelis

Caelis was both the god personifying the sky, and the Latin word meaning 'sky.' The Greek equivalent of Caelis was Uranus (Οὐρανός), which was used in the Septuagint as a translation for the Hebrew term Shamayim (שָׁמַיִם).

4 Codex Sangermanensis: Hieremihel archangelus.
Translation: Jeremiel archangel

• Manuscript B.21: Rmzyl mlåkå wamr oryn (ܠܐܠܡ ܠܣܕܪܒܙ ܘܐܡܪ ܐܘܪܝܢ). Translation: Remashel messenger and command (or order) watcher

• Manuscript Add. 1570: Åiyamiåel måliåäk (ኢየማያኤል መልአክ). Translation: Yomiel commander (or angel)

The Latin archangelus and Old Slavonic arxangεlɯ (ᲜᲮᲑᲮᲠᲜ:ᲠᲚᲘᲛᲬᲝᲒ) are both transliterations of the Greek term archangelos (ἀρχάγγελος), meaning 'ruling messenger.' The Georgian term mtavarangelozi (მთავარანგელოზი), meaning 'chief angel' is also based on the lost Greek translation, with the term angelozi (ანგელოზი) transliterated from the Greek angelos (ἄγγελος), and mtavar (მთავარ) translated from the Greek arch- (ἀρχ-). Likewise, the Old Armenian hreštakapet (Հրեշտակապետ), meaning 'messenger commander' was probably a direct translation from either a Greek or Syriac manuscript.

The Latin, Syriac, and Ge'ez translations do not agree on the name of the archangel, and the name is often substituted with Uriel in English translations. Jeremiel, Remashel, and Yomiel are the names of three of the commanders of the watchers who rebelled with Shemyaza in the Books of the Watchers (1st Enoch). Jeremiel was also a messenger in the Apocalypse of Zephaniah, which only survives is Coptic, and is universally rejected by Jews and Christians. The Syriac manuscript supports the original designation of the being in question as a watcher, suggesting that the Apocalypse may have been preserved in Juduhite, and then translated into Hebrew, by one of the heretical Judean movements that used the Enochian literature. This translation follows uses Jeremiel, however, it is unclear which of the Watcher-Commanders were originally intended.

Judahite Apocalypse of Ezra: Chapter 3

"Nevertheless, for the coming signs, look, the days will come when those who live on Earth will be taken in a great number, and the way of truth will be hidden, and the land will be barren of faith. But the iniquity will be increased more than what you see now, or that you have heard of long ago. The land that you see now with roots, you will observe suddenly become a desert. If the Highest allows you to live, you will see after the third trumpet, that the sun will suddenly rise again in the night, and the moon three times a day. Blood will drop out of wood, and the stone will speak, and the people will be troubled."

"He will rule, who those that live on the earth don't elect. The birds will fly away together. The Sea of Edom[1] will throw out fish, and speak at night, which many have not heard, but they will all hear its voice. There will be confusion in many places, and the fire will be sent out again often, and the wild beasts will change their places, and menstruating women will give birth to monsters. Salt waters will be found to be sweet, and all friends will destroy one another. Then sense will hide itself, and understanding will withdraw itself into his secret place and will be searched for by many, and yet will not be found. Then the unrighteousness and incontinence will be multiplied on Earth."

One land also will ask another, 'Has Righteousness, who makes a man righteous gone to you?' and it will answer, 'No.'

"At the same time, men will hope, but obtain nothing. They will labor, but they will not prosper. I have permission to show you these signs, and if you will pray again, and cry like now, and fast for days, you will hear even greater things."

Then I woke up, and extreme fear filled my body, and my mind was so troubled that it fainted. The messenger that had come to talk with me, held me, comforted me, and lifted me to my feet.

On the second night, it happened, that (Phalthihel) the commander of the Israelites (and not the Arameans)[2] came to me, and asked, "Where have you been? Why are you so depressed? Don't you know that Israel is committed to you in the land of their captivity? Get up and eat bread, and don't forget us, like a shepherd that leaves his flock in the hands of cruel wolves."

Then I said to him, "Leave me, and don't come back."

He heard what I said, and left me. I fasted for seven days, mourning and weeping as Uriel the messenger had commanded me. After seven days, the thoughts of my heart were very terrible within me again, and my mind[3] recovered the spirit of understanding, and I began to talk with the Highest again, and said, "Dominating Lord, of every forest of the Earth, and of all the trees, you have chosen only one vine for yourself. Of all lands in the whole world, you have chosen one place, and of all the flowers just one lily. Of all the depths of the sea, you have filled one river, and of all built cities you have made Zion sacred to yourself. Of all the birds that are created, you have named yourself one dove, and of all the livestock that are born you have chosen one sheep. Among all the multitudes of people, you have begotten one people, and to these people, who you loved you gave a law that is approved by all."

"Now, Lord, why have you given this one people over to many? The one root have you chosen from others, and why have you scattered your only people among the many? They who doubted your promises, and didn't believe your covenants, have trodden them down. If you hated your people so much, you should punish them with your own hands!"

Now when I had said these words, the messenger that came to me the night before was sent to me again, and said to me, "Hear me, and I will instruct you. Listen to what I will say, and I will tell you more."

I replied, "Speak, my lord."

Then he said to me, "You are greatly troubled in your mind for Israel's sake. Do you love those people more than he who made them?"

I answered, "No, lord, but from great grief have I spoken, for my duties pain me every hour, while I labor to comprehend the way of the Highest, and to seek out part of his judgment."

He said to me, "You can not."

I asked, "Why, Lord? Why was I born then? Why wasn't my mother's womb my grave then, so I might not have seen the struggle of Jacob and the terrible struggle of the stock of Israel?"

He answered me, "Count for me the things that have not yet come, gather me together the rubbish that has been thrown away, and make the flowers green again that have withered. Open for me the places that are closed, and bring out to me the winds that are locked within them. Show me the image of a voice, and then I will explain to you the things that you struggle to know."

I asked, "Dominating Lord, who can know these things, except he who is not living among men? As for me, I am ignorant. How may I then speak of these things of which you ask me?"

Then he said to me, "Like you can do none of these things that I have mentioned, likewise you cannot learn my judgment, or in the end the love that I have promised to my people."

I replied, "Look, lord. Are you near to those who are reserved until the end? What will they do, those who have been before me, or we now, or those who will come after us?"

He answered me, "I will liken my judgment to a ring. Like there is no slackness at the end, there is no swiftness at the beginning."

I asked, "Could you not make those who have been made, be again now, and those who are still to come, come immediately, so you might show your judgment sooner?"

Then he answered me, "The body may not hurry above the maker, neither may the world hold all them at once that will be created in it."

I replied, "As you have said to your servant, that you, which give life to all, have given life at once to the body that you have created, and the body carried it, likewise might it now also carry those who now are present at once?"

He said to me, "Ask the womb of a woman, and say to her, 'If you bring out children, why not all together, but instead one after another? Beg her, therefore, to birth ten children at once."

I said, "She cannot, but must do it over a length of time."

Then he replied to me, "Likewise, I have given the womb of the Earth to those who are sown in it, in their times. Like a young child may not bring out the things that belong to the old, even so, have I planned the world which I created."

I asked, "Seeing you have now given me the answer, I will proceed to speak before you, for our mother, of whom you have told me, that she is young and now begins to age."

He answered me, "Ask a woman who carries children, and she will tell you. Say to her, 'Why are they who you have now brought out like those who were before, but of a smaller stature?' She will answer you, 'They that are born in the strength of youth are of one kind, and those who are born in the time of age, when the womb fails, are otherwise.' Consider also, therefore, how you are of less stature than those who were before you. So are those who come after you less than you, as the bodies which now begin to be old, and have passed over the strength of youth."

Then I said, "Lord, I beg you if I have found favor in your sight, reveal your body to your servant who you visit."

Judahite Apocalypse of Ezra: Chapter 3 Notes

1 Codex Sangermanensis: mare Sodomitum. Translation: sea Sodomish

- Manuscript B.21: ymmå wSbtå (ﬢﬦﬦﬦﬦ ﬦﬦﬦﬦ). Translation: sea of Sabaites (or rod, spear, meteor, tribe)
- Manuscript Add. 1570: bɨhirä hayɨmanoɨ (ⴼⴷⴹ Yℓ∾ℯℾⴹ). Translation: sea hayemanoe

The term Sea of Sodom is a very unusual way to refer to the Dead Sea, where Sodom once existed according to the Torah. The Dead Sea was generally called the Sea of Araba (מ֥ עֲרָבָה) in the Tanakh (Old Testament), which appears to have been the name used throughout the Second Temple era. The reference to the Sea of Sodom throwing out fish is also curious, as the Dead Sea does not have any fish in it.

It seems likely that the term was a mistranslation of the Judahite term ym hådm (𐤉𐤌 𐤀𐤃𐤌), meaning the Sea of Edom, which was later reinterpreted as the Red Sea. The Sea of Edom was the older name of the Gulf of Aqaba, recorded in Egyptian as ym jdwmô (𓏤𓈖𓏏𓏏𓈖𓈖) during the early iron age. If the name originated in a mistranslation, it was likely a Judahite text that was being translated into Aramaic, as the Canaanite script's H (𐤄) looked similar to its S (𐤔), while the Aramaic H (ח) did not resemble the S (ש). If this was a mistranslation from Judahite, it would support the original text being written by a Judahite who survived the destruction of Jerusalem before Aramaic supplanted Judahite in Judah.

The Ethiopic term hayımanoı (ሃይማኖት) is not proper Ge'ez, and does not correlate with the Latin, but is a transliteration of the Syriac hymynå (ܗܝܡܢܐ), generally meaning 'the right,' but also meaning 'the south' if written by a Judahite. The Ge'ez term for 'right' was yäman (የማን), which shares the same root, but is not the same word, derived independently from the Old South Arabic ymn (𐩺𐩣𐩬). The definition of 'south' is unique to Judahites, as the original god of Jerusalem was the sun god Shalim, and left and right also referred to the north and south based on the rising of the sun. This usage is commonly found in the Masoretic texts, even after the Judahites had stopped worshipping the sun.

The term 'Sea of the South' appears to be an alternate, and later reference to the Gulf of Aqaba and Red Sea, which does support the interpretation of 'Sodom' being a mistranslation of 'Edom.' The Syriac term can be read as the Sea of Sabaites, which was another name for the people living in the kingdom of Hadhramaut between the 1300s BC and 200s AD. Hadhramaut controlled the southern coast of Arabic at the time, meaning this was a reference to the Gulf of Aden and the Arabian Sea.

2 Codex Sangermanensis: Phalthihel dux populi.
Translation: Phalthihel commander of people

• Manuscript B.21: ulinsh dÅisrål puqdnå ula arimt (ܐܪܡܝܐ ܘܠܐ ܦܘܩܕܢܐ ܕܐܝܣܪܠ ܐܘܠܝܢܫ). Translation: the race (or species, type) of Israel and not Arameans

• Manuscript Add. 1570: Filikätyal liqä mälääikitihomu sääiḥizäb (ፈለከጥያል:ሊቃ፥መላእክቲሆሙ:ስእሕዘብ). Translation: Felekatyal chief spokes-person (or correspondent) of the tribe (or people, nation)

The Latin 'dux populi' appears to be a translation of the Aramaic ryšå glwtå (ܐܛܠܓ ܐܫܝܪ), meaning 'head of exiles,' which was used later Jewish works to represent the exiled king. The longer Ge'ez translation of 'chief spokesperson of the tribe' is essentially the same, and could be an older title before the Greek influence.

Based on the conclusion that the titles refer to an exilarch, the name is generally assumed to be a scribal error of Salathihel, as She'alti'el (שְׁאַלְתִּיאֵל) was the exilarch of the Judahites in Babylon. Assuming this is true, the error is unlikely to have originated in Latin or Greek, as the Latin and Greek 'ph' (Φ) and 's' (Σ / C) do not look similar. It is also unlikely to have happened in Hebrew or Imperial Aramaic, as the Hebrew and Aramaic 'sh' (ܫ / שׁ) and 'p' (ܦ / פ) do not look alike. The most likely origin of the error was when the Greek translation was made, by reading a Classical era Estrangēlā Syriac 'sh' (ܫ) as a 'p' (ܦ). Estrangēlā is the oldest form of Syriac, which developed circa 100 AD, suggesting the Greek translation was made between 100 and 200 AD, as the text was recorded as being used in the Greek churches by 200 AD, although the Greek translation was subsequently lost. The Ethiopic name Filikätyal (ፈለከጥያል) contains the same shift from 'sh' to 'fə' as the Greek translation, however, adds a 'kä' sound missing from both the Greek and Syriac. This additional sound likely also resulted from a misreading of the name written in Maḏnhāyā (Eastern) Syriac, as the 'y/i' (ܝ) and 'kh' (ܟ) are easy to misread. The Maḏnhāyā Syriac script developed in the Sasanian Empire between the 3rd and 7th centuries AD, and was the script used by the Church of the East, suggesting the Geʿez translation was made hundreds of years after the lost Greek translation, from a text obtained from the Church of the East.

The only Syriac copy of the Apocalypse is Manuscript B.21 Inf. (fols. 267a-276b) at the Biblioteca Ambrosiana in Milan, which contains a slightly different verse, regarding a 'commander of Israelites but not Arameans.' Manuscript B.21 is dated to the 6th or 7th century, making it the oldest full manuscript of the apocalypse to survive to the present in any language, however, the Latin, Geʿez, Old Armenian, Old Georgian, and Old Slavonic versions of the apocalypse all support there once being an alternate version of the apocalypse in Syriac.

While the scribal errors could account for the exilarch's name changing, it is odd that Shealtiel would be visiting himself, as he was apparently the one who wrote the Apocalypse. This suggests that the original version of the Apocalypse was written by someone else, whom Shealtiel knew, and the Apocalypse was later reattributed to Shealtiel. If so, it reopens the question of who this Ezra was. One theory was that the name Ezra was derived from the name Azariah, as the name Ia was not spoken in Babylonia. Ia was the name of the ancient Mesopotamian god of floods, but he was generally just called the 'terrible god.' While Azariah was the name of one of the three youths who accompanied Daniel in Babylonia in some versions of the Book of Daniel, he was reportedly thrown into a furnace when Jerusalem rebelled from Nebuchadnezzar's authority and subsequently disappeared from the text of Daniel. As it is reported that he was saved from the furnace, by a messenger wearing white, it is possible that he remained in Babylon, and this was his apocalypse.

Alternatively, if the Syriac version is more accurate, this line about the commander visiting the author may have referred to either a Babylonian official or the exilarch Jeconiah before he died. As most manuscripts do include a name like Phalthihel or Fiḷikätyal, Phalthihel is used in this translation, however, as not all manuscripts include a name, the name is in parentheses, as is the 'and not the Arameans' addition found in the Syriac manuscript.

3 Codex Sangermanensis: anima. Translation: life

The Latin term anima was used as a translation of the Greek term psyche (ψυχή), which was itself a translation of the Hebrew term nefesh (נֶפֶשׁ) both of which translate as mind, life, soul, or person.

Judahite Apocalypse of Ezra: Chapter 4

He replied to me, "In the beginning, when the Earth was made, before the edges of the world stood, or the winds ever blew, before it thundered and lightninged, or the foundations of paradise were laid, before beautiful flowers were seen, or even the movable powers were established. Before the innumerable multitude of messengers were gathered together, or the heights of the air were lifted. Before the measures of the firmament were named, or the chimneys in Zion were hot. Before the present years were planned out, and the inventions of those who now sin had started. Before they were sealed, who have gathered faith as a treasure, then I considered these things, and they all were made through me alone, and through none other. By me also, they will be ended and by none other."

Then I replied, "When will come the dividing of the times? When will be the end of the first, and the beginning of it that follows?"

He answered me, "From Abraham to Isaac when Jacob and Esau were born of him, Jacob's hand held first the heel of Esau. As Esau was the end of the world, and Jacob is the beginning of it that follows. The hand of man is between the heel and the hand. Ezra, do you have another question to ask?"

I answered then and asked, "Dominating Lord, if I have found favor in your sight, I beg you, show your servant the end of your signs, which you showed me part of the previous night."

So he answered and said to me, "Stand up on your feet and hear a mighty-sounding voice. It will be like a great motion, but the place where you stand will not be moved. When it speaks do not be afraid, for the word is about the end, and the foundation of the earth is understood. Why? Because the speech of these things trembles and is moved. It knows that the end of these things must be changed."

It happened, that when I had heard it I stood up on my feet, and listened, and, look, there was a voice that spoke, and the sound of it was like the sound of many waters. It said, "Look, the days approach that I will begin to draw near and to visit those who live on the land and will begin to make inquiries of them, who they are that have hurt unjustly with their unrighteousness, and then the affliction of Zion will be fulfilled. When the world begins to vanish away and will be finished, then I will show these signs: the books will be opened before the firmament, and they will see all together. The children a year old will speak with their voices, the pregnant women will give birth to premature children of three or four months old, and they will live, and be raised.

Suddenly, the farmed lands appear wild, and the full storehouses will be found empty. The trumpet will sound, and when every man hears, they will suddenly be afraid. At that time, friends will fight one against another like enemies, and the Earth will stand in fear with those who live on it. the springs of the fountains will stand still, and for three hours they will not run."

"Whoever remains from all these that I have told you will escape, and see my salvation, and the end of your world. The men that are received will see it, who have not tasted death from their birth, and the heart of the inhabitants will be changed, and turned into another meaning, for evil will be put out, and deceit will be quenched. As for faith, it will flourish, corruption will be overcome, and the truth, which has been so long without fruit, will be declared."

When he talked with me, look, I glanced little by little at him before whom I stood. These words he said to me, "I have come to show you the time of the night to come. If you will still pray more, and fast for seven more days, I will tell you greater things that day that I have heard. For your voice is heard before the Highest. The Mighty has seen your righteous dealing, he has seen also your chastity, which you have had ever since your youth. Therefore he has sent me to show you all these things, and to say to you, 'Be of good comfort and don't be afraid. Don't rush to think vain things about the times that are past, or you may rush from the latter times.'"

It happened after this, that I wept again, and fasted seven days like before, so I might fulfill the three weeks that he had told me. During the eighth night, my heart was troubled within me again, and I began to speak before the Highest. My mind was greatly inflamed, and my mind was in distress.

I said, "Lord, you spoke from the beginning of the creation, even the first day, and said 'Let the sky and earth be made,' and your word was a perfect work. Then, the spirit and darkness and silence were everywhere, and the sound of man's voice was not yet formed. Then you commanded a beautiful light to come out of your treasures, that your work might appear."

"On the second day, you made the spirit of the firmament, and commanded it to part and to make a division between the waters, that the one part might go up, and the other remain beneath."

"On the third day you commanded that the waters should be gathered in the seventh part of the earth, six parts have you dried up, and kept them, intending that some of these would be planted by God, and farmed to serve you. As soon as your word went out the work was made. For immediately there was great and innumerable fruit, and many and diverse pleasures for the taste, and flowers of unchangeable color, and odors of wonderful smell, and this was done on the third day."

"On the fourth day, you commanded that the Sun should shine, and the moon to give her light, and the stars should be organized, and ordered them to serve man, who was yet to be made."

"On the fifth day, you said to the seventh part, where the waters were gathered that it should bring out living bodies, the birds and fishes, and so it came to pass. For the water without life brought out living things at the commandment of God, that all people might praise your wondrous works. Then you ordained two types of living creatures, the one you called lizard,[1] and the other Leviathan.[2] You separated the one from the other, for the seventh part, namely, where the water was gathered together, might not hold them both. To the lizard, you gave one part, which was dried on the third day, that he should live in the region in which there are a thousand hills, but to Leviathan you gave the seventh part, namely, the water, and have kept him to devour whomever you want."

"On the sixth day, you gave a commandment to the Earth that it should bring out beasts, livestock, and creeping things. After these, Adam also, whom you made lord of all your creatures. From him, we all come, and also people whom you have chosen. All this have I spoken before you Lord, because you made the world for our sake. As for the other people, which also come from Adam, you have said that they are nothing, but are like spit, and have compared the abundance of them to a drop that falls from a vessel."

"Now, Lord, see these heathens, which have forever been reputed as nothing and have begun to be lords over us and to devour us. We, your people, whom you have called your firstborn, your only begotten, and your fervent love, are given into their hands. If the world now is made for our sake, why do we not have an inheritance within the world? How long will this last?"

Judahite Apocalypse of Ezra: Chapter 4 Notes

1 Codex Sangermanensis: Enoch

- Manuscript Add. 1570: Åimišidiliti (አምሽድሊት)

Enoch was the Latin translation of the Greek Enôch (Ενωχ) and the Hebrew Chanoch (חֲנוֹךְ). Several people were known as Enoch in the Torah. There was no evidence of a monster named Enoch, and normally Leviathan is paired with Behemoth, suggesting the author had confused the two names. This assumption is so accepted that some modern translations, like the Standard Revised Edition of the Christian Bible, substitute the name 'Behemoth' for 'Enoch.'

Based on the context and phonetics, it is likely that the word mistransliterated as Enoch (Ενωχ) was ånq (ዋነቀ), meaning 'lizard' or 'reptile' in ancient Canaanite and Aramaic dialects. This appears to be an interpretation or alternate reading of the term remes (רֶמֶשׂ), meaning 'insects,' found in the first creation narrative of Bereshit. The Greek translation in Cosmic Genesis used the term herpetà (έρπετὰ), which translates as 'reptiles,' suggesting the Aramaic version of Bereshit the Greeks translated referred to 'reptiles' and not 'insects.' This mistranslation could not have happened later than the Greek translation, as the Latin translator could not have misread the Greek word herpetà (έρπετὰ) as Enôch (Ενωχ). It probably took place when the Greek translation was made, as a word is found in both Canaanite and Aramaic dialects, and therefore a Semitic translator is unlikely to have made the error.

The Ge'ez manuscripts use the name Åimišɨdɨlitɨ (እምሽድሊት) in Manuscript Add. 1570, which could be the result of a scribal error that switched a ni (ን) with a mɨ (ም) and a la (ላ) with a dɨ (ድ), meaning the earlier Ethiopic word was åinišɨlalitɨ (እንሽላሊት), meaning 'lizard.' The only surviving Syriac manuscript has a shorter chapter 4, which does not mention Enoch, a reptile, or Leviathan.

2 Codex Sangermanensis: Leviathan

- Manuscript Add. 1570: Lewiyatanɨ (ለዊይታን)

Leviathan was the Latin translation of the Aramaic Lwytn (𐡋𐡅𐡉𐡕𐡍), and Hebrew Livyatan (לִוְיָתָן), both terms based on the bronze age Canaanite sea monster Ltn (𐤋𐤕𐤍). The Latin spelling indicates the text was previously translated into Greek as Lewiathan (Λευιάθαν), however, that name was not used in the Septuagint, which substitutes the word 'dragon' (δράκων) or the name Cetus (Κῆτος). The Greek transliteration of the name used in modern Bibles is Lebiathan (Λεβιάθαν), however, that transliteration is fairly recent. The only surviving Syriac manuscript has a shorter chapter 4, which does not mention Leviathan.

Judahite Apocalypse of Ezra: Chapter 5

When I had finished speaking these words, the messenger who had been sent to me the previous nights returned, and he said to me, "Get up, Ezra, and hear the words that I have come to tell you."

I answered, "Speak, my god."

Then he said to me, "The sea is set in a wide place, that it might be deep and great. But if the entrance were narrow, and like a river, then who could go to the sea to look at it, and to rule it? If it did not go through the narrow, how could he come into the broad area? There is also another thing: a city is built, and set on a broad field, and is full of all good things, yet the entrance of it is narrow and is set in a dangerous place for one to fall as if there were a fire on the right hand, and on the left deep water. Only one path runs between them both, between the fire and the water, so small that only one man could go there at a time. If this city now were given to a man for an inheritance, and if he will never pass the danger set outside it, how will he receive this inheritance?"

I said, "It is so, lord."

Then he replied to me, "Likewise is Israel's portion also. Because for their sake, I made the world, and when Adam transgressed my statutes, then I decreed that which has been until now. Then were the entrances of this world made narrow, full of sorrow and struggle.

They are but few and evil, full of perils, and very painful. For the entrances of the elder world were wide and sure, and brought immortal fruit. If then those who live don't labor to enter these strait and vain things, they can never receive that which is laid up for them. Now, therefore, why disturb yourself, seeing you are but a corruptible man? Why are you moved, when you are only mortal? Why have you not thought about that which is to come, rather than that which is present?"

Then I answered, "Dominating Lord, you have ordained in your law, that the righteous should inherit these things, but that the ungodly should perish. Nevertheless the righteous will allow narrow things, and hope for wide, for those who have done wickedly have permitted the straight things, and yet will not see the wide."

He replied to me, "There is no judge above God and none that has understanding above the Highest. For there are many that perish in this life because they despise the law of God that is set before them. God has given commandments to those who came, what they should do to live, even as they came, and what they should observe to avoid punishment. Nevertheless, they were not obedient to him, but spoke against him, and imagined vain things, and deceived themselves by their wicked deeds, and said of the Highest, that he does not exist, and did not know his ways."

"His law they have hated, and denied his covenants. They have not been faithful to his statues, and have not performed his works. Therefore, Ezra, for the empty are empty things, and for the full are the full things. Look, the time will come, that these signs which I have told you will come to pass, and the bride will appear, and she will be seen coming out, but that is now removed from the Earth. Whoever is delivered from the aforementioned evils will see my wonders."

("My descendant Joshua[1] will be revealed along with those who are with him, and those who remain will rejoice for four hundred years. After these years my anointed[2] descendant[3] will die, and all men that have life.")[4]

"The world will be returned to the old silence for seven days, like as in the former judgments, so that no man will remain. After seven days the world, that still does not awaken will be raised up, and that which is corrupt will die. The earth will restore those who are asleep in her, and so will the dust restore those who live in silence, and the secret places will deliver those minds that were committed to them. The Highest will appear on the seat of judgment, and misery will pass away, as the long patience has ended. Yet judgment will remain, truth will stand, and faith will become strong. The work will follow, and the reward will be shown, and the good deeds will be empowered, and wicked deeds will no longer rule."

Then I replied, "Abraham prayed first for the Sodomites, and Moses for the fathers that sinned in the wilderness, and Joshua after him for Israel in the time of Achan, and Samuel in the days of Saul, and David for the plague, and Solomon for those who should come to the sanctuary, Elijah for those who received rain, and for the dead, that he might live, Hezekiah for the people in the time of Sennacherib, and many others for many others. Even so, now, seeing corruption has grown up, and wickedness increased, and the righteous have prayed for the ungodly, why will it not be so now also?"

He answered me, "This present life is not the end where much glory abides, therefore, they have prayed for the weak. But the day of doom will be the end of this time, and the beginning of the immortality to come, in which corruption has passed. Intemperance is at an end, infidelity is cut off, righteousness is grown, and the truth has sprung up. Then no man will be able to save he who is destroyed, or to oppress he who has achieved victory."

I replied, "This was my first and is my last statement, that it would have been better to have given the Earth to Adam, or else, when it was given him, to have stopped him from sinning. What benefit is it for men now in this present time to live in struggle, and after death to look for punishment? Adam, what have you done? Though it was you who sinned, you have not fallen alone, but all us who come from you. What benefit is it to us, if there is promised us an immortal time, but we have done the works that bring death? Or, that there is promised to us an everlasting hope, but we ourselves being most wicked are made vain?"

"That there are stored up for us, homes of health and safety, but we have lived wickedly? That the glory of the Highest is kept to defend them who have led a wary life, but we have walked in the most wicked ways of all? That there should be shown us a paradise whose fruit endures forever, in which is security and medicine, but we can not enter into it? (For we have walked in unpleasant places.) That the faces of those which have been abstinent will shine above the stars, whereas our faces will be blacker than darkness? For while we lived and committed iniquity, we did not consider that we should begin to expect it after death too."

Then he answered me, "This is the state of the battle which man who is born on the Earth will fight. That, if he is overcome, he will expect what you have said, but if he is victorious, he will receive that which I said. For this is the life of which Moses spoke to the people while he lived, when he said, 'Choose life, that you may live.' Nevertheless, they did not believe him, or even the prophets after him, or me who has also spoken to them. Otherwise, there would not be such heaviness in their destruction, and would be joy over those who are persuaded to salvation."

I replied then, "I know, lord, that the Highest is called merciful, in that he has mercy on those who have not yet come into the world and on those also who follow his law. He is patient, and long permits those who have sinned as his people. He is bountiful, for he is ready to give where it is needed. That he is of great mercy, for he multiplies more and more mercies to those who are present, and those who are past, and also those which are to come. For if he will not multiply his mercies, the world would not continue with those who inherit it. He pardons, for if he did not do so of his goodness, that those who have committed iniquities might be eased of them, and a ten-thousandth division of men should not remain living. Being judge, if he should not forgive those who are cured by his word, and put out the multitude of contentions, there would be very few left from in an innumerable multitude."

Judahite Apocalypse of Ezra: Chapter 5 Notes

1 Codex Ambianensis: Iesus

The Latin name Iesus is a transliteration of the Greek name Iēsoûs (Ἰησοῦς), which is generally assumed to be a Christian addition to the Apocalypse, and sometimes dropped from translations. Nevertheless, the name is used in the Septuagint and therefore could have been in the pre-Christian version of the Apocalypse. According to the books of Ezra, one of these Jesuses was Jesus ben Jehozadak, who accompanied Zerubbabel to Jerusalem, and was the first High Priest of the Second Temple Zerubbabel built according to the writings of Zechariah.

The Hebrew translation of the name was Yeshua (יֵשׁוּעַ) in Ezra-Nehemiah and Yehoshua (יְהוֹשֻׁעַ) in Zechariah. Both these names appear to be popular Judahite names, although there is no specific reference to a descendant of Shealtiel being named one of these names until Jesus ben Joseph. As the original text appears to have been written in Judahite, the name Joshua is used, as it is the common translation of the Hebrew Yehoshua (יְהוֹשֻׁעַ).

2 Codex Ambianensis: Christus

The Latin term is a translation of the Greek word Christos (Χριστός), supporting the text being translated from a Greek copy. The original term is accepted as being either the Judahite mšyt (𐤁𐤆𐤅𐤉), Aramaic meshiah (𐡌𐡔𐡉𐡇), or Hebrew mashach (מְשַׁח), depending on which language one accepts the text as originating in. Both the Greek translation and

71

Semitic terms mean 'anointed,' indicating that this would have been read as a prophecy of a future king of Judah before the Christian era. As the messiah in question was prophesied to be dead for seven days before the dead returned to the earth, this cannot be a reference to Jesus ben Joseph, the Christian messiah, however, was almost certainly a prediction of a king in Jerusalem from the line of Shealtiel. As the author of the Gospel of Luke placed Jesus in the line of Shealtiel via his human father Joseph, it strongly suggests the Apocalypse of Ezra was in use in Judea at the beginning of the 1st century AD.

Based on the internal dating of the text to 557 BC, and the prediction of the era in question being 400 years later, this indicates a date of 157 BC, implying it was reworked in the early Hasmonean dynasty. The Hasmonean dynasty was not descended from the royal family, or the tribe of Judah, which suggests the Apocalypse was used but an anti-Hasmonean faction. If so, this would explain why they never translated a Hebrew copy of the book.

3 Codex Ambianensis: filius

The Latin term translates as 'son,' however, also denotes any male heir. The word is likely a translation of the Greek word huios (υἱός), which also translates as 'son.' The original term was likely either the Judahite word bn (𐤁𐤍), Aramaic word brå (ברא), or Hebrew word ben (בֶּן), depending on which language the book was composed in. All the Semitic versions of the word refer to either a 'son,' or 'male descendant' like the Latin term, and as the prophecy was related to a 400-year reign, it is translated as 'descendant,' in this verse. If the verse was added by Jesus/Jason the son of Simon II, then it would have been read as a scribal note attributed to Simon II, and the word would have been intended as 'son.'

4 As the verse is not found in all versions of the Apocalypse, this sentence is generally accepted as being a Christian era addition, however, the sentence does not make sense in a Christian context. Jesus did not live for 400 years, and as the Apocalypse was translated into Greek circa 100 AD, it is very unlikely to be a prophecy of Jesus being resurrected in 400 AD. Jesus also didn't build a mountain, and scream fire and lightning on the armies of heathens, or bring the lost tribes of Israel back Judea and Samaria. Likely, the sentence was originally part of another prediction of some kind that has been misinterpreted due to the inclusion of the name Jesus.

Based on the concept of a 400-year period, this could have been an edit made by Jesus the son of Simon II, who bribed Greek officials into making him the high priest of the Second Temple in Jerusalem in 175 BC. Simon II was the high priest until his death, which different sources place in 199 or 196 BC, following which his son Onias III became high priest. Both Simon and Onias were recorded as being good high priests, however, Jesus, who changed his name to Jason, disputed Onias' priesthood, and when Onias died in 175 BC, was accepted as the new high priest by the Greek authorities.

In order for Jason to have been accepted by the Greeks, he would have needed to have a significant following in Judea while Onias was still alive, which he is recorded as having. This suggests he had found or manufactured a prophecy that supported his claim over his brother's.

If the 400-year period is read as a reference to the time since the fall of Jerusalem in 587 BC, then the 'prophecy' would have been released at the time of Simon's death in 199/196 BC, suggesting a restoration of the temple would come in 187 BC. This would have likely been added to the existing Judahite copy of the Apocalypse as a scribal note attributed to Simon II, which would have then been interpreted as Simon II's appointment of Jesus over Onias as his heir. Jesus/Jason held very contrary views to Simon and Onias, supporting the Hellenization of the Judeans, and the interpretation of the Greek god Dionysus and Phrygian god Sabazious as the ancestral god of the Israelites Saboath. These views were not widely accepted, and ultimately led to the Maccabbean Revolt, which drove the Greeks and other non-Israelites from Judea.

Judahite Apocalypse of Ezra: Chapter 6

He replied to me, "The Highest has made this world for many, but the world to come for few. I will tell you a riddle, Ezra: When you ask the Earth, it will tell you that it gives a lot of mud which earthen vessels are made of, but very little gold dust comes from it. This is like the pattern of this present world. There will be many created, but few will be saved."

I replied, "May my mind swallow down under-standing and devour wisdom! For you have agreed to listen, and are willing to prophesy, for you no longer have time to live. Lord, if you don't allow your servants to pray before you, and give seed to our heart, and culture to our understanding, that there may come fruit from it, how will each man live who is corrupt? Who bears the place of a man? You are alone, and we are all one work from your hands, as you have said. When the body is created now in the mother's womb, and you give it limbs, your body is preserved in fire and water, and nine months your workmanship endures your body, which is created in her. But that which survives and is protected will be preserved, and when the time comes, the womb delivers up the things that grew in it. You have commanded out of the parts of the body, that is to say, out of the breasts, milk to be given, which is the fruit of the breasts, so that the thing which is created may be nourished for a time, as you dispose it to your mercy. You brought it up with your righteousness, nurtured it in your law, and reformed it with your judgment. You will mortify it like your body, and quicken it like your work. Therefore if you will destroy him, who with such great labor was created, it is an simple thing to be ordained by your command, that the thing which was made might be saved."

"Now, therefore, Lord, I will speak about man in general. You know best, but regarding your people, for whose sake I am sorry, your inheritance, for whose cause I mourn, for Israel, for whom I am heavy, and for Jacob, for whose sake I am troubled, I will begin to pray before you, for myself and for them, for I see the fall of us who live in the land. I have heard the swiftness of the judge which is to come. Therefore, hear my voice, and understand my words, and I will speak to you."

This is the beginning of the words of Ezra before he was taken up.

I said, "Lord, you who live immortally, who sees from above things in the sky and the air, whose throne is inestimable, and whose glory may not be comprehended, before whom the armies of messengers stand with trembling, whose service is conversant in wind and fire, whose word is true, and sayings constant, whose commandment is strong, and ordinance fearful, whose look dries up the depths, and indignation makes the mountains melt away, who witnesses the truth, hear the prayer of your servant, and listen to the petition of your body."

"While I live, I will speak, and if I understand, I will answer. Don't look on the sins of your people, but on those who serve you in truth. Don't consider the wicked inventions of the heathens, but the desire of those who keep your testimonies during plagues. Don't think of those who have pretended to walk before you, but remember them who have feared you. Don't let your will destroy those who have lived like animals, but see those who have clearly taught your law. Don't take indignation at those who are deemed worse than animals, but love those who always put their trust in your righteousness and glory."

"We and our fathers struggle with such diseases, but because of us sinners, you will be called merciful. If you have mercy on us, you will be called merciful to us, who have done no works of righteousness. For the just, which have many good works stored up with you, will out of their own deeds receive the reward. What is man, that you should take displeasure at him? What is a corruptible generation, that you should be so bitter toward it? In truth, no man among them is born that has not dealt wickedly, and among the faithful, there are none which have not done incorrectly. For in this, Lord, your righteousness and your goodness will be declared, if you are merciful to those which have no confidence in good works."

Then he answered me, and said, "Some things you have said are correct, and according to your words it will be. For indeed, I will not think about the disposition of those who have sinned before death, before judgment, and before destruction. I will rejoice over the disposition of the righteous, and I will remember also their pilgrimage, and the salvation, and the reward, that they have. As I have spoken now, so will it come to pass. As the farmer sows much seed on the ground, and plants many trees, yet the thing that is sown well in his season does not come up, neither does all that is planted take root. Likewise are those who are sown in the world. They will not all be saved."

I replied, "If I have found grace, let me speak. As the farmer's seed perishes, if it does not come up and does not receive your rain in due season, or, if there comes too much rain, and destroys it, likewise man also perishes, who is formed with your hands, and is created in your own image, because you are likewise for him, for whose sake you have made all things, and compared him to the farmer's seed. Do not be angry with us but spare your people, and have mercy on your own inheritance, for you are merciful to your body."

Then he answered me, and said, "Things that are present are for the present and things to come, for that which will come. You fall short that you should be able to love my body more than I, but I have oftentimes drawn near to you, and to it, but never to the unrighteous. In this, also, you are marvelous before the Highest. Because you have humiliated yourself, as it becomes you, and have not judged yourself worthy to be greatly glorified among the righteous. For many great miseries will be done to those in the latter times who will live in the world, because they have walked in great pride. But understand yourself, and seek out the glory for those who are like you. Paradise is opened to you. The tree of life is planted. The time to come is prepared. Abundance is made ready. A city is built, and peace is allowed. Yes, perfect goodness and wisdom. The root of evil is sealed up from you, weakness and the moth are hidden from you, and corruption has fled into the depths of the Earth to be forgotten. Sorrows are passed, and in the end, is shown the treasure of immortality."

"Therefore, ask no more questions concerning the multitude of those who perish, for when they had freedom, they hated the Highest, and thought to mock his law, and forgot his ways. Moreover, they have trodden down his righteous, and said in their heart, 'There is no God,' yes, and so they must die. As for the things previously asked, you will receive, but thirst and pain are prepared for them, for it was not his will that men should come to nothing. They who were created have defiled the name of him that made them and were thankful to him who prepared life for them. Therefore, my judgment now at hand. These things have I not showed to all men, but to you, and a few like you."

Then I replied, "Look, Lord, now have you showed me a multitude of the wonders, which you will begin to do in the last times, but when this is, you have not told me."

Judahite Apocalypse of Ezra: Chapter 7

He answered me then, saying, "Measure the time diligently in itself, and when you see some of the signs happen, which I have mentioned before, then you will understand, that it is the time when the Highest will begin to visit the world that he made. Therefore, when there are earthquakes and uproars among the people in the world, then you will understand that the Highest predicted things from the days that were before you, even from the beginning. As all that is made in the world has a beginning and an end, and the end is manifest. Likewise, the times of the Highest also have a beginning to the wonders and powerful works, and an ending to effects and signs."

"Everyone that will be saved, and will be able to escape through his works, and by faith, which you have believed, and will be saved from the said perils and will see my salvation in my land, and within my borders, for I have sanctified them for myself from the beginning. Then those who now abuse, my ways will be in a pitiful place, and those who have thrown them away hatefully will live in torment. Those that in their life have received benefits, and have not known me, and those who have loathed my law while they still had freedom, and, when yet a place of repentance remained for them, did not understood, but hated it, they must know it after death, through suffering. Therefore, don't be curious how the ungodly will be punished, or when, but inquire how the righteous will be saved, who the world is for, and for whom the world was created."

Then I replied, "I have said before, and now state again, and will say it also from now on, that there are many more of them which perish than those which will be saved, much like a wave is greater than a drop."

He answered, "As the field is, so is the seed. As the flowers are, such are the colors. The workman is, also the work is. As the farmer is himself, so his farm is also, for it was the time of the world. When I prepared the world, which was not yet made, for them who now live to live in, no man spoke against me. Then, everyone obeyed, but now the manners of those who are created in this world are corrupted by a perpetual seed, and by a law which is unsearchable, and they rule themselves. So I considered the world, and, look, there was peril because of the devices that came into it. I saw and spared it, and have kept a cluster of grapes, and a plant of a great people."

"Let the multitude perish then who were born in vain, and let my grape be kept, and my plant, for with great labor have I made it perfect. Nevertheless, if you will stop another seven days more, (but you will not fast in them, and go into a field of flowers, where no house is built, and eat only the flowers of the field. Eat no meat and drink no wine, but eat flowers only,) and pray to the Highest continually, then I will come and talk with you."

"So I went into the field which is called Ardat,[1] as he commanded me, and there I sat among the flowers and ate the plants of the field, and the flesh of them satisfied me. After the seven days that I sat on the grass, my heart was troubled within me, like before, and I opened my mouth, and began to talk before the Highest, and said, "Lord, you who showed yourself to us, you were showed to our fathers in the wilderness, in a place where no man treads, in a barren place, when they came out of Egypt. You spoke saying, 'Hear me, Israel, and record my words, seed of Jacob. Look, I sow my law in you, and it will bring fruit in you, and you will be honored in it forever.' But our fathers, which received the law, did not keep it or follow your ordinances, and though the fruit of your law did not die, nor could it as it was yours, they who received it perished because they did not keep that which was sown in them. It is a custom when the ground has received seed, or the sea received a ship, or any vessel food or drink, that, having perished in whatever it was sown or thrown into, that thing which was also sown or thrown into it, or received does also perish, and does not remain with us. Yet with us, it has not happened like this. We who have received the law perish through sin, and our hearts also receive it. Nevertheless, the law does not perish, but remains in force."

As I said these things in my heart, I looked around with my eyes, and to the right, I saw a woman, mourning and weeping loudly, and was greatly grieved in my heart. Her clothes were ripped, and she had ashes on her head. I had thoughts and turned to her, asking, "Why do you cry? Why is your mind so grieved?"

She answered me, "Sir, leave me alone, that I may cry by myself, and add to my sorrow, for I am greatly hurt in my mind, and brought very low."

I asked her, "What ails you? Tell me."

She answered me, "I, your servant, have been barren and had no child, though I had a husband for thirty years. In those thirty years I did nothing else day and night, and every hour, but pray to the Highest. After thirty years God heard me, your handmaid, and looked on my misery, considered my trouble, and gave me a son, and I was very grateful for him, as was my husband, and also all my neighbors, and we greatly praised the Almighty. I nursed him with great trouble. When he grew up, and it came time that he should have a wife, I made a feast."

Judahite Apocalypse of Ezra: Chapter 7 Notes

1 Codex Ambianensis: Ardat

- Manuscript B.21: amdt (ܐܡܕ)

Scholars have debated the meaning of Ardat for over a thousand years. It is not a Hebrew word and it is not Latin or Greek either. It is also mentioned in some medieval Islamic literature, however, those references do not clarify it and could be based on its mention in the Apocalypse of Ezra. The name is probably based on a Judahite transliteration of the name Uruda (ܐܪܘܕ) meaning 'copper.' Proper names were often feminized in Judahite to denote geographical locations, which would explain the -t (ܬ) ending. The one surviving Syriac manuscript has the transliteration of Amdt (ܐܡܕ), which could have resulted from a scribal error of Awrdt (ܐܘܪܕ), which is likely also what the Greek and later translations were based on.

Some believe the term is referring to 'Arzah' mentioned in the Bundahishn, the Zoroastrian book of creation. In the Bundahishn the world is described as being composed of seven 'divisions of land,' the western known as Arzah. There is no clear scholarly consensus that Ardat is based on Azrah, but those who promote the predominance of Persian thought in this text use the Ardat-Arzah connection to validate their claims. The problem with the Ardat-Arzah connection is that the Bundahishn is believed to date to after the 7th century AD, while the Apocalypse of Ezra is believed to date to the 1st century AD at the latest.

The Babylonians are known to have grown large amounts of poppies in the plains around Babylon, which may be the flower that Ezra was eating. Poppies have been used to create opioid-based medicines in the Middle East since at least 1600 BC, however, eating them would give one a significant hallucination. Several cults in the region and across the Mediterranean used poppies and blue lilies to induce visions among their adherents. The idea that Ezra was eating poppies is not new and believed to have been one of the main unwritten reasons the Apocalypse of Ezra was rejected by the Byzantine Orthodox Church, which attempted to remove the use of poppies and blue lilies in religious practices.

Judahite Apocalypse of Ezra: Chapter 8

"It happened, that when my son had entered into his wedding chamber, he fell down, and died. Then we extinguished all the lights, and all my neighbors rose up to comfort me. So I took my rest on the second day at night. It happened when they had all left from comforting me, so I might be quiet, then I got up at night and fled, and came here into this field, as you see. I don't intend to return to the city, but to stay here, and neither to eat or drink, but constantly to mourn and fast until I die."

Then I stopped the meditation I was doing, and yelled at her, "You are a stupid woman! More than any other! Don't you see our mourning, and what happened to us? How Zion our mother is full of all heaviness, and humiliated, mourning very sorely? Now, seeing we all mourn and are sad, we are all in heaviness, you are sad for one son? Ask the Earth, and she will tell you that it is she who should mourn for the fall of so many that grow in number in her. Out of her came all in the beginning, and out of her will all others come, and, see, they walk almost all into destruction, and many of them are completely forgotten. Who then should mourn more than she, that has lost so great a multitude, and not you, who are but sad for one?"

"But if you say to me, 'My lamentation is not like the Earth's, because I have lost the fruit of my womb, which I brought out with pains, and bare with sorrows, but the Earth is not so, for the multitude present in it, according to the course of the Earth has gone as it came,' then I will reply to you, like you have brought out with labor, even so, the Earth also has given her fruit, namely, man, ever since the beginning to he that made her. Now, therefore, keep your sorrow to yourself, and carry with good courage that which has happened to you. For if you will acknowledge the judgment of God is just, you will both receive your sons in time and will be commended among women. Go back to the city, to your husband."

She replied to me, "I will not do that! I will not go to the city, I will die here!"

I continued to speak to her, and said, "Do not, but listen to me, for how many adversities of Zion are there? Be comforted regarding the sorrow of Jerusalem. For you see that our sanctuary is laid waste, our altar broken down, our temple destroyed, our psaltery is laying on the ground, our song is put to silence, our rejoicing is at an end, the light of our candlestick is put out, the ark of our covenant is spoiled, our holy things are defiled, and the name that we are called by is almost profaned. Our children are put to shame, our priests are burnt, our Levites have gone into captivity, our virgins are defiled, our wives raped, our righteous men carried away, our little ones destroyed, our young men are taken into slavery, and our strong men have become weak, and, which is the greatest of all? The seal of Zion has now lost her honor, for she is delivered into the hands of those who hate us. Therefore shake off your great heaviness, and put away the multitude of sorrows, that the Mighty may be merciful to you again, and the Highest will give you rest and ease from your labor."

While I was talking with her, her face suddenly shined brightly, and her countenance glistened, so much that I was afraid of her, and considered what it might be. Suddenly she cried out very fearfully so that the earth shook at the noise of the woman. I looked and saw, and the woman no longer appeared to me, but there was a city built, and a large place showed itself from the foundations, and then I was afraid, and cried with a loud voice, and said, "Where is Uriel the messenger, who came to me before? As he has caused me to fall into many trances, and my end has turned to corruption, and my prayer to be rebuked."

As I was speaking these words look, he came to me and looked at me, and I fell as one that had been dead, and my understanding was taken from me, and he took me by the right hand, and comforted me, and set me on my feet, and said to me, "What troubles you? Why are you so disturbed? Why is your understanding troubled, and the thoughts of your heart?"

I answered, "Because you have forgotten me, yet I did according to your words, and I went into the field, and I have seen, and still see, that which I am not able to express."

He replied to me, "Stand up bravely, and I will advise you."

Then I said, "Speak, my lord, through me. Only don't forsake me, in case I die frustrated in my hope, for I have seen what I didn't understand, and hear what I do not understand. Or is my sense deceived, or my mind in a dream? Now, therefore, I beg that you explain to your servant this vision."

He answered me then, "Hear me, and I will inform you, and tell you, and therefore you are afraid for the Highest will reveal many secret things to you. He has seen that your way is correct, for you mourn continually for your people, and make great lamentation for Zion. This, therefore, is the meaning of the vision which you recently saw."

"You saw a woman mourning, and you began to comfort her, but now you no longer see the image of the woman, but there appears to you a built city. When she told you of the death of her son, this is the explanation:

this woman who you saw is Zion, and when she said to you, even she who you see as a built city. When I say, she said to you, that she has been thirty years barren, those are the thirty years in which there was no offering made in her. But after thirty years, Solomon built the city and offered sacrifices, and then carried the barren son. When she told you that she nursed him with labor, that was the living in Jerusalem. But when she said to you, 'That my son coming into his marriage chamber happened to fall, and died, this was the destruction that came to Jerusalem. See, you saw her likeness, and because she mourned for her son, you began to comfort her, and of these things which have chanced, these are to be opened to you. For now, the Highest sees that you are grieved honestly, and from your whole heart for her, so he has shown you the brightness of her glory, and the comeliness of her beauty."

"Therefore I commanded you to remain in the field where no house was built, for I knew that the Highest would show this to you. Therefore, I commanded you to go into the field, where no foundation of any building was. For in the place in which the Highest begins to show his city, no man's building can stand. Therefore, don't be afraid, don't let your heart be in fear, but go on your way, and see the beauty and greatness of the building, as much as your eyes can see. Then you will hear as much as your ears may understand. You are blessed above many others and are called by the Highest. Only a few are. But tomorrow at night you will remain here, so the Highest showed you visions of the high things, which the Highest will do for those who lived on the Earth in previous days."

So I slept that night and another, as he had commanded me.

Judahite Apocalypse of Ezra: Chapter 9

Then I saw a dream and saw there came up from the sea an eagle, which had twelve feathered wings, and three heads. I watched, and she spread her wings over all the earth, and all the winds of the air blew on her and were gathered together. I saw out of her feathers there grew other contrary feathers, and they became little feathers and small. But her heads were at peace, and the head in the middle was greater than the others yet it rested with the others. Moreover, I saw the eagle fly with her feathers and reigned on earth, and over those who dwelt on it. I saw that all things under the sky were subject to her, and no man spoke against her, no, not one body on earth. I watched, and the eagle rose on her talons, and said to her feathers, "Don't watch all at once. Everyone sleeps in his own place and watches in turns. But let the heads be saved for the last."

I saw, and, the voice did not come out of her head, but from the middle of her body. I counted her contrary feathers, and there were eight of them. I looked, on the right side and there arose another feather, and reigned over all the earth. It was so, that when it reigned the end of it came, and the place of it appeared no longer, so the next one following it stood up and reigned, and had a great time. It happened, that when it reigned the end of it also came, like as the first so that it appeared no longer.

Then a voice came to it there, and said, "Hear, those of you who have ruled over the Earth for so long, this I say to you before you begin to disappear, there will be none after you to rule as long as your time, not even half of it."

Then the third arose and reigned like the others before, and appeared no more also. So it went with all the rest, one after another, and everyone that reigned, appeared no longer. Then I saw, in the passage of time, the feathers that followed stood up on the right side that they might rule also, and some of them ruled, but after a while, they appeared no more for some of them were set up but did not rule.

After this, I saw the twelve feathers appeared no longer, nor the two little feathers. There were no more on the eagle's body, but three heads that rested, and six little wings. Then I saw also that two little feathers divided themselves from the six, and remained under the head that was on the right side, for the four continued in their place. I saw the feathers that were under the wing, thought about setting up themselves to rule. I saw there was one set up, but shortly it appeared no more. The second was sooner gone than the first. I saw the two that remained also thought themselves to reign. When they so thought, one of the heads that were at rest woke, specifically, the middle one, as it was greater than the two other heads. Then I saw that the two other heads joined with it. And the head turned with the others and ate up the two feathers under the wing that would have reigned. This head put the whole Earth in fear and ruled over it and all those who dwelt on the Earth with much oppression, and it had greater governance of the world than all the wings that had been."

After this, I saw the head that was in the middle suddenly disappear like the wings had, but there remained the two heads, which also in similar kind ruled over the earth, and over those who dwelt in it. I saw the head on the right side devoured the one that was on the left. Then I heard a voice, which said to me, "Look before you, and consider the thing that you see."

I saw as it were, a roaring lion run out of the forest, and I saw that he said in a man's voice to the eagle, "Listen, I will talk with you, and the Highest will say to you, 'Are you not it that remains of the four beasts that I made to reign in my world, that the end of times might come through them?"

The fourth came and conquered the beasts that were before, and had power over the world with great fearfulness, and over the whole compass of the Earth with a great deal of wicked oppression, and so, for a long time, he lived on the Earth with deceit, for the Earth you have not judged with truth. You have afflicted the meek, you have hurt the peaceable, you have loved liars and destroyed the dwellings of those who brought out fruit, and have thrown down the walls of those that did you no harm. Therefore, your wrongful dealings come up to the Highest, and your pride to the Mighty. The Highest has also looked on the proud times, and they are ended and his abominations are fulfilled. Therefore, appear no more, you eagle, nor your horrible wings, nor your wicked feathers nor your malicious heads, nor your hurtful claws, nor all your vain body, so that all the Earth may be refreshed, and may be restored, being delivered from your violence, and that she may hope for the judgment and mercy of him that made her."

Judahite Apocalypse of Ezra: Chapter 10

It happened, while the lion said these words to the eagle, I saw the head that remained and the four wings disappear, and the two went to it and set themselves up to reign, and their kingdom was small, and filled with uproar. I saw they appeared no longer, and the whole body of the eagle was burned so that the Earth was in great fear. Then I awoke out of the troubled trance of my mind, and from great fear, and asked my spirit, "This you have done to me, in that you search out the ways of the Highest? Yet am I weary in my mind, and very weak in my spirit, and little strength is there in me, for the great fear where I was afflicted this night. Therefore, I will now beg the Highest that he will comfort me to the end."

I said, "Dominating Lord, if I have found grace before your sight, and if I am justified with you before many others, and if my prayer indeed has come up before your face, comfort me and show me, your servant, the interpretation and understanding of this fearful vision, that you may perfectly comfort my mind. You have judged me worthy to show me the last times."

He said to me, "This is the interpretation of the vision. The eagle that you saw come up from the sea, is the kingdom which was seen in the vision of your brother Daniel. But it was not explained to him, therefore now I explain it to you. Look, the days will come, that there will rise up a kingdom on Earth, and it will be feared above all the kingdoms that were before it. In this land, twelve kings reigned, one after another.[1] When the second begins to reign, he has more time than any of the twelve. This is what the twelve wings that you saw mean."

"As for the voice which you heard speak, and that you didn't see go out from the heads but from the middle of the body, this is the interpretation: After the time of that kingdom, there will come great struggle, and it will stand in peril of failing, nevertheless it will not fall then but will be restored again like its beginning." [2]

"When you saw the eight small under feathers sticking to her wings, this is the interpretation: That in it there will arise eight kings,[3] whose times will be short and their years swift. Two of them will perish, the middle time approaching, four will be kept until their end begins to approach, but two will be kept to the end."

"When you saw three heads resting, this is the interpretation: In the last days the Highest will raise up three kingdoms,[4] and renew many things within them, and they will have dominion over the Earth, and of those who live on it through much oppression, greater than those who who were before them, therefore they are called the heads of the eagle. These are those who will accomplish his wickedness, and that will finish his last end. When you saw the great head disappear, it signified that one of them would die on his bed, but in pain. The two that remain will be slain with the sword, as the sword of the one will devour the other, but the last will fall through the sword himself."[5]

"When you saw two feathers under the wings passing over the head that is on the right side, it signifies that these are those who the Highest has kept to their end. This is a small kingdom and full of trouble, as you saw. The lion that you saw rising up out of the forest, and roaring and speaking to the eagle, and rebuking her for her unrighteousness, with all the words you heard. This is the anointed, which the Highest has saved for them and for their wickedness to the end, and he will reprimand them and will find them guilty of their cruelty. He will set them before him alive in judgment and will rebuke them, and correct them. He will deliver with mercy the rest of my people, those who have been pressed on my borders, and he will make them joyful until the coming of the day of judgment when I have spoken to you from the beginning."

"This is the dream that you saw, and these are the interpretations. Only you have been allowed to know this secret of the Highest, therefore, write all these things that you have seen in a book, and hide them. Teach them to the wisest of the people, whose hearts you know may comprehend and keep these secrets. But wait here another seven days, that it may be shown to you whatever it pleases the Highest to tell you."

With that, he went his way. It happened when all the people saw that the seven days had passed, and I had not come back to the city, they gathered all together, from the least to the greatest, and came to me, and said, "How have we offended you? What evil have we done against you, that you forget us, and sit here in this place? Of all the prophets, only you are left to us, like a grape cluster to the wine, and like a candle in a dark place, and like a haven to save a ship from the storm. Are the evils that have come against us not sufficient? If you forsake us, how much better had it been for us, if we also had been burned in Zion? We are not better than those who died there."

They wept in a loud voice, and then I answered them, and said, "Be of good comfort, Israel, and do not be heavy, you house of Jacob. For the Highest has you in his memory, and the Mighty has not forgotten you in temptation. As for me, I have not forgotten you, nor have I departed from you, but have come into this place to pray regarding the desolation of Zion, that I might seek mercy for the low state of your sanctuary. Now, go back home everyone, and after these days I will return to you.

So the people went their way into the city, as I commanded them, but I remained in the field another seven days as the messenger had commanded me, and ate only the flowers of the field in those days, and had my food from the plants.

Judahite Apocalypse of Ezra: Chapter 10 Notes

1 The reference to the kingdom that ruled the world which was ruled by a succession of 12 kings, is likely the Persian Empire. Not counting the interloper Gaumata, whom Darius I killed, there were twelve recognized kings of the Achaemenid Persian Empire: Cyrus II, Cambyses II, Darius I, Xerxes I, Artaxerxes I, Xerxes II, Darius II, Artaxerxes II, Artaxerxes III, Artaxerxes IV, Darius III, and Artaxerxes V. The later kings did generally have shorter reigns than the earlier kings, however, Cambyses II's reign was not the longest.

2 This is likely a reference to the Great Satraps' Revolt of 372 to 362 BC, when King Artaxerxes II recalled Nehemiah, the military commander of Jerusalem, to help suppress the rebellion. During the Great Satraps' Revolt, most of Anatolia and Armenia became independent, under the control of the former Persian satraps (governors), backed by the king of Egypt. The revolt threatened to spread to the rest of Persia and took ten years to suppress. Ultimately, Artaxerxes II managed to restore Persian authority to Armenia and Anatolia, however, for several years it appeared that the Persian empire was breaking up.

3 The reference to the eight little kings appears to be a reference to the brief government of Alexander's empire after his death. At the time, the most powerful men in the empire were Alexander's mentally challenged brother

Arridaeus, and the seven Somatophylakes, Alexander's bodyguards. There was great debate on whether Arridaeus or Alexander's unborn child was the rightful heir, and the Somatophylakes debated whether to wait for the child to be born or make Arridaeus the king. Ultimately the debate, and long-established rivalries within the army led to the government collapsing into the Wars of the Diadochi (successors).

4 The reference to the three kingdoms that would rise up after the collapse of Alexander's empire, would be the kingdoms of Lysimachus, Ptolemy, and Seleucus, the three generals who fought for control of the former Persian Empire in the Wars of the Diadochi, ultimately forming their own empires. There was a fourth general, Cassander, however, his kingdom was limited to Macedonia, and never seriously challenged the other three.

5 The three major Diadochi kings all died around the same time, in 282 and 281 BC. Ptolemy I Soter, who was the oldest, died in 282 BC at the age of 85. It isn't clear if he died in bed, but that is a likely scenario, as he had established a secure kingdom for his heirs, and his authority had been passed to his son Ptolemy II Philadelphus. Lysimachus and Seleucus I Nicator both died the following year in battle, suggesting that either this prophecy, or this interpretation of the prophecy, dates to shortly after that, as there are no additional kings mentioned after that.

The small struggling kingdom that is predicted to follow suggests an independence movement in Judea circa 280 BC, which would have been during the time of the High Priest Onias I. The books of the Maccabees refer to letters exchanged between Onias and the Spartans and Romans, supporting an attempt to forge an independent Judea, however, the attempt appears to have failed, as Judea appears to have been firmly part of the Ptolemys' empire until 200 BC.

Judahite Apocalypse of Ezra: Chapter 11

It happened after seven days, I dreamed a vision at night, "And, there arose a wind from the sea, that moved all the waves. I saw that a man came, strong as the thousands of the sky, and when he turned his countenance to look, all the things that were seen under him trembled. Whenever the voice came out of his mouth, all those who heard his voice burned like the Earth fails when she feels the fire. After this I saw there was gathered together a multitude of men beyond counting, from the four winds of the sky, to subdue the man that came out of the sea. But I saw he had created himself a great mountain, and flew up onto it. I would have seen the region or land where the hill was created, but I could not. After this, I saw all those who were gathered together to subdue him were greatly afraid and yet fought. And as he saw the violence of the multitude that came, he neither lifted his hand nor held a sword or any weapon of war.

But I saw that he only sent out of his mouth a blast of fire, and out of his lips a flaming breath, and out of his tongue, he threw out sparks and lightning. They were all mixed together; the blast of fire, the flaming breath, and the great lightning, and fell with violence on the multitude which was prepared to fight, and burned them up, everyone, so that suddenly an uncountable multitude disappeared, but only dust and smell of smoke remained. When I saw this I was afraid. Afterward, I saw the same man come down from the mountain, and call to himself a peaceful multitude. Many people came to him, some of whom were glad, some were sorry, some of them were bound, and others brought from those who were offered.

Then I was sick through great fear, and I awoke, and said, "You have shown your servant these wonders from the beginning, and have counted me worthy that you should receive my prayer. Show me now the interpretation of this dream, for as I consider it in my understanding, woe to those who will be left in those days, and much more woe to those who are not left behind! Those who were not left, were in heaviness. Now I understand the things that are planned for the latter days, what will happen to them, and to those who are left behind. Therefore, they have come into great perils and many necessities, as these dreams show. Yet it is easier for he who is in danger to come into these things than to pass away out of the world like a cloud, and not to see the things that happen in the last days."

He answered me, "The interpretation of the vision I will show you, and I will explain to you the thing that you have required. You have asked of those who are left behind, and this is the interpretation: He who will endure the peril in that time has kept himself. They who are fallen into danger are such as have works and faith toward the Almighty. Know this, therefore, that they who are left behind are more blessed than those who are dead."

"This is the meaning of the vision: When you saw a man coming up from the middle of the sea, he is who the Highest God has saved a long time, who by his own self will deliver his body, and he will organize those who are left behind."

"When you saw, that out of his mouth there came as blast of wind, fire, and lightning, that he held neither sword, nor any weapon of war, but that the blast from him destroyed the whole multitude that came to subdue him, this is the interpretation: The days come, when the Highest will begin to save those who are on the Earth. He will come to the astonishment of those who live on the Earth. One will fight against another, one city against another, one place against another, one people against another, and one realm against another."

"The time will be when these things will come to pass, and the signs will happen which I showed you before, and then my son will be declared, whom you saw as a man ascending. When all the people hear his voice, every man will leave the battle they have one against another in their own land. An uncountable multitude will be gathered together, as you saw them, willing to come and overcome him by fighting. But he will stand on the top of Mount Zion. Zion will come and will be shown to all men, being prepared and built, as you saw the hill built without hands. My son will rebuke the wicked inventions of those nations, which for their wicked life, will fallen to the tempest, and will lay before them their evil thoughts, and the torments where they will begin to be tormented, which are like a flame, and he will destroy them without trouble through the law which is like fire."

"When you saw that he gathered a peaceable multitude to him, those are the ten tribes, which were carried away prisoners out of their own land in the time of Hoshea the king, who Shalmaneser[1] the king of Assyria led away captive, and he carried them over the waters, and so they came into another land. But they took this counsel among themselves, that they would leave the multitude of the heathens, and go out into a further country, where mankind never lived before, that they might keep their laws there, which they never kept in their own land."

"They entered the Euphrates by the narrow places of the river. For the Highest showed signs for them then, and held still the water until they were passed over. Through that country, there was a great road to follow, a year and a half long, and the same region is called the land of Herat.[2] Then they lived there until the latter times, and now when they will begin to return, the Highest will stop the springs of the stream again, that they may go through, therefore you saw the multitude in peace. But those who are left behind of your people, are those who are found within my borders. When he destroys the multitude of the nations that are gathered together, he will defend his people that remain. Then he will show them great wonders."

Then I asked, "Dominating Lord, show me this. Why have I seen the man coming up from the middle of the sea?"

He answered me, "As you can neither search out nor understand the things that are in the deep of the sea, even so, can no man on Earth see my son or those who are with him, except in those days. This is the interpretation of the dream which you saw, and which you only are now enlightened. You have forgotten your own way, and applied your diligence to my law, and researched it. Your life you have centered on wisdom, and have searched for understanding about your mother. Therefore, I have shown you the treasures of the Highest. After another three days, I will speak other things to you, and tell you of mighty and wondrous things."

Then I went out into the field, praising and thanking greatly the Highest because of the wonders which he did over time, and because he governs the same way and things happen in their seasons.

I sat there for three days.

Judahite Apocalypse of Ezra: Chapter 11 Notes

1 Codex Sangermanensis: Salmanassar rex Assyriorum

This king is commonly considered to be Shalmaneser V today. King Shalmaneser V, was the son and heir to King Tiglath-Pileser III, who ruled the Assyrian Empire between 727 and 722 BC. Prior to becoming king, he was the governor of Zimirra in Phoenicia.

2 Codex Sangermanensis: Arzaret

It is unclear where or even if this country existed. The land of Arzaret, often anglicized as Arsareth was historically identified by Christians as being in the Northern Caucasus mountains on the Black Sea coast, in the vicinity of modern Abkhazia, Krasnodar Kray, and Adygea. The traditional Jewish interpretation is that this is a corruption of another word such as 'eretz (אָרֶץ) meaning Earth or land. Nevertheless, wherever they would have gone, there would have already been people there by the 700s BC. It is plausible that the name originated in the term 'land of Herat,' which should have been rendered as års hråt (𐤕𐤀𐤓𐤄 𐤓𐤀𐤑) in Judahite. Herat is a city in western Afghanistan that has existed for thousands of years, however, it is unclear when it was founded. The earliest Old Persian records of the land called it Haraiva (𐎛𐎼𐎈𐎺𐎡𐎹), and date to around 500 BC, however, it is not clear if a city was in the region at the time. The region is named after the Hari (𐤄𐤓𐤉) river, which is generally accepted as being the Hari river from the Vedic

111

Texts, meaning the name would have been established before the Neo-Babylonian era.

Judahite Apocalypse of Ezra: Chapter 12

It happened on the third day, as I sat under an oak, a voice came out of a bush to me, and called, "Ezra, Ezra."

I answered, "I am here, Lord," and I stood up.

Then he said to me, "Through a bush, I revealed myself to Moses, and talked with him when my people served in Egypt. I sent him and led my people out of Egypt, and brought him up to the mountain where I kept him with me a long time and told him many wondrous things, and showed him the secrets of the times, and the end, and commanded him, 'These words you will tell others, but these others you will keep to yourself.' Now I say to you, that you lay up in your heart the signs that I have shown, and the dreams that you have seen, and the interpretations which you have heard. You will be taken away from all, and from now on you will remain with my son, and with others like you, until the end times. The world has lost his youth, and time begins to grow old. The world is divided into twelve parts, and the ten parts of it are gone already, and half of a tenth part. What remains is that which is after the half of the tenth part. Now, therefore, set your house in order, reprove your people, comfort those who are in trouble, renounce corruption, and let go of mortal thoughts, throw away the burdens of man, put off the weak nature, and set aside the thoughts that are most heavy to you, and rush to escape these times."

"Yet greater evils than those which you have seen happen will be done from now on. Look how much the world will be weakened through age, so that much more evil will increase against those who live on it. Time is fled far away, and work is hard at hand. As is, the vision of that to come, which you have seen."

Then I answered, "Look, Lord, I will go as you have commanded, and chastise the people which are present today, but they who will be born afterward, who will admonish them? So the world is set in darkness, and those who live within it are without light. Your law is burnt, and therefore no man knows the things that are done by you or the work that will begin. But, if I have found grace before you, send holy spirit into me, and I will write all that has been done in the world since the beginning, which was written in your law, that men may find your path, and that they who will live in the latter days may live."

He answered me, saying, "Go on your way, gather the people together, and say to them that they should not seek you for forty days. Prepare many box trees, and take with you Sarea, Dabria, Selemia, Ecanus, and Asiel, the five who are ready to write quickly. Come here, and

I will light a candle of understanding in your heart, which will not be put out until the things have happened which you will begin to write. When you have done this, some things you will publish, and some things you will reveal secretly to the wise. Tomorrow, at this hour you will begin to write."

Then I went out, as he commanded, and gathered all the people together, and said, "Hear these words, Israel. Our fathers, in the beginning, were foreigners in Egypt, which they were delivered from, and received the law of life, which they did not keep, and which you have also transgressed like them. Then the land of Zion was divided among you by lot, but your fathers and you yourselves, have acted unrighteousness, and have not kept the ways which the Highest commanded you. As he is a righteous judge, after some time he took back the thing that he had given you. Now you are here, and your brothers among you. Therefore, if you will subdue your own understanding, and reform your hearts, you will be kept alive and after death, you will obtain mercy. After death, the judgment will come when we live again, and then the names of the righteous will be known, and the works of the ungodly will be declared. Let no man, therefore, come to me now, or seek me for these forty days."

I took the five men, as he commanded me, and we went into the field and remained there. The next day, a voice called to me, "Ezra, open your mouth, and drink the drink that I give you."

Then I opened my mouth, and he handed me a cup full of something like water, but its color was like fire. I took it and drank, and after I had drunk of it, my heart spoke understanding, and wisdom grew in my chest, for my spirit strengthened my memory, and my mouth was opened and shut no longer. The Highest gave understanding to the five men, and they wrote down the wonderful visions that were shown that night, which they did not previously know. They sat for forty days and they wrote all day, and at night they ate bread. As for me. I spoke all day, and I did not stop at night. Over forty days they wrote nine hundred and four books.

It happened, when the forty days were over, that the Highest said, "The first that you have written publish openly, that the worthy and unworthy may both read it. However, keep the last seventy, that you may give them only to those who are wise among the people, for in them is the spring of understanding, the fountain of wisdom, and the stream of knowledge."

This I did.

Forward to the Latin Apocalypse of Ezra

In 1592, Pope Clement VIII's creation of a Catholic Bible added a version of the Apocalypse of Ezra to the Catholic Bible under the name 4th Esdras. Esdras was the direct Latin transliteration of the Greek version of Ezra's name: Ἔσδρας. During the Protestant Reformation, the Catholic book of 4th Esdras was renamed 2nd Esdras, as it continues to be listed in Protestant Bibles that include it.

Unfortunately, the Latin translation of the Apocalypse of Ezra that Clement added to the Catholic Vulgate included the shorter Latin Apocalypse of Ezra, resulting in the Catholic and Protestant Bibles having longer, and self-contradicting versions of the apocalypse in comparison to Orthodox Bibles. The Latin translation of the Judahite Apocalypse of Ezra did circulate for centuries without the addition of the shorter Latin Apocalypse of Ezra, as evidenced by the Slavonic translation, which is believed to have been translated from Latin and not Greek.

The shorter Latin Apocalypse of Ezra has become fused with the Judahite Apocalypse of Ezra in most Catholic and Protestant translations, however, scholars divide the Catholic version of 4th Esdras (Protestant 2nd Esdras) into three sections, with only the core twelve chapters that correspond to the Orthodox and Ethiopian versions of the book labeled as 4th Ezra. The opening two chapters, which are only found in the Catholic version, are labeled as 5th Ezra, while the last 2 chapters found in the Catholic version, as well as fragments surviving in an ancient Greek translation, are labeled 6th Ezra. 5th Ezra and 6th Ezra appear to have originally been one document, which is commonly called the Latin Apocalypse of Ezra, although it was almost certainly not written in Latin.

There is no consensus of when the Latin Apocalypse of Ezra was written, however, it appears to be an early Christian era reworking of an Aramaic Apocalypse. The Apocalypse's claim to being the second book of the prophet Ezra implies that the author was positioning it as the sequel to the Judahite Apocalypse of Ezra, and as such it does not repeat the same material as the Judahite Apocalypse, unlike some of the other apocalypses. 5th and 6th Ezra appear to have been in circulation together before being united with the Judahite apocalypse but do not appear to have originated as one text. 5th Ezra appears to be a Greco-Roman era introduction to the older 6th Ezra prophecy, which reattributes it to Ezra the scribe as the author does not appear to have understood that they were two different people who lived centuries apart.

In chapters 1 and 2 of the apocalypse, which is 5th Ezra, the author claims to be Ezra the scribe and gives his genealogy, which is found in the books of Ezra from the

Masoretic text and Septuagint, however, then claims he had been held captive in Media during the time of Artaxerxes. While Ezra the scribe did live during the reign of a king named Artaxerxes, neither of the Ezras were recorded as being held captive in Media. The Shealtiel that was also called Ezra from the Judahite Apocalypse is usually considered the same Shealtiel who returned from Babylon to rebuild Jerusalem after the Persians conquered Babylon, while Ezra the scribe also reported living in the city of Babylon before returning to Jerusalem.

Chapter 3 and the beginning of chapter 4 of the apocalypse, the bulk of 6th Ezra, appear to be much older and describe a world that the author of the longer apocalypse did not seem to understand. The prophecy itself was focused on the fall of the Assyrian Empire, which fell in 609 BC. The Assyrian Empire fell to a large alliance of its enemies, including the Medes, Scythians, and the rebelling Babylonians. The prophet, whoever it was, did not know this would happen and did not mention the Medes or Scythians. He prophesied that after defeating the Assyrians, the conquerors would besiege Babylon, demonstrating the prophecy was made before Babylon revolted in 626 BC.

The prophecy specifically mentions the Carmanians as coming to attack Assyria. The Carmanians are a Persian people from the province of Kerman, in southeast Iran. The name of the region was recorded in Old Persian as Karmanā (𐎣𐎼𐎶𐎴). The Greeks transliterated the Persian name in several ways including Carmanioe (Καρμάνιοι), Carmanitoe (Καρμανιτοι), or Germanioe (Γερμάνιοι). Carmania had been inhabited continuously since the bronze age, however, the Iranian Carman tribe is believed to have arrived in the region in the 8th century BC. Cyrus the Great conquered Carmania shortly before he conquered Babylonia in the mid 6th century BC. According to the 3rd century BC Babylonian historian Berossus, Cyrus the Great granted Nabonidus, the last King of Babylon, Carmania as a vassal kingdom after conquering Babylonia.

The Carmanians were a semi-legendary people by the early Christian era, who were considered a warlike people who practiced cannibalism, according to Strabo (Στράβων) in his Geographica (Γεωγραφικά), published between 7 and 18 AD. It isn't clear if this is true, however, the region was civilized throughout the Greek era, and kings were recorded as ruling there. As the prophecy indicates the Carmanians were independent, it suggests the original prophecy was first recorded in the Neo-Assyrian or Neo-Babylonian era, before the Medes conquered Carmania.

As the Medes and Persians were not mentioned at all after the introduction, this suggests this prophecy was made before the Medes became politically significant circa 625 BC. Prior to that, Media was nominally part of the Neo-Assyrian empire, and then the Scythian empire, however, Carmania was still beyond its reach. The fact that Elam was not mentioned, which had been a great southern rival to Assyria, suggests the prophecy was made after 640 BC, when Ashurbanipal annexed the country. At that point, Carmania was the most powerful country on the eastern frontier.

To the south, the Arab Kingdom of Lihyan dominated northern Arabia, however, the author of the introduction does not appear to have recognized the name. Instead, the prophecy now reads that tribes of dragons would drive chariots out of Arabia. If the Latin Apocalypse was based on the Greek version, the term translated as 'dragons' should have been drákontes (δράκοντες), a word found in the Septuagint, and generally mirrored by lwytn (לויתן) in the Masoretic text. Lwytn means 'crocodile' in modern Hebrew, and generally anglicized as Leviathan. The documented Aramaic spelling is identical, lwytn (לחݩתך), however, the earlier spelling in the Ugaritic text from the 1300s BC, was Ltn (𐎍𐎚𐎐), the name of a sea monster commonly anglicized as Lotan. The term lwytn is used in early Israelite texts, which were written before the adoption of the Aramaic script, and the development of Classical Hebrew, so there must have been a Canaanite (Judahite and Samaritan form), however, it has not survived. It could have been any variation of ltn (𐤉𐤕𐤋), lwtn (𐤉𐤕𐤅𐤋), or lwytn (𐤉𐤕𐤆𐤅𐤋), or perhaps several, as different Canaanite dialects spelled some words differently.

If one accepts that something has been lost in the translation of 'nations of Arabian dragons riding chariots,' the most likely explanation is that the original Semitic text read Lhyn (לחין / 𐤉^𐤍𐤋 / 𐤉𐤆𐤁𐤋), which was misread as a variation of lwytn by the author of the introduction. If so, the prophecy was about 'tribes of Arabian Lihyans riding chariots.' The Lihyans became the most powerful tribe in northern Arabia during the Neo-Assyrian era. They established their capital in the city of Dedan, which the Israelite prophet Ezekiel reported trading with Tyre in the 7th century BC. During the late Neo-Babylonian era, the Nabonidus Chronicle records that the Lihyans had a king, however, most of northwest Arabia was occupied by the Babylonians.

When the Neo-Babylonian empire fell, the Kingdom of Lihyan expanded quickly, occupying most of north-west Arabia. At the time, the Gulf of Aqaba became known as the Gulf of Lihyan. The culture thrived during the Persian era and reached its peak between 552 and 353 BC, however, went into decline as the Persian economy contracted, and then Greek merchants took over Persian trade routes. It struggled economically for a couple of centuries, as more powerful Arab states arose that had close trade ties to the Greeks, and was finally defeated by the Nabateans in a series of battles in the 1st century BC. It is accepted that it lost most of its power in 65 BC and then was conquered in 24 BC. This supports the opening chapters, and concluding paragraphs as dating to the early Christian era, after Lihyan had been forgotten.

The beginning of chapter 4 lists Babylon, Asia, Egypt, and Syria, as the lands that would be destroyed after Assyria, which also indicates the era of the original prophecy. The Kingdom of Aram, later known as Syria by the Greeks, was conquered incrementally by the Neo-Assyrian Empire in a series of wars spanning a century, culminating in Hama, the capital, being conquered in 738 BC. Egypt was not conquered by the Neo-Assyrian Empire until 671 BC. Before that, it had been part of the Kushite Empire for centuries and was, therefore, part of Assyria's greatest rival. Asia was also mentioned earlier, in chapter 3, where it was prophesied that it would suffer the same fate as Babylon.

Asia (Ἀσία) was originally the name of western Anatolia, however, later became the name of the Asian continent in Greek geography. The name is documented in the bronze age as the name of western Anatolia as the Mycenaean Greek Asiwija (𐀀𐀯𐘖𐀹𐀊), and in Neshite, the language of the Hittite Empire, as Aššuwa (𒀸𒋗𒉿). The Kingdom of Aššuwa developed into the Kingdom of Lydia during the early Iron Age, which became an ally of Assyria during the Cimmerian invasions of the 8th century BC and continued to be an ally during the Scythian invasions of the early 7th century. After Assyria fell in 615 BC, the Lydians and Medes became enemies, which lasted until the Battle of the Eclipse circa 590 BC. The battle is named after a solar eclipse that happened during the battle, and which both sides viewed as an omen. The Lydians and Medes signed a peace agreement, and the royal families were united by the Mede king Cyaxares's son Astyages marrying the Lydian king Alyattes's daughter Aryenis.

There is a reference to a 'wind' coming from the east to destroy Assyria, which seems to confirm the dating of the original prophecy to earlier than 625 BC, as based on the context, this 'wind' was the name of a people. The term 'wind' almost certainly originated in a mistranslation when the Greek translation was made, where the translator misinterpreted another Aramaic word as rwḥå (אחור), meaning 'wind,' 'breath,' or 'spirit.' Based on the description of 'rwcha' being east of Assyria, this was almost certainly the city of Ragā, today known as Ray (ری). Ray was an ancient city that existed since at least 6000 BC, which has now been absorbed into modern Greater Tehran.

The exact Median pronunciation is unknown, but accepted as being close to the Old Persian Ragā (𒀹𒅗𒈜-𒈨), the Neo-Assyrian name Raga (𒂊𒈨𒂊𒐊𒑖𒀸𒉺), and the older Elamite name Rakkaan (𒀹𒀹𒀹). The city played a major role in the Book of Tobit, the story of a Samaritan who lived in Assyria during the decline of the empire, and fled to Ray several years before the empire fell. At the time indicated in the prophecy, Ray was outside of the Neo-Assyrian empire, and arguably the closest thing the rebel Medes had to a capital city between 652 and 625 BC. In 652 BC, the Scythians occupied the Medes' capital Ecbatana along with most of western Media, and in 625 BC Cyaxares led the Medes in a successful revolt against the Scythians and took back that territory. This, therefore, would have been an indirect prophecy of the rebel Medes coming to defeat Assyria, which ultimately did happen, however, the prophet did not seem to know who exactly they were.

Considering the prophecy was the destruction of Assyria at the hands of Carmanians, Lihyans, and rebel Medes of Ray, while Babylon, Egypt, and Lydia were treated as subjects or allies of Assyria, this prophecy could only have been made sometime between 640 and 625 BC. If it was earlier than 640 BC, the Elamites would have been mentioned, and if it was later than 625 BC, the Medes would have been named rather than their city of Ray. The Greek translator, who may or may not have been the author of the extended opening and concluding paragraphs, clearly did not understand the political geography of the era when the prophecy was written. As only fragments of the old prophecy have been found in Greek, it is plausible that the extended content was written after the translation, either in Greek or Thracian, before being translated into Latin.

No fragments of the Thracian translation have been found, however, it is attested by the strange reference to "terrible fire, hail, and flying swords," destroying the fields of crops. The Latin translation reads 'rompheas volantes,' which certainly translates as 'swords (or spears) flying.' The Latin word romphea originally meant javelins, however, later became a word for swords. It is generally accepted as being adopted from the Greek word rhomphaea (ῥομφαία), which was a type of broadsword that the Thracians used. The Thracian language is poorly understood, however, they were the people living in the region that would later become Byzantium. Their language is accepted as being Indo-European, however, it is debated which modern language family it was closest to. Some linguists claim it was Baltic, while others believe it was related to Dacian or Illyrian. Thracian was a language of literature, but little survives. The Italian pilgrim Antoninus of Piacenza reported that Bessian, a Thracian dialect, was one of several used at a monastery in the Sinai in the 7th century AD, along with Greek, Latin, Syriac, and Coptic.

The Thracian term rhomphaea (ῥομφαία), while the name of a type of fighting pike or pole-ax, was derived from the Thracian word meaning 'ripper,' or 'tearer,' and believed to be related to the word rrufé in Albanian, and rofija (рофия) in Bulgarian, both of which mean 'lightning bolt.' This indicates that the source text for the Latin translation was probably a Thracian translation, therefore, the extended opening and conclusion could have originated in Thracian. The reason for the extension is not clear, as the core prophecy seems highly heretical to both Christianity and Judaism. The prophecy, while predicting the fall of Assyria, is focused on a power struggle between God and the constellations, so it may have been reworked to discredit astrology.

The astrological focus of the prophecy targets Leo, which is called both the 'constellation terrible' (sidus terribile) and 'constellation prolific' (sidus copiosum). In Old Babylonian star charts the asterism today called Leo was known as ^{mul}Ur Gula (✷✳ 𒇻𒄒𒈨𒆪), meaning

ᶜasterismGreat Dog.' By the Neo-Assyrian era it was still
mulUr Gula (𒀯𒌨𒄖𒆷), however, the name translated as ᶜasterismGreat Beast,' which later became the
mulUrgula (𒀯𒌨𒃲) of the Neo-Babylonian era, by
which time the name was simply interpreted as
ᶜconstellationLion.' During the Middle Assyrian and Neo-
Assyrian eras, Leo was recorded as being the asterism
that the sun rose in during the summer solstice. Due to
the precession of the equinoxes, by the Greek era,
Cancer was the constellation the sun rose in during the
summer solstice, and it has subsequently shifted to
Gemini as of 1990. Sometime late in the Neo-Assyrian
era, Leo stopped rising just before the sun, as the solstice
shifted into the cusp between asterisms, which seems to
be what this prophecy was about.

Being the asterism that presided over summer, they
viewed Leo as causing the best weather and allowing
the crops to grow, and the empire to thrive. The
prophecy claimed that because the constellation was no
longer rising, there would be extreme rains, floods, and
lightning storms, which would destroy the fields and
cities. Eastern tribes would see it as an omen and invade
Assyria.

This prophecy about the 'Prolific constellation' being
knocked down from the sky, parallels the Judahite
prophet Isaiah's claim that Heilel ben-Shachar (הֵילֵל

בֶּן־שָׁחַר) had been thrown from the sky. Heilel ben-Shachar translates directly as 'Exalt son of Dawn,' which has often been read as a name, although it is not clear what he was talking about. The Greeks translated the name as Heôsphoros ho prôi anatellôn (Ἐωσφόρος ὁ πρωὶ ἀνατέλλων), meaning 'Eosphorus which the morning makes bright.' Eosphorus was the Greek concept of the morning star, which the Romans translated as Lucifer, their name for the morning star. The Rabbinical interpretation was that Isaiah was referring to an arrogant king, while the Christian interpretation has traditionally been that he was speaking about the devil.

Isaiah's writing is broadly dated to between 740 BC and 686 BC, meaning that he lived through the Assyrian conquests of Samaria and Babylonia in the 720s BC and the relatively peaceful era that followed, when Judah was a vassal state of the Neo-Assyrian Empire. If 'Exalt son of Dawn' was a reference to the sun's rising in Leo at the summer solstice, then Leo must have moved into the cusp before 686 BC. This would mean that the prophecy, which likely dates to between 640 and 625 BC, was not prophesying the shift itself, but using it as an ill omen that others would take as a sign the gods had turned against Assyria.

The later decades of the Neo-Assyrian Empire were chaotic, with constant rebellions and repeated coup attempts. Historians debate the reason for the sudden loss of authority by the kings, however, the world turned against Assyria. Armies of revolting Medes and Babylonians, supported by Cimmerians and Scythians swarmed across the empire, and in 614 BC, Assur, the ancestral capital of the Assyrians, fell to the combined forces of the Medes and Scythians. Two years later, in 612 BC, Nineveh, the largest city in Assyria fell, and the empire was gone. The remnants of the Assyrian forces held out around Carchemish with the aid of the Egyptians until 605 BC, when they were finally defeated.

While the prophet later claims that God will destroy all the high and prominent constellations, the focus on Leo is clearly based on the connection between the Neo-Assyrians and the 'Great Beast' constellation. The prophet refers to the prolific constellation, as being 'their constellation,' a reference to each nation having a constellation that served as their 'guardian' and 'guide,' in Neo-Assyrian astrology. The term used in the early Iron Age was ^{deity}lamassu (𒀭𒆗) in the Neo-Assyrian Empire, meaning protector deity/star. This belief was well established in the Judahite culture of the era and was cited as the reason that the Persians rose to power after the Babylonians instead of the Judahites forming an empire. The Talmud (Yoma 77a:5), records a belief from the Persian era, that the Judahites' guardian messenger Gabriel intervened when Babylon fell to the Persians, by protecting the Judahites in Babylon, and was subsequently stripped of power briefly. During this period, the Persians' guardian messenger Dobiel guided them in establishing their empire. Dobiel, which translates as 'bear god,' was also a name for the constellation Ursa Major, indicating that the guardians/guides of the astrologers of the era were the constellations themselves. In the Judean astrology of the late Second Temple era, there had been 72 of these guardian messengers, one for each nation in the world, but 70 had become corrupt, and only Gabriel, the guardian messenger of the Judahites, and Michael, the guardian messenger of the Samaritans had not been corrupted.

A similar claim about God dividing the tribes of humans among the messengers is found in the Song of Moses, near the end of Deuteronomy, however, in the Masoretic version the messenger that received the Israelites as his inheritance was Yhwh. This is likely a Hasmonean-era mistranslation, as the Hasmoneans attempted to repair the Torah by putting the name Yhwh back into it, as King Manasseh was believed to have removed it. It is unclear when the Song of Moses was itself created, however, it appears to be a late addition to the Samaritan Torah, likely added after the Assyrians conquered Samaria, as it includes the Curse of Moses, which prophesied that would happen, but promised redemption if the Israelites returned to worshiping Moses' god.

The Neo-Assyrian Empire closely associated itself with the asterism now called Leo, which they did not envision as a giant Lion, like later cultures, but like the lamassu statues they carved, with the body of a lion, wings of an eagle, and head of a man. The kings of the Neo-Assyrian empire also viewed themselves, and Assyria itself, as lions upon the Earth that could devour whatever they pleased. The kings engaged in annual lion hunts which were celebrated, and elaborate relief carvings depicting the hunts have survived. In this apocalypse, the prophet is associating the Assyrians with Leo, their lamassu, and prophesying that, like Leo, who has fallen from the sky, the Neo-Assyrian summer is over, and the stormy season is coming against the empire.

Unfortunately, while most of the strange references in the core prophecy (6th Ezra), can be accounted for as translation errors, these errors have existed for close to two thousand years, since the original Greek translation was made. The extended material (5th Ezra) found in chapters 1 and 2 of the apocalypse appears to have been added by the Thracian translator, who already believed the prophecy was about dragons riding chariots, and clouds knocking stars out of the sky. Therefore, two copies are included here, a translation, and a restoration.

Latin Apocalypse of Ezra: Chapter 1

The second book of the prophet Ezra, the son of Seraiah, the son of Azariah, the son of Hilkiah, the son of Sadamias, the son of Zadok, the son of Ahitub, the son of Achias, the son of Phinehas, the son of Eli, the son of Omri, the son of Aziei, the son of Marimoth, the son of Arna, the son of Uzziah, the son of Borith, the son of Abishua, the son of Phinehas, the son of Eleazar, the son of Aaron, of the tribe of Levi, who was captive in the land of the Medes,[1] in the reign of Artaxerxes[2] king of the Persians.

The word of the Lord[3] came to me, saying, "Go your way and show my people their sinful deeds, and their children their wickedness which they have done against me, so they may tell their children's children. The sins of their fathers are increased in them, for they have forgotten me and have sacrificed to foreign gods. Am I not he who brought them out of the land of Egypt, from the house of slavery? Yet they have provoked me to anger and hated my counsel. Pull your hair off your head, and throw all evil on them, for they have not been obedient to my law, but are a rebellious people. How long will I restrain myself from them, to whom I have done so much good?"

"I have destroyed many kings for their sake. Pharaoh with his servants and all his power I have destroyed. All the nations I have destroyed before them, and to the east I have scattered the people of two provinces: Tyre and Sidon. I have killed all their enemies."

"Therefore say to them, 'The Lord says, I led you through the sea, and from the beginning gave you a large and safe passage. I gave you Moses as a leader and Aaron as a priest. I gave you light as a pillar of fire, and great wonders I have done among you, yet you have forgotten me.'

The Almighty Lord[4] said, "The quails were a sign for you. I gave you tents for your safety. Nevertheless, you murmured there, and did not celebrate my name or the destruction of your enemies, but still to this day you murmur. Where are the benefits that I have done for you? When you were hungry and thirsty in the wilderness, didn't you cry out to me saying, 'Why have you brought us into this wilderness to kill us? It had been better for us to have served the Egyptians than to die in this wilderness.' Then I pitied your grieving, and gave you manna to eat and so you ate messengers' food."

"When you were thirsty, didn't I split the rock and waters flowed out to fill you? For the heat, I covered you with the leaves of the trees. I divided among you a fruitful land, and I drove out the Canaanites,[5] Perizzites,[6] and Pelesets,[7] from before you. What more can I still do for you?"

The Almighty Lord said, "When you were in the wilderness, in the bitter river, being thirsty, and blaspheming my name, I did not incinerate you for your blasphemies, but threw a tree in the water, and made the river sweet. What will I do for you, Jacob? You, Judah, would not obey me. I will turn to other nations, and I will give my name to those so they may keep my statutes. Seeing you have forgotten me, I will forsake you also. When you desire me to be gracious to you, I had no mercy on you. Whenever you call on me, I will not hear you, for you have defiled your hands with blood, and your feet are swift to murder. You have not forgotten me, but yourselves."

The Almighty Lord says, "Have I not treated you like a father for his sons, like a mother for her daughters, and a nurse for her young babes, so you would be my people, and I should be your God, so you would be my children, and I should be your father? I gathered you together, as a hen gathers her chicks under her wings, but now, what will I do to you? I will throw you out from before my face. When you sacrifice to me, I will turn my face from you, as your solemn holidays, your new moons, and your circumcisions, I have forgotten. I sent to you my servants the prophets, who you have captured and murdered, and ripped their bodies into pieces, and whose blood I will require of your hands."

The Almighty Lord says, "Your house is desolate, and I will cast you out as the wind drives stubble. Your children will not be fruitful, for they have despised my commandment, and done that which is evil before me. Your houses I will give to a people that will come, which not having heard of me yet will believe me, and to whom I have shown no signs, yet, they will do what I have commanded them. They have seen no prophets, yet, they will remembrance their sins, and acknowledge them. I take as witness the grace of the people to come, whose little ones rejoice in gladness, and though they have not seen me with bodily eyes, yet, in spirit, they believe the thing that I say."

Now, brother, look what glory and see the people that come from the east, to whom I will give for leaders, Abraham, Isaac, Jacob, Hosea, Amos, Micah, Joel, Obadiah, Jonah, Nahum, Habakkuk, Zephaniah, Haggai, Zachariah, and Malachi (who is also called a messenger of the Lord).

Latin Apocalypse of Ezra: Chapter 1 Notes

1 Codex Sangermanensis: Medorum

• Translation: Media

Media was the name of the land of the Medes, an ancient Iranian people who lived in northern Iran before the rise of the Persian Empire.

2 Codex Sangermanensis: Artaxersis

• Translation: Artaxerxes

It is not specified which Artaxerxes this was. King Artaxerxes I ruled the Persian Empire between 465 and 424 BC. King Artaxerxes II ruled the Persian Empire between 404 and 358 BC. King Artaxerxes III ruled the Persian Empire between 358 and 338 BC. King Artaxerxes IV ruled the Persian Empire between 338 and 336 BC.

3 Codex Sangermanensis: Domini

• Translation: Lord

The term 'Lord' is treated as a proper name in the Latin translation.

4 Codex Sangermanensis: Dominus omnipotens.

• Translation: Lord omnipotent (of almighty)

This is generally a translation of the Greek cyrios pantokrátor (κύριος παντοκράτωρ), which was a translation of the Judahite ȧdny šdy (𐤆𐤀𐤅 𐤆𐤉𐤀𐤈) meaning Lord powerful.

5 Codex Sangermanensis: Chananeos

• Translation: Canaanites

The Canaanites were the ancient people of Israel, Palestine, Lebanon, and western Syria. The name Canaan is derived from the Canaanite/Phoenician word Knôn (𐤊𐤍𐤏𐤍), which itself appears to be derived from the Old Babylonian name of the region ᵏᵘʳKinaḫnum (𒆳𒆠𒈾𒄴𒉏). The Old Babylonian name is believed to have been derived from the word kinaḫnu (𒆠𒈾𒄴𒉏), meaning 'red dye' or 'purple dye.' Canaan was a major source of textiles throughout its history, especially wool dyed red and purple. They were also known as Phoenicians (Φοίνικες), based on the Greek term meaning 'purple people' which appears to have been inherited from the Mycenaean ponikijo (𐀡𐀛𐀑𐀍), itself derived from the ancient Egyptian fnḫw (𓂋𓄿𓈖𓏥), which meant 'carpenter' or 'lumberjack,' likely due to Canaan being the source for most wood used in ancient Egypt. This alternate name for the region continued to be used by Canaanites as well in, as Pt (𐤐𐤕) and its people as the Pnym (𐤐𐤍𐤉𐤌). The older term for the region used which was used in the Ugaritic texts, was ådm (𐎀𐎄𐎎), which also means 'red.'

6 Codex Sangermanensis: Ferezeos

• Translation: Perizzites

The Perizzites are mentioned in the Torah as having lived in Canaan before the Israelites settled in the region. The word Perizzites (פרזי) means people 'that live in the country,' or 'rural people,' which modern Israeli archeologists believe were assimilated into the ancient Israelite population.

7 Codex Sangermanensis: Philistheos

• Translation: Philistines.

The equivalent term in the Masoretic texts is pelishti (פְּלִשְׁתִּי), which translates as Philistine or Palestinian. The Peleseti were an ancient people based in the region of the modern Gaza Strip of the Palestinian Territories. The earliest surviving mention of them is from the reliefs of the Temple of Ramses III at Medinet Habu in Egypt which dates back to some time between 1186 and 1155 BC, in which they were called Pelesets (𓊪 𓍿 𓍯 𓈉 𓀀𓏥). They were also known in cuneiform as the ᵏᵘʳPalastu (𒆳𒉿𒆷𒀸𒌇).

It is unclear where they came from, however, one theory is that they were the Pala, a Luwian people from the Black Sea coast of Anatolia. The region was an independent country called Palaa (𒉺𒆷𒀀) in the Neshite (Hittite) records from the 1600s BC, however, had become part of the Neshite Empire by the 1500s BC. Around the time the Pelesets invaded Canaan, the Pala were driven from their homeland by the neighboring Kaskians from northeast Anatolia, which supports the connection between the groups, however, it has yet to be proven conclusively.

While the term is generally found in the Masoretic texts related to the time of Joshua, centuries before the Peleseti migrated into the region, this appears to be an Iron Age interpretation, and not universal. Some of the Targums use the phrase 'those who lived in the land of the Pelishti,' while in some places the writers of the Targums substitute the word 'fires' for Pelishti. The term fires is likely a relic of the original term, as the Amorites occupied the region before the time of Joshua, and the Egyptians referred to them derisively as fires. This reference to the Pelesets instead of the Amorites, is dependent on the translation of Joshua from the early Iron Age, which was later translated into both Judahite and Aramaic, and then into Hebrew and Greek.

Latin Apocalypse of Ezra: Chapter 2

The Lord said, "I brought these people out of slavery, and I gave them my commandments through my servants the prophets, who they would not listen to, and they hated my counsel. The mother that carried them said to them, 'Go on your own, you children, for I am a widow and forgotten. I raised you in joy, but with sorrow and heaviness have I lost you, for you have sinned before the Lord your god, and done that thing that is evil before him. But what will I now do to you? I am a widow and forgotten, go on your own, my children, and ask mercy of the Lord.'"

"As for me, Father, I call on you as a witness over the mother of these children who would not keep my covenant, that you bring them to confusion, and their mother to ruin, that there may be no offspring of them. Let them be scattered abroad among the heathens. Let their names be left out of the Earth, as they have despised my covenant. Woe to you Assyria,[1] you who hide the unrighteous among you! You, wicked people, remember what I did to Sodom and Gomorrah, whose land lies in clods of pitch and heaps of ashes. I will do the same to those that will not listen," said the Almighty Lord.

The Lord said to Ezra, "Tell my people that I will give them the kingdom of Jerusalem, which I would have given to Israel. Their glory I will also take to myself, and I will give to these the everlasting tabernacles which I had prepared for them. They have the tree of life for a sweet smelling ointment, and they will not work or get tired. Go, and you will receive."

"Pray for the few days left for you, that they may be shortened. The kingdom is already prepared for you. Take the Sky[2] and Earth[3] as witnesses, for I have broken the evil in pieces, and created the good, as I live," the Lord said.

"Mother, embrace your children and bring them up with joy. Make their feet as steady as a pillar, for I have chosen you," the Lord said.

"Those who are dead, I will raise up again from their places, and bring them out of the graves, for I have known my name in Israel. Don't be afraid, mother of the children, for I have chosen you," the Lord said.

"For your help, I will send my servants Esau and Jeremiah, whose counsel I have sanctified and prepared for you twelve trees loaded with diverse fruits, and as many fountains flowing with milk and honey, and seven mighty mountains where there grow roses and lilies, through which I will fill your children with joy. Do right by the widow. Judge the fatherless, and give to the poor. Defend the orphan, and clothe the naked, heal the broken and the weak, and don't laugh at a lame man to shame him. Defend the maimed, and let the blind man come into the sight of my clearness."

"Keep the old and young within your walls. Wherever you find the dead, take them and bury them, and I will give you the first place in my resurrection. Stay still, my people, and take your rest, for your quietness still comes. Feed your children, good nurse, and establish their feet. As for the servants that I have given you, not one of them will perish for I will require them from among your number. Do not be weary, for when the day of trouble and heaviness comes, others will cry and be sad, but you will be merry and have abundance. The heathens will envy you, but they will be able to do nothing against you," the Lord said.

"My hands will cover you so that your children will not see Hades. Be joyful, you mother with your children, for I will deliver you," the Lord said.

"Remember, your children that sleep, for I will bring them out of the sides of the earth, and show mercy to them, for I am merciful," said the Almighty Lord. "Embrace your children until I come and show mercy to them, for my wells run over, and my grace will not fail."

I, Ezra, received an order from the Lord on Mount Horeb, that I should go to Israel, but when I came to them, they considered me like nothing and despised the commandments of the Lord. Therefore I say to you, you heathens that hear and understand, look for your shepherd, he will give you everlasting rest, for he is near at hand, who will come at the end of the world. Be ready for the reward of the kingdom, for the everlasting light will shine on you forever. Flee the shadow of this world, and receive the joyfulness of your glory. I testify of my savior openly. Receive the gift that is given you, and be glad, giving thanks to he who has led you to the heavenly kingdom. Rise up and stand, and see the number of those that be sealed in the feast of the Lord, which are departed from the shadow of the world, and have received glorious garments from the Lord. Count your number, Zion, and shut up those of you who are clothed in white; who have fulfilled the law of the Lord. The number of your children, who you longed for, is fulfilled. Beg the power of the Lord, that your people, which have been called from the beginning, may become sacred.

I, Ezra, saw on Mount Zion a great people, who I could not count, and they all praised the Lord with songs. Among them, there was a young man of high stature, taller than all the rest, and on every one of their heads, he set crowns and was more exalted, which I marveled at greatly. So I asked the messenger, and said, "Lord, what are these?"

He answered and said to me, "These are those that have taken off the mortal clothing, and put on the immortal, and have confessed the name of God. Now they are crowned, and receive palms."

Then I asked the messenger, "Who is that young person that crowns them, and places palms in their hands?"

He answered me, "It is the son of God, whom they have confessed in the world." Then I began to greatly commend those who stood so stiffly for the name of the Lord, and the messenger said to me, "Go on your way, and tell my people what manner of things, and of the great wonders of the Lord your god, you have seen."

Latin Apocalypse of Ezra: Chapter 2 Note

1 Codex Sangermanensis: Assur

- Translation: Assyria

Assur, also called Ashur or Qal'at Sherqat, was the name of the ancient Assyrian capital city from the Old Kingdom era to the early Neo-Assyrian era, when King Ashur-nasir-pal II moved the capital to the city of Kalhu, also called Nimrud, in 879 BC. The apocalypse mentions Assyria many times, and prophecies the fall of Assyria repeatedly, which is odd, as the Neo-Assyrian Empire fell in 609 BC, and the remnants of the Assyrian population have never exerted political power over the region.

The apocalypse also prophecies the siege of Babylon, which fell in 539 BC, indicating the author viewed the Carmanians as independent even though they had not been since before the fall of Babylon, and suggests the Lihyan tribes were a major power in Arabia, which was accurate from the Neo-Assyrian through Persian eras, but not when the Apocalypse is believed to have originated. This all paints a map of an older world and suggests the apocalypse was not simply the invention of someone in the early Christian era that attributed it to Ezra, but the translation of a much older prophecy, which was reattributed to Ezra.

2 Codex Sangermanensis: Caelum

- Translation: sky (or Caelus)

The older Israelite text called on the sky and earth to act as witnesses between God and man many times. Both were considered gods in their own right in Aramaen religions, and this does support the author being a Syrian. In the Masoretic texts, the sky was called Shamayim (שָׁמַיִם), and in the Septuagint he was called Uranus (οὐρανὸν). In both cases depicted as being intelligent.

The Canaanites worshiped Baʻal Shamin (𐤔𐤌𐤔 𐤋𐤏𐤁) as one of their gods, whose name means Lord of the Sky. The Aramaic version was Baʻal Samin (ܒܥܠ ܫܡܝܢ), who continued to be worshiped in Lebanon and Syria until at least the 1st century AD. These Canaanite gods were virtually identical to the Greek primordial deity Uranus. This idea of calling the Earth and Sky as witnesses was likely an archaic expression by the time this apocalypse was written, suggesting it may have been written as early as the first century.

3 Codex Sangermanensis: terram

• Translation: land (or dirt, Earth, Terra)

The older Israelite text called on the sky and earth to act as witnesses between God and man many times. Both were considered gods in their own right in Aramaen religions, and this does support the author being a Syrian.

In the Masoretic texts, the earth was called Eretz (אֶרֶץ) and in the Septuagint, she was called Ge (Γῆ). In both cases depicted as being intelligent. It is unclear if the Canaanites worshiped an Earth-goddess called Eretz, however, it is theorized that Asherah may have been an Earth-goddess due to her connection to sacred groves of trees. She was considered the wife of El (𐤀 / 𐎛𐎍 / 𐤋𐤀) by Canaanites, and the mother of Yahw (𐤉𐤄𐤅) by the early Israelites. Her name appears many times in the Tanakh as one of the goddesses worshiped by the early Israelites before the Babylonian captivity.

In Edom, the Earth goddess Adamah was worshiped, who appears in the Masoretic version of Numbers to eat Korah and his followers. In the Septuagint, it was Ge who ate Korah. The Greek concept of Ge (also called Gaia) is equally unclear, as she was a primordial deity, but there were no temples dedicated to her. This idea of calling the Earth and Sky as witnesses was likely an archaic expression by the time this apocalypse was written, suggesting it may have been written as early as the first century.

Latin Apocalypse of Ezra: Chapter 3

"Tell my people the words of the prophecy that I will put in your mouth," the Lord said. "Have them written on paper, for they are faithful and true. Don't be afraid of the thoughts directed against you, don't let the disbelief of those who speak against you trouble you. All the unfaithful will die in their unfaithfulness."

"Look," the Lord said, "I will bring plagues on the world, the sword, famine, death, and destruction, for wickedness has exceedingly polluted the whole earth, and their hurtful works are fulfilled."

"Therefore," the Lord said, "I will hold back my tongue no longer regarding their wickedness, which they profanely commit, neither will I allow them to do those things, in which they wickedly exercise themselves. See the innocent and righteous blood grows before me, and the minds of the just complain constantly."

"Therefore," the Lord said, "I will certainly avenge them, and receive to myself all the innocent blood from among them. Look, my people are led like a flock to the slaughter, and I will not allow them now to live in the land of Egypt, but I will bring them with a mighty hand and a stretched-out arm, and destroy Egypt with plagues, like before, and will destroy all the land. Egypt will mourn, and the foundation of it will be destroyed with the plague and punishment that God will bring on it. Those who till the ground will mourn, for their seeds will fail through the blasting and hail, and under the terrible constellation."[1]

"Woe to the world, and those who live in it! The sword, and their destruction draws near. One people will stand up and fight against another with swords in their hands. There will be sedition among men, and the invading of one another. They will not consider their kings or princes, and the decisions regarding their actions will be their own. A man will desire to go into a city, and will not be able to. Because of their pride, the cities will be troubled, the houses will be destroyed, and men will be afraid. A man will have no pity on his neighbor, but will destroy their houses with the sword, and plunder their goods because of the lack of food, and from the great tribulation."

"Look," God said, "I will call together all the kings of the Earth to revere me, which are from the rising sun, from the south, from the east, and Lebanon, to turn themselves one against another, and repay the things that they have done to them, as they do yet today to my chosen, so I will also do, and repay them in the chest."

The god Lord said, "My right hand will not spare the sinners, and my sword will not stop over those who shed innocent blood on the earth. The fire has gone out from his anger and has consumed the foundations of the earth, and the sinners, like the straw that is ignited. Woe to those who sin, and don't keep the commandments!"

The Lord said, "I will not spare them. Go on your way, you children, from the power, don't defile my sanctuary, for the Lord knows all those that sin against him, and therefore he delivers them to death and destruction. Now the plagues have come against the whole Earth, and you will remain among them, for God will not deliver you, as you have sinned against him."

"Look, a horrible vision and the appearance of those in the east. I bring out tribes of dragons from Arabia[2] who will come out with many chariots, and the cloud of them will be carried as the wind on earth, that all they which hear them may fear and tremble. Also, the Carmanians[3] raging in anger will go out like the wild boars of the forest, and with great power will they come, and enter the battle with them, and will destroy a portion of the land of the Assyrians. Then the dragons will have the upper hand, remembering their nature, and if they will turn to themselves, conspiring together in great power to persecute them, then these will be troubled and bleed, and keep silent through their power, and will flee. From the land of the Assyrians, the enemy will besiege them, and consume some of them, and in their armies will be fear and dread, and strife among their kings."

"Look, a cloud[4] from the east, from the north to the south, and they are very horrific to see, full of anger and storms.[5] They will attack one another, and they will knock down the prolific constellation[6] to the earth, their own constellation, and blood will come from the sword to the belly, and femurs of men, and the camel's hind legs. There will be fear and great trembling across the land, and horrified will be those who see their rage, and trembling will take hold of them. Then I will arouse many clouds from the south, and from the north, and another group from the west. They will be overpowered by wind[7] from the east, and discover the multitude raised in anger. The constellation will cause the corruption to be known in the east, and the west will be violated.

"I will raise multitudes, big and strong, full of fury and constellation,[8] as they will come from all the earth and the inhabitants of her, and I will destroy more than every high and prominent constellation.[9] Terrible fire, hail, and flying swords,[10] and so much water that all fields will flood and all the rivers will overflow with water, which will break down the cities and walls, mountains and hills, trees of the wood, and grass of the meadows, and their grain."

"They will go steadfastly to Babylon,[11] and make her afraid. They will come to her and besiege her, and will unleash rebellion and all fury against her,[12] and then the dust and smoke will go up to the sky, and all they who are near her will mourn her. Those who remain under her, will service those who have put her in fear. You, Asia,[13] who shares of the hope of Babylon and her glory, woe to you, you wretch, because you have made yourself like her, and have dressed your daughters like whores, that they might please and glory in your lovers who have always desired to commit prostitution with you. You have followed her who is hated in all her works and inventions."

"Therefore," God said, "I will send plagues on you, widowhood, poverty, famine, sword, and pestilence, to waste your houses with destruction and death. The glory of your power will be dried up like a flower, the heat will rise that is sent over you. You will be weakened like a poor woman who has been whipped, and like one punished with wounds so that the mighty and her lovers will not be able to receive her. Would I, with jealousy, have so proceeded against you?"

The Lord said, "If you had not always killed my chosen, exalting the stroke of your hands, and saying over their dead when you were drunk, 'point out the beauty of your countenance.' The reward of your prostitution will be in your chest, and therefore you will receive repayment."

"As you have done to my chosen," the Lord said, "Even so, God will do to you and will deliver you into trouble. Your children will die of hunger, and you will fall to the sword. Your cities will be broken down, and you all will perish with the sword in the fields. They who are in the mountains will die of hunger, eat their own bodies, and drink their own blood because of their hunger for bread and thirst for water. You will come through the sea in misery, and receive plagues again. In the passage, they will rush on the idle city and will destroy some portion of your land, and consume part of your glory, and will return to Babylon which was destroyed. You will be thrown down by them like rubble, and they will be to you like fire and will consume you, your cities, your land, and your mountains, and they will burn up all your forests and your orchards with fire. They will carry your children away as slaves, and what you have, they will plunder, and damage the beauty of your face."

Latin Apocalypse of Ezra: Chapter 3 Notes

1 Codex Sangermanensis: sidus terribile

• Translation: constellation (or asterism, star) terrible (or terrific, horrible, awful)

The Latin 'constellation terrible' (sidus terribile) is being used as an alternate translation of the 'constellation prolific' (sidus copiosum) found later in the text, suggesting one was the name, and the other a reference to its importance to the Assyrians. The most likely explanation was that this was a reference to the constellation today called Leo. In Old Babylonian star charts the asterism was known as ᵐᵘˡUr Gula (𒀭 [cuneiform]), meaning ᵃˢᵗᵉʳⁱˢᵐGreat Dog.' By the Neo-Assyrian era was still ᵐᵘˡUr Gula ([cuneiform]), however, the name translated as ᵃˢᵗᵉʳⁱˢᵐGreat Beast,' which later became the ᵐᵘˡUrgula ([cuneiform]) of the Neo-Babylonian era, by which time the name was simply interpreted as ᶜᵒⁿˢᵗᵉˡˡᵃᵗⁱᵒⁿLion.' During the Middle Assyrian and Neo-Assyrian, Leo was recorded as being the asterism that the sun rose in during the summer solstice. Due to the precession of the equinoxes, by the Greek era, Cancer was the constellation the sun rose in during the summer solstice, and it has subsequently shifted to Gemini as of 1990. Sometime late in the Neo-Assyria era, Leo stopped rising just before the sun as the solstice shifted into the cusp between asterisms, which seems to be what this prophecy was about.

Being the asterism that presided over summer, they viewed Leo as causing the best weather and allowing the crops to grow, and the empire to thrive. The prophecy claimed that because the constellation was no longer rising, there would be extreme rains, floods, and lightning storms, which would destroy the fields and cities. Eastern tribes would see it as an omen and invade Assyria. This prophecy about the 'Prolific constellation' being knocked down from the sky, parallels the Judahite prophet Isaiah's claim that Heilel ben-Shachar (הֵילֵל בֶּן־שָׁחַר) had been thrown from the sky. Heilel ben-Shachar translates directly as 'Exalt son of Dawn,' which has often been read as a name, although it is not clear what he was talking about. The Greeks translated the name as Heôsphoros ho prôi anatellôn (Ἑωσφόρος ὁ πρωὶ ἀνατέλλων), meaning Eosphorus which the morning makes bright. Eosphorus was the Greek concept of the morning star, which the Romans translated as Lucifer, their name for the morning star. The Rabbinical interpretation was that Isaiah was referring to an arrogant king, while the Christian interpretation has traditionally been that he was speaking about the devil.

Isaiah's writing is broadly dated to between 740 BC and 686 BC, meaning that he lived through the Assyrian conquests of Samaria and Babylonian in the 720s BC and the relatively peaceful era that followed, when Judah was a vassal state of the Neo-Assyrian Empire. If 'Exalt son of Dawn' was a reference to the sun's rising in Leo at the summer solstice, then Leo must have moved into the cusp before 686 BC. This would mean that the prophecy, which likely dates to between 640 and 625 BC, was not prophesying the shift itself, but using it as an ill omen that others would take as a sign the gods had turned against Assyria.

The later decades of the Neo-Assyrian Empire were chaotic, with constant rebellions and repeated coup attempts. Historians debate the reason for the sudden loss of authority by the kings, however, the world turned against Assyria. Armies of revolting Medes and Babylonians, supported by Cimmerians and Scythians swarmed across the empire, and in 614 BC, Assur, the ancestral capital of the Assyrians, fell to the combined forces of the Medes and Scythians. Two years later, in 612 BC, Nineveh, the largest city in Assyria fell, and the empire was gone. The remnants of the Assyrian forces held out around Carchemish with the aid of the Egyptians until 605 BC, when they were finally defeated.

2 Codex Sangermanensis: nationes draconum Arabum

• Translation: nations of dragons Arabian

If the Latin Apocalypse was based on a Greek version, the term translated as draconum should have been drákontes (δράκοντες), a word used in the Septuagint. However, nations of Arabian dragons riding chariots is an unusual prophecy to saw the least. The word most commonly translated as 'dragon' in the Septuagint, is mirrored by lwytn (לויתן) in the Masoretic text, a word that means 'crocodile' in modern Hebrew, and generally anglicized as Leviathan. The documented Aramaic spelling is identical, lwytn (לן^לL), however, the earlier spelling in the Ugaritic text from the 1300s BC, was Ltn (𐎍𐎚𐎐), the name of a sea monster commonly anglicized as Lotan. The term lwytn is used in early Israelite texts, which were written before the adoption of the Aramaic script, and development of Classical Hebrew, so there must have been a Canaanite (Judahite and Samaritan form), however, it has not survived. It could have been any variation of ltn (𐤟𐤟𐤟), lwtn (𐤟𐤟𐤟), or lwytn (𐤟𐤟𐤟𐤟), or perhaps several, as different Canaanite dialects spelled some words differently.

If one accepts that something has been lost in the translation of 'nations of Arabian dragons riding chariots,' the most likely explanation is that the original Semitic text read Lḥyn (/ 𐤟𐤟𐤟 לחין / 𐤟𐤟𐤟), which was misread as a variation of lwytn by the Greek translation. If so, the prophecy was about 'tribes of Arabian Lihyans riding chariots.' The Lihyans became the most powerful tribe in northern Arabia during the Neo-Assyrian era. They established their capital in the city of Dedan, which the Israelite prophet Ezekiel reported trading with Tyre in the 7th century BC.

During the late Neo-Babylonian era, the *Nabonidus Chronicle* records that the Lihyans had a king, however, most of northwest Arabia was occupied by the Babylonians. When the Neo-Babylonian empire fell the Kingdom of Lihyan expanded quickly, occupying most of northwest Arabia. At the time, the Gulf of Aqaba became known as the Gulf of Lihyan. The culture thrived during the Persian era, and reached its peak between 552 and 353 BC, however, went into decline as the Persian economy contracted, and then Greek merchants took over Persian trade routes. It struggled economically for a couple of centuries, as more powerful Arab states arouse that had close trade ties to the Greeks, and was finally defeated by the Nabateans in a series of battles in the 1st century BC. It is accepted that it lost most of its power in 65 BC, and then was conquered in 24 BC.

As this is before the Apocalypse is generally dated to, it makes an early Christian era prophecy of tribes of Lihyans riding chariots as unlikely as nations of dragons riding chariots. If the origin of the dragons was a misreading of 'Lihyans' it points to an era much earlier, during the Neo-Assyrian, Neo-Babylonian, or Persian era for the origin of the prophecy. It also supports the prophecy as originating with someone other than Ezra the Scribe, as he arrived in Jerusalem to reorganize the city and rebuild the walls in 351 BC, when the Persian Empire was already beginning to collapse economically. This was the time the Lihyan economy began to weaken, and, moreover, Ezra the Scribe did not make any claims of being a prophet. Therefore, the name at the beginning of the prophecy was likely an addition made later, when the prophecy was reattributed to 'Ezra.' This earlier dating would also explain how the word Lihyan could have been easily misread by a Greek translator, especially in the early Christian era, after the civilization no longer existed.

3 Codex Sangermanensis: Carmonii

• Translation: Carmanians

The Carmanians are a Persian people from the province of Kerman, in southeast Iran. The name of the region was recorded in Old Persian as Karmanā (𒅗𒅕𒈠𒈾𒀀). The Greeks transliterated the Persian name several ways including Carmanioe (Καρμάνιοι), Carmanitoe (Καρμανιτοι), or Germanioe (Γερμάνιοι). Carmania had been inhabited continuously since the bronze age, however the Iranian Carman tribe is believed to have arrived in the region in the 8th century BC. Cyrus the Great conquered Carmania shortly before he conquered Babylonia in the mid 6th century BC. According to the 3rd century BC Babylonian historian Berossus, Cyrus the Great granted Nabonidus, the last King of Babylon, Carmania as a vassal kingdom after conquering Babylonia.

The Carmanians were a semi-legendary people by the early Christian era, who were considered a warlike people that, according to Strabo (Στράβων) in his *Geographica* (Γεωγραφικά), published between 7 and 18 AD, practiced cannibalism. It isn't clear if this is true, however, the region was civilized throughout the Greek era, and kings were recorded as withering there. As the prophecy indicates the Carmanians are independent, it suggests the original prophecy was first recorded in the Neo-Assyrian or Neo-Babylonian era, before Cyrus conquered Carmania. The fact that the Medes and Persians were not mentioned at all after the introduction, which appears to be a later addition, suggests this prophecy was made before the Medes became politically significant in the late-7th century BC.

4 Codex Sangermanensis: nubs

• Translation: multitude (or swarm, haze, smoke, cloud, phantom, gloom)

The Latin word 'nubs' can be read as the singular form for 'cloud,' 'smoke,' 'dust' or 'haze,' however, the verse refers to nubs in the plural, and it is therefore often translated as 'clouds.' In this translation, the word 'could' is used, however, 'multitude' is used in the restoration as a multitude can be expressed in either a singular or plural form. While 'clouds' knocking stars from the sky is more evocative than a multitude knocking a constellation from the sky, the reference to one of the constellations being their constellation confirms that this is a reference to a nation.

5 Codex Sangermanensis: procellae

• Translation: aggression (or invasion, incursion, assult, storms, winds)

If the word 'multitude' (nubs) is translated as 'cloud,' the term 'storms' is generally used here.

6 Codex Sangermanensis: sidus copiosum

• Translation: constellation (or asterism, stars) prolific (or abundant, abundant)

The form of sidus is singular, suggesting the term translated as copiosum was a name or description, not a reference to 'many' as often translated. In Neo-Assyrian and Neo-Babylonian astrology, each nation had a constellation that served as their 'guardian' and 'guide.' The term used in the early Iron Age was ^{deity}lamassu (⊢+⊨⫼⫼) in the Neo-Assyrian Empire, meaning protector deity/star. This belief was well established in the Judahite culture of the era and was cited as the reason that the Persians rose to power after the Babylonians instead of the Judahites forming an empire.

The Talmud (Yoma 77a:5), records a belief from the Persian era, that the Judahite's guardian messenger Gabriel intervened when Babylon fell to the Persians, by protecting the Judahites in Babylon, and was subsequently stripped of power briefly. During this period, the Persians' guardian messenger Dobiel guided them in establishing their empire. Dobiel, which translates as bear-god, was also a name for the constellation Ursa Major, indicating that the guardians/guides of the astrologers of the era were the constellations themselves. In the Judean astrology of the late Second Temple era, there had been 72 of these guardian messengers, one for each nation in the world, but 70 had become corrupt, and only Gabriel, the guardian messenger of the Judahites, and Michael, the guardian messenger of the Samaritans had not been corrupted.

A similar claim about God dividing the tribes of humans among the messengers is found in the Song of Moses, near the end of Deuteronomy, however, in the Masoretic version the messenger that received the Israelites as his inheritance was Yhwh. This is likely a Hasmonean-era mistranslation, as the Hasmoneans attempted to repair the Torah by putting the name Yhwh back into it, as King Manasseh was believed to have removed it. It is unclear when the Song of Moses was itself created, however, it appears to be a late addition to the Samaritan Torah, likely added after the Assyrians conquered Samaria, as it includes the Curse of Moses, which prophesied that would happen, but promised redemption if the Israelites returned to worshiping Moses' god.

The Neo-Assyrian Empire closely associated itself with the asterism now called Leo, which they called [mul]Ur Gula (𒀯𒌨𒄖𒆷), meaning the '[asterism]Great Beast.' They did not envision it as a giant Lion, like later cultures, but like the lamassu statues they carved, with the body of a lion, wings of an eagle, and head of a man. During the Middle Assyrian and early Neo-Assyrian era, the constellation Great-Beast rose with the sun during the summer solstice and was therefore seen as controlling the summer weather. The kings of the Neo-Assyrian empire also viewed themselves, and Assyria itself, as lions upon the Earth that could devour whatever they pleased. The kings engaged in annual lion hunts which were celebrated, and elaborate relief carvings depicting the hunts have survived. In this verse, the prophet is associating the Assyrians with Leo, their lamassu, and prophesying that, like Leo, who has fallen from the sky, the Neo-Assyrian summer is over, and the stormy season is coming against the empire.

7 Codex Sangermanensis: venti

• Translation: wind

If this was mistranslated when the Greek translation was made, it was likely an error that resulted from an Aramaic word being misread as rwḥå (אחור), meaning 'wind,' 'breath,' or 'spirit.' Based on the description of 'rwḥå' being east of Assyria, this was almost certainly the city of Ragā, today known as Ray (ری). Ray was an ancient city that existed since at least 6000 BC, which has now been absorbed into modern Greater Tehran. The exact Median pronunciation is unknown, but accepted as being close to the Old Persian Ragā (𐎼𐎥𐎠), the Neo-Assyrian name Raga (𒊏𒂵𒀀𒍑), and the older Elamite name Rakkaan (𐎠𐎹𐎺).

The city played a major role in the Book of Tobit, the story of a Samaritan who lived in Assyria during the decline of the empire, and fled to Ray several years before the empire fell. At the time, Ray was outside of the Neo-Assyrian empire, and arguably the closest thing the rebel Medes had to a capital city between 652 BC, when the Scythians occupied the Medes' capital Ecbatana, and 625 BC when Cyaxares led the Medes in a successful revolt against the Scythians.

8 Codex Sangermanensis: irae et sidus

• Translation: anger and constellation (or asterism, meteors)

This is almost certainly a translation of the Greek oestros cae sidêros (οἶστρος καί σίδηρος), which are the closest Greek phonetically. The Greek term oestros (οἶστρος), which can be translated as 'anger,' more accurately translates as 'agonizing pain,' 'furious passion,' 'madness,' or 'frenzy.' Although the Latin term sidus is almost phonetically identical to the Greek term sidêros (σίδηρος), the Greek term had a different meaning, generally related to the metal iron. The Latin also appears to have meant 'iron' at a very early stage, however, transitioned to 'meteor,' and then 'constellation,' during the early Greco-Roman era. In Greek, sidêros (σίδηρος) was also used figuratively to denote anyone who was being 'stubborn,' 'obstinate,' 'disobedient,' 'insubordinate,' 'insolence,' or 'rebellious' which means the Greek translation read something to the effect 'fury and insolence.'

9 Codex Sangermanensis: fundent super omnem altum eminentem sidus.

• Translation: I will overthrow (or I will pour out, I will smelt out, I will secure, I will establish, I will scatter, I will vanquish) more than (or above, top, upward, beyond, also, regarding) every (or all) high (or tall, deep) eminent (or distinguished, lofty, towering, prominent) constellation

10 Codex Sangermanensis: rompheas volantes

• Translation: swords (or spears) flying (or birds)

The Latin word romphea originally meant javelins, however, later became a word for swords. It is generally accepted as being adopted from the Greek word rhomphaea (ῥομφαία), which was a type of broadsword that the Thracians used. The Thracian language is poorly understood, however, they were the people living in the region that would later become Byzantium. Their language is accepted as being Indo-European, however, it is debated which modern language family it was closest to. Some linguists claim it was Baltic, while others believe it was related to Dacian or Illyrian. Thracian was a language of literature, but little survives. The Italian pilgrim Antoninus of Piacenza reported that Bessian, a Thracian dialect, was one of several used at a monastery in the Sinai in the 7th century AD, along with Greek, Latin, Syriac, and Coptic.

The Thracian term rhomphaea (ῥομφαία), while the name of a type of fighting pike or pole-ax, was derived from the Thracian word meaning 'ripper,' or 'tearer,' and believed to be related to the word rrufé in Albanian, and rofija (рофия) in Bulgarian, both of which mean 'lightning bolt.' As 'lightning bolts' makes more sense than 'flying swords,' it is used in the restoration. However, this indicates that the source text for the Latin translation was probably a Thracian translation, not a Greek translation.

11 Codex Sangermanensis: Babylonem

• Translation: Babylon

Babylon was occupied by the Neo-Assyrian Empire until 609 BC when it successfully rebelled with Median help. There were several earlier attempts to rebel, such as Marduk-apla-iddina II's rebellions, which took control of Babylon between 722 and 710 BC, and again briefly for nine months in 703 and 702 BC. Marduk-apla-iddina II's first independent Babylon forged alliances with Samaria, Aram, and Elam, all of which were conquered or devastated in retaliation by the Assyrian king Sargon. This prophecy treats Babylon as part of the Assyrian empire, suggesting it was made either earlier than 722 BC or after 710 BC.

12 Codex Sangermanensis: effundent sidus et omnem iram super eam

• Translation: will release (or will pour out, will drive out, will yield to, will squander, will give up, will loosen, will scatter) constellation (or asterism, meteors) and all (or every) anger on (or above, top, upward, beyond, also, regarding, more) her (or it, this)

This verse appears to have been the Greek term sidêros (σίδηρος) and oestros (οἶστρος), translated as sidus and iram, the same as earlier in the chapter. Sidêros (σίδηρος) which can be translated as 'anger,' more accurately translates as 'agonizing pain,' 'furious passion,' 'madness,' or 'frenzy.' Although the Latin term sidus is almost phonetically identical to the Greek term sidêros (σίδηρος), the Greek term had a different meaning, generally related to the metal iron. The Latin also appears to have meant 'iron' at a very early stage, however, transitioned to 'meteor,' and then 'constellation,' during the early Greco-Roman era. In Greek, sidêros (σίδηρος) was also used figuratively to denote anyone who was being 'stubborn,' 'obstinate,' 'disobedient,' 'insubordinate,' 'insolence,' or 'rebellious' which means the Greek translation read something to the effect 'will unleash rebellion and all fury against her.'

13 Codex Sangermanensis: Asia

The Latin name Asia was a translation of the Greek name Asia (Ἀσία), which originally referred to western Anatolia, however, later became the name of the Asian continent in Greek geography. The name is documented in the bronze age as the name of western Anatolia the Mycenaean Greek Asiwija (𐀀𐀯𐀹𐀊) and Neshite (Hittite) Aššuwa (𒀸𒋗𒉿).

The Kingdom of Aššuwa developed into the Kingdom of Lydia during the early Iron Age, which became an ally of Assyria during the Cimmerian invasions of the 8th century BC and continued to be an ally during the Scythian invasions of the early 7th century. After Assyria fell in 615 BC, the Lydians and Medes became enemies, which lasted until the Battle of the Eclipse in 590 BC. The battle is named after a solar eclipse that happened during the battle, and which both sides viewed as an omen. The Lydians and Medians signed a peace agreement, and the royal families were united by the Mede king Cyaxares's son Astyages marrying the Lydian king Alyattes's daughter Aryenis. This suggests the prophecy was originally written in the 7th or 6th century BC.

Latin Apocalypse of Ezra: Chapter 4

Woe to you, Babylon and Asia! Woe to you, Egypt and Syria![1] Dress yourselves with clothes of sack and hair, mourn your children, and be sorry, for your destruction is at hand. A sword is sent on you, and who may turn it back? A fire is sent among you, and who may quench it? Plagues are sent to you, and who is he who may drive them away? May any man drive away a hungry lion in the forest? May anyone quench the fire in the stubble, when it has begun to burn? May one turn back an arrow that is already shot by a strong archer?

The mighty Lord sends the plagues and who is he who can drive them away? A fire will go out from his anger, and who is he who may quench it? He will hurl lightning, and who will not fear? He will thunder, and who will not be afraid? The Lord will threaten, and who will not completely crumble to powder in his presence? The earthquakes and the foundations of the sea will rise up with waves from the deep, and the waves in it will be troubled, and the fish also, before the Lord and before the glory of his power.

Strong is his right hand that bends the bow. His arrows that he shoots are sharp, and will not miss when they are shot, even to the edges of the world. Look, the plagues are sent, and will not turn back until they come on the Earth. The fire is started, and will not be put out until it consumes the foundation of the Earth. Like an arrow that is shot by a mighty archer does not turn back, likewise, the plagues that will be sent on Earth will not turn back.

Woe to me! Woe to me! Who will deliver me in those days?

The beginning of sorrow and great mourning, the beginning of famine and great death, the beginning of wars, and the powers will stand in fear and the beginning of evils! What will I do when these evils will come? Look, the plague of famine is released, and tribulation is like his whip, and punishment his discipline, yet for all these things they will not turn from their wickedness, nor remember their punishment. Look, food will be so cheap on Earth, that they will think themselves to be in a good place, and even then evil will grow on Earth, and sword, famine, and great confusion. Many of those who live on Earth will perish of famine, and others who escape the hunger will be destroyed by the sword. The dead will be thrown out like dung, and there will be no man to comfort them, for the land will be devastated, and the cities will be torn down. There will be no man left to farm the land or to sow it. The trees will give fruit, and who will gather them? The grapes will ripen, and who will tread them? All places will be deserted of men so that one man will desire to see another, and to hear his voice.

In a city, there will be left ten, and two in the field, who will hide themselves in the thick groves, and in the clefts of the rocks. In an orchard of olives, on every tree, there are left three or four olives. When a vineyard is gathered, there are some clusters left by those who diligently search through the vineyard. Even so, in those days there will be three or four left by those who search their houses with the sword. The Earth will be laid waste, and the fields will grow old, and her paths and all her roads will grow full of thorns because no man will travel through them. The virgins will mourn, having no bridegrooms. The women will mourn, having no husbands. Their daughters will mourn, having no helpers. In the wars, their bridegrooms will be destroyed, and their husbands will perish from famine.

Now hear these things and understand them, you servants of the Lord. Look at the word of the Lord. Receive it. Don't worship the gods of whom the Lord spoke. Look, the plagues draw near and are not lazy. Like when a pregnant woman in the ninth month births her son, with for two or three hours of delivery causes great pain to her womb, yet when birthing they cannot stop for a break. Likewise, the plagues will not stop coming on the Earth, and the world will mourn, and sorrows will come on it on every side.

My people, hear my word. Prepare for battle, and those evils will be like pilgrims on the land. He who sells let him be like he who flees away, and he who buys like one that will lose. He who stores merchandise like he who has no profit from it, and he who builds like he who will not live in it. He who sows as if he should not reap, so also he who plants the vineyard, as he who will not gather the grapes. Those who marry will be like those who will have no children, and those who don't marry will be like the widowers. Therefore, those who work, labor in vain, and strangers will reap their fruits, and plunder their goods, overthrow their houses, and take their children as slaves.

"In slavery and famine they will have children. Steal their property! The more they beautify their cities, their houses, their possessions, and their own bodies, the more I will be angry with them for their sin," Lord said.

Like when a whore envies a right honest and virtuous woman, so will the righteousness hate iniquity when she dresses herself and will accuse her to her face. When he comes, who will defend against he who diligently searches out every sin on Earth? Therefore, don't be like them, or do their works. In a short time, iniquity will be taken away out of the land, and righteousness will reign among you.

Let no sinner say that he has not sinned, for coals of fire will burn[2] above his head who says, "I have not sinned before God and his glory."

Look, the Lord knows all the works of men, their imaginations, their thoughts, and their hearts. He who spoke only the words, 'Let the Earth be made,' and it was made, and 'Let the sky be made,' and it was made. Through his words, the stars were made, and he knows the number of them. He searched the deep and the treasures of it. He has measured the sea, and what it contains. He has shut the sea among the waters, and with his words, he has placed the earth on the waters. He spread out the heavens like a vault. Above the waters, he has built it. In the desert, he has made springs of water, and pools on the tops of the mountains that the floods might pour down from the high rocks to water the Earth.

He made man, and put his heart in his body, and gave him breath, life, and understanding. Yes and the breathing omnipotent God,[3] which made all things, and searches out all hidden things in the secrets of the Earth. Certainly, he knows your thoughts, and what you think in your hearts, even those who sin, and would hide their sin. Likewise the Lord has precisely examined all your works, and he will put you all to shame. When your sins are found out, you will be ashamed before men, and your own sins will be your accusers on that day. What will you do? How will you hide your sins before God and his messengers?

Look, God himself is the judge. Fear him. Stop sinning and forget your iniquities, and never again dabble with them so the God will lead you out, and deliver you from all trouble. Look, the burning anger of a great multitude has started over you, and they will take away some of you, and feed you, being idle, with things offered to idols. Those who consent to them will be included in derision and in reproach and trodden underfoot.

There will be, in every place, and in the cities, a great insurrection against those that fear the Lord. They will be like madmen, sparing none, but still spoiling and destroying those who fear the Lord. They will waste and take away their goods, and throw them out of their houses. Then they will be known, who are my chosen, and they will be tested like the gold in the fire.

"Hear, my beloved," Lord said, "Look, the days of trouble are at hand, but I will deliver you from it. Do not be afraid or have doubt, for God is your guide."

"The guide of those who keep my commandments and precepts," said the god Lord, "Don't let your sins weigh you down, and don't let your iniquities lift themselves up. Woe to those who are bound with their sins, and covered with their iniquities, like when a field is covered over with bushes, and a path covered with thorns that no man may travel it! It is left undressed, and is thrown into the fire to be consumed with it."

Latin Apocalypse of Ezra: Chapter 4 Notes

1 Codex Sangermanensis: Aegypte et Syria.

- Translation: Egypt and Syria (or Aram)

The Kingdom of Aram, later known as Syria by the Greeks, was conquered incrementally by the Neo-Assyrian Empire in a series of wars spanning a century, culminating in Hama, the capital, being conquered in 738 BC. Egypt was not conquered by the Neo-Assyrian Empire until 671 BC. Before that, it had been part of the Kushite Empire for centuries. and was therefore part of Assyria's greatest rival. As the prophecy seems to be directed at the Assyrian Empire and its ally Lydia, this suggests the original prophecy was written after 671 BC.

2 Codex Sangermanensis: carbones ignis conburet.

- Translation: I will burn coals fire (or signal)

The Latin carbones was almost certainly a translation of the Greek anthrax (ἄνθραξ), which also means coal. However, the Greek anthrax also referred to a mythical glowing stone, which was used as a translation of an unknown gemstone in the Septuagint's book of Isaiah, where the Masoretic text uses the name ekdach (אֶקְדָּח). The modern Hebrew word ekdach means 'handgun,' however, Isaiah used the word as the name of a stone that would be used in rebuilding the gateway of Jerusalem. The term is not otherwise used in the Masoretic Text, however, the commentary on Isaiah in the Talmud (Bava Batra 75a:10, Sanhedrin 100a:7) confirms that it has traditionally been viewed as a gemstone. The Torah commentary of Rabbi Bahya (Shemot 28:15:3) claims that the light that Noah used in his ark was an ekdach stone, and disputes the correlation of the ekdach and 'turquoise of Nubia,' which the Greeks also translated as anthrax in the Septuagint.

The Sanhedrin tractate (103b:12) in the Talmud, tells the story of King Jehoiakim's heresy when claiming that man no longer needed God, as men had glowing stones that created light. The god he was talking about was clearly the sun, however, it's not clear what the glowing stones were. The tractate uses the term zhb prwyym (זהב פרויים), and while zhb translates as 'gold,' the meaning of prwyym is debated. A virtually identical term, zehav parvayim (זָהָב פַּרְוָיִם), was used in the description of King Solomon's temple found in the Masoretic book of Divrei-hayyamim, which claims the temple walls were decorated with this precious stone.

The parallel verse in the Septuagint's book of 2nd Paralipomenon interprets this as 'gold of the Pharouaem' (χρυσίου τοῦ ἐκ Φαρουάιμ), however, that simply appears to be a Greek transliteration of the same term. It is generally interpreted as the name of a land, however, a simpler explanation is that prwym (𐤐𐤓𐤅𐤉𐤌) was the Canaanite term for 'pharaohs.' Solomon was described as deeply involved with trade in northern Egypt at the time, and his first wife was recorded as being an Egyptian princess. The era was one of chaos, referred to as the Third Intermediate Period by Egyptologists. The Egyptian empire had collapsed a couple of centuries earlier, and the Libyans had occupied northern

Egypt. Nevertheless, this 'gold of the Pharaohs,' is described as being a gemstone, and not gold itself.

The gemstone in question was likely calcite, a stable carbonate mineral that may occasionally show phosphorescence or fluorescence. Calcite-alabaster, also called Egyptian alabaster, is a gemstone that the Egyptians were using in the New Kingdom era. Several Egyptian alabaster perfume jars were discovered in the tomb of Tutankhamun from circa 1323 BC, however, the gemstone was mainly used to carve figures of the guardian goddess Bast, from which the name 'alabaster' is ultimately derived.

Calcite stones that glow in the dark are somewhat rare, however, can glow in a variety of colors. The Greek legends about the anthrax gemstone referred to it had a reddish-orange hue, while the term 'gold of the pharaohs' suggests it was a yellowish-orange. It suggests that all the glowing stones the ancient Egyptians had access to came from the same mine, however, it is not clear where that would have been. As Egypt was already thousands of years old, it could have imported the stones at any point during its history. There is evidence of an orange calcite mine in Bronze Age Iberia, and so it is possible that they imported the stones from there.

All the Judahite references to the glowing stones are found in the era of Solomon's temple. Solomon imported the stones in the 10th century BC and used them to decorate the temple walls. Later, in the 8th century BC, Isaiah envisions huge gemstones would be used at the top of the new gate, and later Jehoiakim commits heresy against the sun god, by claiming that humanity no longer needs him, as we have the stones. King Jehoiakim had been appointed to rule Egypt after King Necho of the Egyptian Empire had killed his father, King Josiah, in 609 BC. His heresy against the sun god was likely inspired by his hatred of Necho, who was a sun worshipper. Four years into his rule, in 605 BC, the Babylonians defeated the Egyptian army at Carchemish and besieged Jerusalem, following which Jerusalem switched from being an Egyptian vassal to a Neo-Babylonian vassal.

Three years later, the Babylonians launched a failed invasion of Egypt, which weakened their military, and Jehoiakim rebelled from Babylon, and allied with Egypt as a nominally independent kingdom. Three years later, in 598 BC, the Babylonians returned and besieged Jerusalem, and their Egyptian allies did not send aid. Jehoiakim is reported as dying in the siege or right after it, and King Nebuchadnezzar II took his son and heir Jeconiah, who was also known as Jehoiachin, captive to Babylon, along with other members of the nobility. Nebuchadnezzar appointed Jehoiakim's brother Zedekiah to rule Judah, who also revolted in 589 BC, after forming an alliance with the Egyptians. Again the Babylonians laid siege to Jerusalem, however, this siege lasted much longer than the earlier sieges, approximately 30 months, ending in 586 BC. The Judahites were waiting for an Egyptian army to break the siege, but it never arrived. According to the Judahite records, the people inside the city had eaten everything, including the unclean animals, and had turned to cannibalizing each other before the end of the siege.

After the city surrendered, the Babylonians decided to destroy the kingdom. They shackled King Zedekiah, blinded him, and dragged him to Babylon, where he later died. Most of the survivors from the city were sold as slaves, although Jeremiah and a few members of the royal family did escape to Egypt. The city of Jerusalem was razed, and the temple was demolished. The valuables in the temple were taken to Babylon, which is presumably where the glowing stones would have also ended up. Babylon was itself conquered by the Persians a few decades later, and the Greek myths of the anthrax gemstones sometimes claimed that the Persian magi had them. The magi were the priestly caste of the Zoroastrian religion, the religion the Persian royal family followed, so it is plausible that they received the stones when Persia sacked Babylon. The stones later appeared in medieval myths of alchemists, however, it is unknown where the stones would be today.

As the Judahites only appear to have referenced the stones during the era of King Solomon's temple, it is unlikely that this prophecy would have been written later. It is also worth noting that the stones were on the interior of the temple walls, so only someone who had been to Jerusalem, and considered worthy to enter the temple would have seen them. This suggests a priest, prophet, or noble made the original prophecy.

3 Codex Sangermanensis: spiramentum Dei omnipotentis

- Translation: breathing God omnipotent

Latin Apocalypse of Ezra Restoration: Chapter 1

The second book of the prophet Ezra, the son of Seraiah, the son of Azariah, the son of Hilkiah, the son of Sadamias, the son of Zadok, the son of Ahitub, the son of Achias, the son of Phinehas, the son of Eli, the son of Omri, the son of Aziei, the son of Marimoth, the son of Arna, the son of Uzziah, the son of Borith, the son of Abishua, the son of Phinehas, the son of Eleazar, the son of Aaron, of the tribe of Levi, who was captive in the land of the Medes,[1] in the reign of Artaxerxes[2] king of the Persians.

The word of the Lord[3] came to me, saying, "Go your way, and show my people their sinful deeds, and their children their wickedness which they have done against me, so they may tell their children's children. The sins of their fathers are increased in them, for they have forgotten me and have sacrificed to foreign gods. Am I not he who brought them out of the land of Egypt, from the house of slavery? Yet they have provoked me to anger and hated my counsel. Pull your hair off your

---

1 See note 1 on page 143

2 See note 2 on page 143

3 See note 3 on page 143

head, and throw all evil on them, for they have not been obedient to my law, but are a rebellious people. How long will I restrain myself from them, to whom I have done so much good? I have destroyed many kings for their sake. Pharaoh with his servants and all his power I have destroyed. All the nations I have destroyed before them, and to the east I have scattered the people of two provinces: Tyre and Sidon. I have killed all their enemies."

"Therefore say to them, 'The Lord says, I led you through the sea, and from the beginning gave you a large and safe passage. I gave you Moses as a leader and Aaron as a priest. I gave you light as a pillar of fire, and great wonders I have done among you, yet you have forgotten me.'

The Almighty Lord[4] said, "The quails were a sign for you. I gave you tents for your safety. Nevertheless, you murmured there, and did not celebrate my name or the destruction of your enemies, but still to this day you murmur. Where are the benefits that I have done for you? When you were hungry and thirsty in the wilderness, didn't you cry out to me saying, 'Why have you brought us into this wilderness to kill us? It had been better for us to have served the Egyptians than to die in

---

4 See note 4 on page 143

this wilderness.' Then I pitied your grieving, and gave you manna to eat and so you ate messengers' food. When you were thirsty, didn't I split the rock and waters flowed out to fill you? For the heat, I covered you with the leaves of the trees. I divided among you a fruitful land, and I drove out the Canaanites,[5] Perizzites,[6] and Pelesets,[7] from before you. What more can I still do for you?"

The Almighty Lord said, "When you were in the wilderness, in the bitter river, being thirsty, and blaspheming my name, I did not incinerate you for your blasphemies, but threw a tree in the water, and made the river sweet. What will I do for you, Jacob? You, Judah, would not obey me. I will turn to other nations, and I will give my name to those so they may keep my statutes. Seeing you have forgotten me, I will forsake you also. When you desire me to be gracious to you, I had no mercy on you. Whenever you call on me, I will not hear you, for you have defiled your hands with blood, and your feet are swift to murder. You have not forgotten me, but yourselves."

---

5 See note 5 on page 144

6 See note 6 on page 144

7 See note 7 on page 145

The Almighty Lord says, "Have I not treated you like a father for his sons, like a mother for her daughters, and a nurse for her young babes, so you would be my people, and I should be your God, so you would be my children, and I should be your father? I gathered you together, as a hen gathers her chicks under her wings, but now, what will I do to you? I will throw you out from before my face. When you sacrifice to me, I will turn my face from you, as your solemn holidays, your new moons, and your circumcisions, I have forgotten. I sent to you my servants the prophets, who you have captured and murdered, and ripped their bodies into pieces, and whose blood I will require of your hands."

The Almighty Lord says, "Your house is desolate, and I will cast you out as the wind drives stubble. Your children will not be fruitful, for they have despised my commandment, and done that which is evil before me. Your houses I will give to a people that will come, which not having heard of me yet will believe me, and to whom I have shown no signs, yet, they will do what I have commanded them. They have seen no prophets, yet, they will remembrance their sins, and acknowledge them. I take to witness the grace of the people to come, whose little ones rejoice in gladness, and though they have not seen me with bodily eyes, yet, in spirit, they believe the thing that I say."

Now, brother, look what glory and see the people that come from the east, to whom I will give for leaders, Abraham, Isaac, Jacob, Hosea, Amos, Micah, Joel, Obadiah, Jonah, Nahum, Habakkuk, Zephaniah, Haggai, Zachariah, and Malachi (who is also called a messenger of the Lord).

Latin Apocalypse of Ezra Restoration: Chapter 2

The Lord said, "I brought these people out of slavery, and I gave them my commandments through my servants the prophets, who they would not listen to, and they hated my counsel. The mother that carried them said to them, 'Go on your own, you children, for I am a widow and forgotten. I raised you in joy, but with sorrow and heaviness have I lost you, for you have sinned before the Lord your god, and done that thing that is evil before him. But what will I now do to you? I am a widow and forgotten, go on your own, my children, and ask mercy of the Lord.'"

"As for me, Father, I call on you as a witness over the mother of these children who would not keep my covenant, that you bring them to confusion, and their mother to ruin, that there may be no offspring of them. Let them be scattered abroad among the heathens. Let their names be left out of the Earth, as they have despised my covenant. Woe to you Assyria,[8] you who hide the unrighteous among you! You, wicked people, remember what I did to Sodom and Gomorrah, whose land lies in clods of pitch and heaps of ashes. I will do the same to those that will not listen," said the Almighty Lord.

---

8 See note 1 on page 152

The Lord said to Ezra, "Tell my people that I will give them the kingdom of Jerusalem, which I would have given to Israel. Their glory I will also take to myself, and I will give to these the everlasting tabernacles which I had prepared for them. They have the tree of life for a sweet smelling ointment, and they will not work or get tired. Go, and you will receive."

"Pray for the few days left for you, that they may be shortened. The kingdom is already prepared for you. Take Shamayim[9] and Eretz[10] as witnesses, for I have broken the evil in pieces, and created the good, as I live," the Lord said.

"Mother, embrace your children and bring them up with joy. Make their feet as steady as a pillar, for I have chosen you," the Lord said.

"Those who are dead, I will raise up again from their places, and bring them out of the graves, for I have known my name in Israel. Don't be afraid, mother of the children, for I have chosen you," the Lord said.

"For your help, I will send my servants Esau and Jeremiah, whose counsel I have sanctified and prepared for you twelve trees loaded with diverse fruits, and as

---

9 See note 2 on page 152

10 See note 3 on page 153

many fountains flowing with milk and honey, and seven mighty mountains where there grow roses and lilies, through which I will fill your children with joy. Do right by the widow. Judge the fatherless, and give to the poor. Defend the orphan, and clothe the naked, heal the broken and the weak, and don't laugh at a lame man to shame him. Defend the maimed, and let the blind man come into the sight of my clearness. Keep the old and young within your walls. Wherever you find the dead, take them and bury them, and I will give you the first place in my resurrection. Stay still, my people, and take your rest, for your quietness still comes. Feed your children, good nurse, and establish their feet. As for the servants that I have given you, not one of them will perish for I will require them from among your number. Do not be weary, for when the day of trouble and heaviness comes, others will cry and be sad, but you will be merry and have abundance. The heathens will envy you, but they will be able to do nothing against you," the Lord said.

"My hands will cover you so that your children will not see Hades. Be joyful, you mother with your children, for I will deliver you," the Lord said.

"Remember, your children that sleep, for I will bring them out of the sides of the earth, and show mercy to them, for I am merciful," said the Almighty Lord.

"Embrace your children until I come and show mercy to them, for my wells run over, and my grace will not fail."

I, Ezra, received an order from the Lord on Mount Horeb, that I should go to Israel, but when I came to them, they considered me like nothing and despised the commandments of the Lord. Therefore I say to you, you heathens that hear and understand, look for your shepherd, he will give you everlasting rest, for he is near at hand, who will come at the end of the world. Be ready for the reward of the kingdom, for the everlasting light will shine on you forever. Flee the shadow of this world, and receive the joyfulness of your glory. I testify of my savior openly. Receive the gift that is given you, and be glad, giving thanks to he who has led you to the heavenly kingdom. Rise up and stand, and see the number of those that be sealed in the feast of the Lord, which are departed from the shadow of the world, and have received glorious garments from the Lord. Count your number, Zion, and shut up those of you who are clothed in white; who have fulfilled the law of the Lord. The number of your children, who you longed for, is fulfilled. Beg the power of the Lord, that your people, which have been called from the beginning, may become sacred.

I, Ezra, saw on Mount Zion a great people, who I could not count, and they all praised the Lord with songs. Among them, there was a young man of high stature, taller than all the rest, and on every one of their heads, he set crowns and was more exalted, which I marveled at greatly. So I asked the messenger, and said, "Lord, what are these?"

He answered and said to me, "These are those that have taken off the mortal clothing, and put on the immortal, and have confessed the name of God. Now they are crowned, and receive palms."

Then I asked the messenger, "Who is that young person that crowns them, and places palms in their hands?"

He answered me, "It is the son of God, whom they have confessed in the world." Then I began to greatly commend those who stood so stiffly for the name of the Lord, and the messenger said to me, "Go on your way, and tell my people what manner of things, and of the great wonders of the Lord your god, you have seen."

Latin Apocalypse of Ezra Restoration: Chapter 3

"Tell my people the words of the prophecy that I will put in your mouth," the Lord said. "Have them written on paper, for they are faithful and true. Don't be afraid of the thoughts directed against you, don't let the disbelief of those who speak against you trouble you. All the unfaithful will die in their unfaithfulness."

"Look," the Lord said, "I will bring plagues on the world, war, famine, death, and destruction, for wickedness has exceedingly polluted the whole earth, and their hurtful works are fulfilled."

"Therefore," the Lord said, "I will hold back my tongue no longer regarding their wickedness, which they profanely commit, neither will I allow them to do those things, in which they wickedly exercise themselves. See the innocent and righteous blood grows before me, and the minds of the just complain constantly."

"Therefore," the Lord said, "I will certainly avenge them, and receive to myself all the innocent blood from among them. Look, my people are led like a flock to the slaughter, and I will not allow them now to live in the land of Egypt, but I will bring them with a mighty hand and a stretched-out arm, and destroy Egypt with plagues, like before, and will destroy all the land. Egypt will mourn, and the foundation of it will be destroyed with the plague and punishment that God will bring on it. Those who till the ground will mourn, for their seeds will fail through the blasting and hail and under the constellation Leo."[11]

"Woe to the world, and those who live in it! War and destruction draw near, and one people will stand up and fight against another with swords in their hands. There will be sedition among men, and the invading of one another. They will not consider their kings or princes, and the decisions regarding their actions will be their own. A man will desire to go into a city, and will not be able to. Because of their pride, the cities will be troubled, the houses will be destroyed, and men will be afraid. A man will have no pity on his neighbor, but will destroy their houses with the sword, and plunder their goods because of the lack of food, and from the great tribulation."

"Look," God said, "I will call together all the kings of the Earth to revere me, which are from the rising sun, from the south, from the east, and Lebanon, to turn themselves one against another, and repay the things that they have done to them, as they do yet today to my chosen, so I will also do, and repay them in the chest."

---

11 See note 1 on page 161

The god Lord said, "My right hand will not spare the sinners, and my sword will not stop over those who shed innocent blood on the earth. The fire has gone out from his anger and has consumed the foundations of the earth, and the sinners, like the straw that is ignited. Woe to those who sin, and don't keep the commandments!"

The Lord said, "I will not spare them. Go on your way, you children, from the power, don't defile my sanctuary, for the Lord knows all those that sin against him, and therefore he delivers them to death and destruction. Now the plagues have come against the whole Earth, and you will remain among them, for God will not deliver you, as you have sinned against him."

"Look, a horrible vision and the appearance of those in the east. I bring out tribes of Lihyans from Arabia[12] who will come out with many chariots, and the multitude of them will be carried as the wind on earth, that all they which hear them may fear and tremble. Also, the Carmanians[13] raging in anger will go out as the wild boars of the forest, and with great power will they come, and enter the battle with them, and will destroy a portion of the land of the Assyrians. Then the Lihyans will have the upper hand, remembering their nature,

---

12 See note 2 on page 163

13 See note 3 on page 165

and if they will turn to themselves, conspiring together in great power to persecute them, then these will be troubled and bleed, and keep silent through their power, and will flee. From the land of the Assyrians, the enemy will besiege them, and consume some of them, and in their armies will be fear and dread, and strife among their kings."

"Look, a multitude[14] from the east, from the north to the south, and they are very horrific to see, full of anger and aggression.[15] They will attack one another, and they will knock down the constellation Leo[16] to the earth, their own constellation, and blood will come from the sword to the belly, and femurs of men, and the camel's hind legs. There will be fear and great trembling across the land, and horrified will be those who see their rage, and trembling will take hold of them. Then I will arouse many multitudes from the south, and from the north, and another group from the west. They will be overpowered by Ray[17] from the east, and discover the multitude raised in anger. The constellation will cause the

---

14 See note 4 on page 167

15 See note 5 on page 167

16 See note 6 on page 167

17 See note 7 on page 170

corruption to be known in the east, and the west will be violated."

"I will raise multitudes, big and strong, full of fury and insolence,[18] as they will come from all the earth and the inhabitants of her, and I will destroy more than every high and prominent constellation.[19] Terrible fire, hail, and lightning bolts,[20] and so much water that all fields will flood and all the rivers will overflow with water, which will break down the cities and walls, mountains and hills, trees of the wood, and grass of the meadows, and their grain."

"They will go steadfastly to Babylon,[21] and make her afraid. They will come to her and besiege her, and will unleash rebellion and all fury against her,[22] and then the dust and smoke will go up to the sky, and all they who are near her will mourn her. Those who remain under her, will service those who have put her in fear. You, Lydia,[23] who shares of the hope of Babylon and her

---

18 See note 8 on page 170

19 See note 9 on page 171

20 See note 10 on page 171

21 See note 11 on page 172

22 See note 12 on page 173

23 See note 13 on page 174

glory, woe to you, you wretch, because you have made yourself like her, and have dressed your daughters like whores, that they might please and glory in your lovers who have always desired to commit prostitution with you. You have followed her who is hated in all her works and inventions."

"Therefore," God said, "I will send plagues on you, widowhood, poverty, famine, sword, and pestilence, to waste your houses with destruction and death. The glory of your power will be dried up like a flower, and the heat will rise that is sent over you. You will be weakened like a poor woman who has been whipped, and like one punished with wounds so that the mighty and her lovers will not be able to receive her. Would I, with jealousy, have so proceeded against you?"

The Lord said, "If you had not always killed my chosen, exalting the stroke of your hands, and saying over their dead when you were drunk, 'point out the beauty of your countenance.' The reward of your prostitution will be in your chest, and therefore you will receive repayment."

"As you have done to my chosen," the Lord said, "Even so, God will do to you and will deliver you into trouble. Your children will die of hunger, and you will fall to the sword. Your cities will be broken down, and you all will perish with the sword in the fields. They who are in the mountains will die of hunger, eat their own bodies, and drink their own blood because of their hunger for bread and thirst for water. You will come through the sea in misery, and receive plagues again. In the passage, they will rush on the idle city and will destroy some portion of your land, and consume part of your glory, and will return to Babylon which was destroyed. You will be thrown down by them like rubble, and they will be to you like fire and will consume you, your cities, your land, and your mountains, and they will burn up all your forests and your orchards with fire. They will carry your children away as slaves, and what you have, they will plunder, and damage the beauty of your face."

Latin Apocalypse of Ezra Restoration: Chapter 4

Woe to you, Babylon and Lydia! Woe to you, Egypt and Syria![24] Dress yourselves with clothes of sack and hair, mourn your children, and be sorry, for your destruction is at hand. A sword is sent on you, and who may turn it back? A fire is sent among you, and who may quench it? Plagues are sent to you, and who is he who may drive them away? May any man drive away a hungry lion in the forest? May anyone quench the fire in the stubble, when it has begun to burn? May one turn back an arrow that is already shot by a strong archer?

The mighty Lord sends the plagues and who is he who can drive them away? A fire will go out from his anger, and who is he who may quench it? He will hurl lightning, and who will not fear? He will thunder, and who will not be afraid? The Lord will threaten, and who will not completely crumble to powder in his presence? The earthquakes and the foundations of the sea will rise up with waves from the deep, and the waves in it will be troubled, and the fish also, before the Lord and before the glory of his power.

Strong is his right hand that bends the bow. His arrows that he shoots are sharp, and will not miss when they are shot, even to the edges of the world. Look, the

---

24 See note 1 on page 182

plagues are sent, and will not turn back until they come on the Earth. The fire is started, and will not be put out until it consumes the foundation of the Earth. Like an arrow that is shot by a mighty archer does not turn back, likewise, the plagues that will be sent on Earth will not turn back.

Woe to me! Woe to me! Who will deliver me in those days?

The beginning of sorrow and great mourning, the beginning of famine and great death, the beginning of wars, and the powers will stand in fear and the beginning of evils! What will I do when these evils will come? Look, the plague of famine is released, and tribulation is like his whip, and punishment his discipline, yet for all these things they will not turn from their wickedness, nor remember their punishment. Look, food will be so cheap on Earth, that they will think themselves to be in a good place, and even then evil will grow on Earth, and war, famine, and great confusion. For many of those who live on Earth will perish in famine, and the others who escape starving will be destroyed by the sword. The dead will be thrown out like dung, and there will be no man to comfort them, for the land will be devastated, and the cities will be torn down. There will be no man left to farm the land or to sow it. The trees will give fruit, and who will gather them? The grapes will ripen, and who will tread them? All places will be deserted of men so that one man will desire to see another, and to hear his voice.

In a city, there will be left ten, and two in the field, who will hide themselves in the thick groves, and in the clefts of the rocks. In an orchard of olives, on every tree, there are left three or four olives. When a vineyard is gathered, some clusters are left by those who diligently search through the vineyard. Even so, in those days there will be three or four left by those who search their houses with the sword. The Earth will be laid waste, and the fields will grow old, and her paths and all her roads will grow full of thorns because no man will travel through them. The virgins will mourn, having no bride-grooms. The women will mourn, having no husbands. Their daughters will mourn, having no helpers. In the wars, their bridegrooms will be destroyed, and their husbands will perish from famine.

Now hear these things and understand them, you servants of the Lord. Look at the word of the Lord. Receive it. Don't believe the gods of whom the Lord spoke. See, the plagues draw near and are not lazy. Like when a pregnant woman in the ninth month gives birth to her son with two or three hours of delivery that causes great pain to her womb, yet when is birthing they cannot stop for a break. Likewise, the plagues will not stop coming on the Earth, and the world will mourn, and sorrows will come on it on every side.

My people, hear my word. Prepare for battle, and those evils will be like pilgrims on the land. He who sells let him be like he who flees away, and he who buys like one that will lose. He who stores merchandise like he who has no profit from it, and he who builds like he who will not live in it. He who sows as if he should not reap, so also he who plants the vineyard, as he who will not gather the grapes. Those who marry will be like those who will have no children, and those who don't marry will be like the widowers. Therefore, those who work, labor in vain, and strangers will reap their fruits, plunder their goods, overthrow their houses, and take their children as slaves.

"In slavery and famine they will have children. Steal their property! The more they beautify their cities, their houses, their possessions, and their own bodies, the more I will be angry with them for their sin," Lord said.

Like when a whore envies a right honest and virtuous woman, so will the righteousness hate iniquity when she dresses herself and will accuse her to her face. When he comes, who will defend against he who diligently searches out every sin on Earth? Therefore, don't be like them, or do their works. In a short time, iniquity will be taken away out of the land, and righteousness will reign among you.

Let no sinner say that he has not sinned, for coals of fire will burn[25] above his head who says, "I have not sinned before God and his glory."

Look, the Lord knows all the works of men, their imaginations, their thoughts, and their hearts. He who spoke only the words, 'Let the Earth be made,' and it was made, and 'Let the sky be made,' and it was made. Through his words, the stars were made, and he knows the number of them. He searched the deep and the treasures of it. He has measured the sea, and what it contains. He has shut the sea among the waters, and with his words, he has placed the earth on the waters. He spread out the heavens like a vault. Above the waters, he has built it. In the desert, he has made springs of water, and pools on the tops of the mountains that the floods might pour down from the high rocks to water the Earth.

He made man and put his heart in his body, and gave him breath, life, and understanding. Yes and the breathing omnipotent God,[26] which made all things, and searches out all hidden things in the secrets of the Earth. Certainly, he knows your thoughts, and what you think

---

25 See note 2 on page 182

26 See note 3 on page 186

in your hearts, even those who sin, and would hide their sin. Likewise the Lord has precisely examined all your works, and he will put you all to shame. When your sins are found out, you will be ashamed before men, and your own sins will be your accusers on that day. What will you do? How will you hide your sins before God and his messengers?

Look, God himself is the judge. Fear him. Stop sinning and forget your iniquities, and never again dabble with them so the God will lead you out, and deliver you from all trouble. Look, the burning anger of a great multitude has started over you, and they will take away some of you, and feed you, being idle, with things offered to idols. Those who consent to them will be included in derision and in reproach and trodden underfoot.

There will be, in every place, and in the cities, a great insurrection against those that fear the Lord. They will be like madmen, sparing none, but still spoiling and destroying those who fear the Lord. They will waste and take away their goods, and throw them out of their houses. Then they will be known, who are my chosen, and they will be tested like the gold in the fire.

"Hear, my beloved," Lord said, "Look, the days of trouble are at hand, but I will deliver you from it. Do not be afraid or have doubt, for God is your guide."

"The guide of those who keep my commandments and precepts," said the god Lord, "Don't let your sins weigh you down, and don't let your iniquities lift themselves up. Woe to those who are bound with their sins, and covered with their iniquities, like when a field is covered over with bushes, and a path covered with thorns that no man may travel it! It is left undressed, and is thrown into the fire to be consumed with it."

Forward to the Greek Apocalypse of Ezra

The Greek Apocalypse of Ezra is a third Apocalypse of Ezra, which has only survived in two copies, both dating to before the 9th century. It is a separate text from the Judahite or Latin Apocalypses of Ezra and appears to be a Christian-era composite of various Ezra and Shadrach related materials. There is no consensus of when the Greek Apocalypse of Ezra was written, however, it is a Christian era Apocalypse, which refers to several Christian Apostles as being in heaven along with the Israelite Patriarchs. This Apocalypse uses a very inconsistent writing style and switches constantly between first-person and third-person as if it is a composite of materials that originated in various earlier Ezra related works. Some of it repeats content found in the Judahite Apocalypse of Ezra, however, the bulk of the material is unique, describing Ezra's journey through the sky (Heaven) and the underworld (Tartarus).

This Apocalypse is one of the earliest surviving texts that include the Antichrist, who is described as being chained in the lowest level of Hades. His description is curious:

> "This is he who claimed 'I am the son of God,' who made stones into bread, and water into wine."

This description points very clearly to the early-2nd century for this section of the Apocalypse, when the majority of Christians still believed there had been an Antichrist around at the same time as the Christ, another Jesus. This Jesus Antichrist was phased out of mainstream Christianity by the mid 3rd century, and those who believed he had existed were ultimately hunted down and exterminated by the Byzantine Orthodox Church in the 5th through 8th centuries. The core of this belief in the Antichrist was the then heretical Gospel of John, which told an entirely different version of Jesus' life from the older synoptic Gospels: Mathew, Mark, and Luke.

The Gospel of John was originally used by the Valentinian Sect of Gnostics, and according to the Agoli sect of Christians, who were in the land it originated, was written by the Gnostic philosopher Cerinthus, who had reworked the actual teachings of John. As the Gospel of Luke claimed that John was illiterate, it is clear that someone else had written the Gospel of John, however, the author is not named anywhere in the gospel. This other Jesus from the Gospel of John had turned water into wine for a bunch of drunks, while most Christians abstained from wine until well into the 3rd century.

This short description from the Greek Apocalypse of Ezra clearly points to the Antichrist as being the Jesus from the Gospel of John, while it endorsed the Jesus from the Gospel of Matthew, who refused to turn the stones into bread when Satan challenged him to do so. As such, this section of the Apocalypse must date to the mid 2nd century when the debates over the Gospel of John, the Antichrist, and the Holy Spirit, were tearing the Christian churches apart across the Roman Empire. In the end, the Orthodox Church of Emperor Constantine forced everyone to just get along, by combining the Christ and the Antichrist into one Jesus and fusing that Jesus into the Trinity with God and the Holy Spirit. Therefore, this simple description of the Antichrist points to a mid 2nd century origin for the description, and likely the composition itself, although other sections were likely copied from older sources.

One of these sources appears to have been the Vision of Ezra, which survives in Latin but was probably composed in Coptic. Both texts describe Ezra's descent into the underworld, however, the Vision goes into more depth and includes more elements drawn from the ancient Egyptian description of the underworld. Both the Vision and the Apocalypse refer to a worm in the underworld, which the Apocalypse refered to as the 'worm that does not sleep,' while the Vision calls it an 'immortal worm, its size he was not able to reckon.' The Greek term rhomos (ῥόμος) and Latin vermis do both mean 'worm,' however, the original term was almost certainly fnt (ϥⲛⲧ), the Coptic word meaning 'worm' or 'snake.'

The giant serpent in the underworld was Ôåpp (𓇋𓇋𓆙) in ancient Egyptian beliefs, who lived in the far western region of the underworld, near the place the sun set each evening. During the early Iron Age, he became known as Åpåp (𐤀𐤐𐤐), a demonic serpent of the underworld in Egyptian beliefs. The Greeks interpreted him as Apophis (Αποφις), an underworld serpent god. In the early Christian era, he was interpreted as Aphoph (ⲁⲫⲱⲫ) by Coptic Christians, the worm/serpent (ϥⲛⲧ) from the Garden of Eden who was sent to live eternally in the underworld. It is unlikely someone other than an early Coptic Christian would have written a vision of the underworld that included this giant worm/serpent.

Greek Apocalypse of Ezra: Chapter 1

It happened in the thirtieth year,[1] on the twenty-second of the month, when I was in my house, that I cried out and said to the Highest,[2] "Lord, give the glory so that I may see your mysteries."

That night an messenger came, Michael the archangel, who said to me, "Prophet Ezra, do not eat food for seventy weeks."

I fasted as he told me, and then the generalissimo[3] Raphael came, and gave me a styrax wand. I fasted twice for sixty weeks, and I saw the mysteries of God and his messengers. I said to them, "I wish to plead before God about the Christian people. It is better for a man to not be born than to come into this world."

I was therefore taken up into the sky,[4] and I saw in the first sky a great army of messengers, and they took me to the judgments. I heard a voice saying to me, "Have mercy on us, Ezra the chosen of God."

Then I said, "Woe to sinners when they see one who is more just than the messengers, and they themselves are in the Gehenna[5] of fire!"

Ezra asked, "Have mercy on the works of your hands, you who are compassionate, and of great mercy. Judge me rather than the souls of the sinners, for it is better that one soul should be punished, and that the whole world should be destroyed."

God replied, "I will give peace in paradise to the righteous because I have become merciful."

Ezra asked, "Lord, why do you give benefits to the righteous? Just as one who has been hired out, and has served out his time leaves, and again works as a slave when he returns to his masters, so also the righteous have received his reward in the skies. But have mercy on the sinners, for we know that you are merciful."

God answered, "I do not see how I can have mercy on them."

Ezra stated, "They cannot endure your anger."

God replied, "This is their fate." God continued, "I want to preserve you like Paul and John, as you have given me a pure treasure that cannot be stolen, the treasure of virginity, the bastion of men."

Ezra replied, "It is better for a man to not be born. It is not good to be alive. The irrational animals are better than man, because they have no punishment, but you have taken us, and given us up to judgment. Woe to the sinners in the world to come! Because their judgment is endless, and the flame unquenchable."

Greek Apocalypse of Ezra: Chapter 2 Notes

1 This is the same year stated in the Judahite Apocalypse of Ezra, which Shealtiel stated was the thirtieth year since the destruction of Jerusalem, which would place the setting of the text in 557 BC. The author of the Latin apocalypse did not know the era of the Judahite apocalypse and dated his apocalypse to circa 350 BC. This indicates that the author of the Greek apocalypse had access to the Judahite apocalypse, supporting the origin of the Greek apocalypse in the early Christian era when the Judahite apocalypse was in circulation among Christians.

2 BnF Gr. 929: ypsístou (υΨφστου)

* Translation: highest

The Highest is a reference to God, or a god, found in many ancient religions in the Middle East. According to the Torah, the ancient people of Jerusalem worshiped El Elyon, which translates as 'Highest God' when Abraham passed through the regions. The term Highest repeats through other early Jewish and Samaritan texts and was continued into Christian texts in the first few centuries. Outside of Hebrew scriptures, Elyon shows up in the Sefire I Treaty as ål wålyn (ᒐᛂ Ꭹ᪾ᒐᛂᒊ), The Sefire Steles are a series of treaties between the Assyrians and the city of Arpad, which date to the 8th century BC. The term Highest God is also found in the religions of neighboring nations, such as the Greek titan Zagreus, who was described as being the 'highest god' in the epic Alcmeonis, in the 6th century BC.

3 BnF Gr. 929: archistrátigos (ἀρχιστραντηγος).

• Translation: generalissimo (or supreme commander of the army)

The same term was used in the Septuagint's translation of the Book of Joshua, mirrored by the Hebrew sar-tzeva (שַׂר־צָבָא) in the Masoretic text, which translates as 'minister of the army.' Joshua encountered this generalissimo at Jericho before he destroyed it. There is no surviving explanation of who this generalissimo was, however, he has traditionally been interpreted as the supreme commander of God's army. This is the interpretation in the Hebrew translation, which calls him the 'Minister of the army of Yehvah' (שַׂר־צָבָא־יְהוָה), and the Targum Jerusalem, which calls him the 'Translation: messenger-agent from before Yah' (מַלְאָךְ שְׁלִיחַ מִן קֳדָם יְ?). This interpretation is less obvious in the Septuagint, as he was simply called the 'generalissimo of the forces of the lord,' and it does not clarify if this lord was a god or a human lord, such as King Thutmose I of Egypt, who was campaigning in Egypt at the time according to Egyptian records.

The identification of Raphael, the old god of the Raphites, as the generalissimo is not made in the surviving versions of the book of Joshua. Nevertheless, it is curious, as the Raphites are mentioned in the Torah as still being in Canaan circa 1548 BC, yet had disappeared by the time of Joshua's invasion, circa 1508 BC, both dates based on the Septuagint's chronology. This suggests that they were remnants of the Hyksos dynasty in Canaan, which the Egyptians were campaigning against. The various versions of the book of Joshua do contain a scribal note that must have been inserted early, which states that the Raphites were the Hinns of the north. As the Greek translation was based on a slightly longer Aramaic version of Joshua, which appears to have originated in Samaria, it suggests the scribal note was added before the separation of the Samaritan and Judahite priesthoods. By the era the note was added, the Raphites were viewed like the Greek Gigantes, an ancient tribe that had fought the gods and lost. The Raphites appear to have been viewed as extinct by the mid 1300s BC, as the Ugaritic texts refer to them as living in the underworld.

4 BnF Gr. 929: ouranòn (ουβλνον).

• Translation: sky (or universe, Uranus)

Uranus (Οὐρανός) / Shomayim (שָׁמַיִם) is depicted as the same type of primordial deity in the Septuagint and early Israelite texts, as Uranus was in the Greek myths, and called on to witness blessings and curses, implying consciousness. The Canaanites considered the sky to be a god, virtually identical to the Greek concept of Uranus. The Canaanites worshiped Ba'al Shamin (𐤔𐤌𐤔 𐤋𐤏𐤁) as one of their gods, whose name means Lord of the Sky. The Aramaic version was Ba'al Shamin (ܫܡܝܢ ܒܥܠ), who continued to be worshiped in Lebanon and Syria until at least the 1st century AD. In this text, the sky is clearly not a god, indicating it was a later composition, dating to some time after the Maccabean Revolt of circa 165-140 BC.

5 BnF Gr. 929: Geenna (ⲅⲉⲟⲛⲛⲁ)

- Translation: Gehenna

Gehenna was the early Christian reinterpretation of the ancient Israelite concept of the underworld. The name Gehenna is based on the Hebrew gy hnm (גי בנם), a shortened version of gy vn hnm (גי בן הנם), meaning 'valley of the sons of Hinns.'

The Septuagint includes a different name in Joshua chapter 18, reading 'Forest of Sonnam' (ναπης Σονναμ) where the Masoretic text reads Valley of the Sons of Hinnom (גֵּי בֶן־הִנֹּם). The misreading of an H (𐤄) for a S (𐤑) indicates a transcription error when a Samaritan or Judahite version of the book was translated into Aramaic, however, the substitution of 'forest' for 'valley of the sons...' is clearly not a translation error. The combination of 'valley/abyss' and 'forest/woodland' suggests it is a reference to a gravesite, and not a physical valley. At the time, Canaanites marked gravesites by planting trees, usually oak, which was known as the 'Asherah' tree, because it could self-pollinate, and was therefore seen as a 'virgin' tree.

The origin of the word is likely a plural of hinn (حِنّ), a reference to an ancient extinct type of being that once lived on the Earth in Semitic folklore. The hinns continue to be part of the Islamic and Druze religions, although their roles in the religions vary. It is agreed that they are extinct, however, it isn't clear what they were. Many sources describe the hinn and binn as powerful, gigantic primordial creatures, suggesting they were influenced by finding the bones of extinct animals. Conversely, the Revelations of

'Abdullah Al-Sayid Muhammad Habib claims the hinns were air creatures, and their enemies the binns were water creatures, while the medieval Islamic historian al-Tabari claimed they were created from poisonous fire (سموم). In most versions of the stories, they fought in part of a series of wars for control of the earth before the creation of humanity, and most of the ancient species became extinct, including the hinns.

In the context of a gravesite, it is likely that the term 'sons of hinns' did not refer to some known people, but an ancient gravesite of a by then unknown people. Oak trees are known to live over 1000 years and reproduce, so the gravesite in question could have already been thousands of years old. Later during the reforms of King Josiah, ancient graves and Asherah groves near Jerusalem were destroyed, and he was specifically recorded as destroying a statue in the valley of the sons of Hinns, implying that this was the gravesite he destroyed.

This verse, referring to the 'Gehenna of fire,' could only be a Christian-era interpretation of Gehenna, based on the Greek concept of Hades. The traditional Semitic interpretation was that the underworld was a place of dryness. The development of the Hinn from giant creatures into fire beings was also based on Greek influence and was not found in Semitic literature earlier than the Greek era.

Greek Apocalypse of Ezra: Chapter 2

While I was saying this to him, Michael and Gabriel came, and all the apostles and they said, "Rejoice, faithful man of God!"

Ezra said, "Rise, and come here with me, Lord, to judgment."

The Lord replied, "Look, I give you my covenant, between you and I, that you may receive it."

Ezra asked, "Let us plead before you."

God replied, "Ask Abraham your forefather how a son pleads with his father, and then come plead with us."

Ezra stated, "As the Lord lives, I will not stop pleading with you on behalf of the Christian people. Where is your ancient compassion, Lord? Where is your patience?"

God answered, "As I have made night and day, I have made the righteous and the sinner, and he should have lived like the righteous."

The prophet asked, "Who made Adam the first-formed?"[1]

God answered, "My undefiled hands. I put him in paradise to guard the food of the tree of life, and then he became disobedient, and in this transgressed."

The prophet asked, "Was he not protected by an messenger? Wasn't his life guarded by the cherubs for endless ages? How was he deceived? Who was guarded by messengers? You commanded all to be present and to do what was commanded by you. Yet, if you had not given him Eve, the serpent would not have deceived her. So who will you save, and who will you destroy?"

The prophet asked, "My Lord, let us have a second judgment."

God replied, "I threw fire on Sodom and Gomorrah."

The prophet said, "Lord, You deal with us like our deserts."

God said, "Your sins transcend my mercy."

The prophet said, "Remember the scriptures, my father. Who measured out Jerusalem and rebuilt her again? Have mercy, Lord, on sinners. Have mercy on your own creatures. Pity your works."

Then God remembered those who he had made, and said to the prophet, "How can I have mercy on them? They gave me vinegar and gall to drink, and they did not even then repent."

The prophet replied, "Reveal your cherubs, and let us go together to judgment, and show me the day of judgment, what it is like."

God stated, "You have been deceived, Ezra, to compare the day of judgment to that when there is no rain on the Earth, for it is a merciful comparison with that day."

The prophet stated, "I will not stop pleading with you unless I see the day of the consummation."

God answered, "Count the stars and the sand of the sea, and if you can count them, you are also able to plead with me."

Greek Apocalypse of Ezra: Chapter 2 Notes

1 BnF Gr. 929: prôtoplastos (πβοοτℽπλϸτοc)

* Translation: first-formed (or prototype)

Greek Apocalypse of Ezra: Chapter 3

The prophet said, "Lord, You know that I wear human flesh, how can I count the stars of the sky and the sand of the sea?"

God stated, "My chosen prophet, no man will know that great day and the appearance that comes to judge the world. For your sake, my prophet, I have told you the day, but I have not told you the hour."

The prophet asked, "Lord, tell me also the years."

God replied, "If I see that the righteousness of the world has grown, I'll have patience with them, but if not, I will stretch out my hand, and grab the world by its four quarters, and bring them all together into the Valley of Jehoshaphat,[1] and will wipe out the people of men so that the world will be no more."

The prophet asked, "How can your right hand be glorified?"

God answered, "I will be glorified by my messengers."

The prophet inquired, "Lord, if you have decided to do this, why did you make man? You said to our father Abraham, 'Multiply. I will multiply your seed like the stars of the sky, and like the sand that is by the seashore,' so where is your promise?"

God answered, "First I will make an earthquake to knock down the animals and men. When you see that brother gives up brother to death, and that children will rise up against their parents, and that a woman forgets her husband, and when nation will rise up against nation in war, then you will know that the end is near. For then, neither brother pities brother, or man wife, or children parents, or friend friends, or a slave his master, for he who is the adversary of men will come up from Tartarus, and will show men many things. What will I make of you, Ezra? Will you continue to plead with me?"

Greek Apocalypse of Ezra: Chapter 3 Notes

1 This is a restatement of the prophecy of Joel, indicating the author had a copy of the Dokeda, or possibly the entire Septuagint. The valley of Jehoshaphat was likely a reference to wherever King Jehoshaphat defeated the Moabites in the 9th century BC.

Greek Apocalypse of Ezra: Chapter 4

The prophet said, "Lord, I will not stop pleading with you."

God replied, "Count the flowers of the earth. If you can count them, you are also able to plead with me."

The prophet answered, "Lord, I cannot count them. I wear human flesh, but I will not stop pleading with you. I wish, Lord, to see also the underworld of Tartarus."[1]

God said, "Go down and see."

He gave me Michael and Gabriel, and another thirty-four messengers and I went down eighty-five steps, and they brought me down five hundred steps, and I saw a fiery throne and an old man sitting on it, and his judgment was merciless. I asked the messengers, "Who is this? What is his sin?"

They answered me, "This is Herod, who for a time was a king, and ordered the children from two years old and under to be put to death."

I replied, "Woe to his mind!"

Again they took me down thirty steps, and there I saw fire boiling up, and in it, there was a multitude of sinners, and I heard their voice but didn't see their forms. They took me down many steps, which I could not measure. There I saw old men with fiery pivots turning in their ears. I asked, "Who are these, and what is their sin?"

They said to me, "These are those who would not listen."

They took me down another five hundred steps, and there I saw the serpent[2] that doesn't sleep, and fire burning up the sinners. They took me down to the lowest part of destruction, and I saw there the twelve plagues of the abyss. They took me away to the south, and I saw there a man hanging by the eyelids, and the messengers kept whipping him. I asked, "Who is this? What is his sin?"

Michael the commander said to me, "This is one who lay with his mother. For having put into practice a small wish, he has been ordered to be hanged."

They took me away to the north, and I saw a man there bound with iron chains. I asked, "Who is this?"

He answered me, "This is he who claimed 'I am the son of God,' who made stones into bread, and water into wine."

The prophet asked, "My lord, let me know what his form is, and I will tell the humans, that they may not believe in him."

He answered me, "His expression is like that of a wild beast. His right eye is like the morning star, and the other is without motion. His mouth was one cubit, his teeth a span long. His fingers were like scythes, and the footmarks were two spans. On his face was an inscription reading 'Antichrist.'[3] He has been praised to the sky, but he will go down to Hades.[4] At one time he will become a child, and at another, an old man."

The prophet asked, "Lord, how do you permit him when he deceives the humans?"

God answered, "Listen, my prophet. He becomes both a child and an old man, and no one believes him that he is my beloved son. After this, a trumpet will sound, and the tombs will be opened, and the dead will be raised incorruptible. Then the adversary, hearing the dreadful threat, will be hidden in the outer darkness. Then the sky, the earth, and the sea will be destroyed. Then I will burn the sky eighty cubits high, and the earth eight hundred cubits deep."

The prophet asked, "How has the sky sinned?"

God answered, "Since there is evil."

The prophet asked, "Lord, how has the earth sinned?"

God replied, "Since the adversary, having heard the dreadful warnings will be hidden. Because of this I will melt the earth, and with it the enemy of humans."

Greek Apocalypse of Ezra: Chapter 4 Notes

1 BnF Gr. 929: Tartaros (Ταρταρος)

- Translation: Tartarus (or underworld)

Tartaros (Τάρτᾰρος) was the ancient Greek underworld, which like the older Egyptian underworld was entered somewhere in the far west. The ancient Greek historian Strabo believed this word had been invented by Homer, based on the city of Tartêssos (Ταρτησσός) in mind, it being west of the Pillars of Heracles, where the sun sank into Oceanus. Tartêssos was an ancient city-state in southwest Spain, recorded in the Neo-Assyrian records of Esarhaddon as Tarsisi (𒋻𒋛𒋛), where it was used as a metaphor for the most distant known land. It was also recorded as Tršš (𐤕𐤓𐤔𐤔), on the Phoenician language Nora Stone discovered in Sardinia, which is also believed to date to the same era. It was later known as Tartêssos (Ταρτησσος) in Greek myths, however, was no longer viewed as being a known land that people sailed to. In the 4th century BC, Aristotle identified Tartêssos as being on the Atlantic coast of Iberia. Around the same time, the Greek geographer and explorer Pytheas reported that the civilization once existed on the Baetis River, the modern Guadalquivir River in southwest Spain.

While the location of the civilization has been debated for thousands of years, it is commonly accepted as being the 'Tartessian' culture of southwest Iberia. During the 1900s, extensive remains of a bronze age civilization were discovered by archaeologists working in southwest Spain and southern Portugal. This civilization existed between approximately 1900 and 700 BC. It controlled extensive mines in southwest Iberia, which produced both metals and gemstones, and it also appears to have traded extensively with both the Phoenicians and Celts.

Tartarus was also the name of the god of Tartarus, whom the Greek poet Hesiod viewed as one of the primordial gods, who had fathered the monster Typhon. The classical era Greek philosophers believed Typhon and the Egyptian Apophis were the same god, supporting the interpretation of the giant worm/serpent in the Apocalypse and Vision, as being Apophis. As there is no god of the underworld present, it is likely that the word was being used in regards to the place, and not the god, meaning these angels of Tartarus were working for God.

2 BnF Gr. 929: rhomos (ῥῶμος)

- Translation: worm

This appears to be a mistranslation of the Coptic word fnt (ϥⲛⲧ), which means both 'worm' and 'snake.' While the terms for snake and worm are the same in many languages, they were not in Greek or Latin, indicating the text originated in another language. In this case, an identical error is found in the Latin translation of the Vision of Ezra, which this Apocalypse appears to be using as a source. The Vision of Ezra includes many references to the ancient Egyptian underworld, reset in a Christian mindset, indicating it was composed in Egypt.

The giant serpent in the underworld was Ôåpp (𝖔𝖔 𝖀𝖒) in ancient Egyptian beliefs, who lived in the far western region of the underworld, near the place the sun set each evening. During the early Iron Age, he became known as Åpåp (𝖪?𝖪?), a demonic serpent of the underworld in Egyptian beliefs. The Greeks interpreted him as Apophis (Αποφις), an underworld serpent god.

In the early Christian era, he was interpreted as Aphoph (ⲁⲫⲱⲫ) by Coptic Christians, the worm/serpent (ϥⲛⲧ) from the Garden of Eden who was sent to live eternally in the underworld. It is unlikely someone other than an early Coptic Christian would have written a vision of the underworld that included this giant worm/serpent.

3 BnF Gr. 929: Antichristos (ⲁⲛⲧⲫⲭⲣⲓⲥⲧⲟⲥ)

• Translation: antichrist (or false messiah)

The term Antichrist is only found within the Bible in the 1st and 2nd Letters of John, within the Johannine Literature. The concept was popular within the early Christian churches of the 2nd century, however, it fell into disuse once the Gospel of John was accepted as canon by the Byzantine Church. In the mid 2nd century, when the Johannine Literature first surfaced in western Anatolia, the Agoli Christians in the region claimed the Letters of John were written to warn Christians to avoid the Gospel of John, which was actually the Gospel of the Gnostic writer Cerinthus, and the gospel being passed off in John's name was actually the gospel of the Antichrist. This view spread quickly across the churches in both the Roman and Parthian Empires, which prohibited their members from reading both the Gospel and Apocalypse of John.

The Gospel of John was nevertheless accepted quickly by some Christians in Western Anatolia, including the influential Christian philosopher Justin Martyr, and the founders of the Montanist sect of Christianity, which was itself excommunicated by most Christian churches in the two empires because it urged its members to channel the spirit Paraclete (Παράκλητος), who would guide them as the voice (or Word) of God.

The Byzantine Orthodox Church ended most of the early schisms within the Christian community by forcing all Christians to accept that the Jesus in the Gospel of John was the same Jesus as in the Gospels of Matthew, Mark, and Luke, even though the stories and miracles were different, and that the spirit Paraclete from the Gospel of John, was the Holy Spirit, and part of the Trinity with God the Father and Jesus. Therefore this reference to the Antichrist, especially as the sentence endorsed the Jesus from the Gospel of Matthew, who refused to turn stones into bread while rejecting the Jesus from the Gospel of John, who turned water into wine, allows this section of the text the be dated fairly conclusively to sometime during the Antichrist controversy, likely towards its beginning as acceptance of the Johannine Literature did spread along with the Montanist heresy, and was widely accepted by the time the Orthodox church canonized it.

4 BnF Gr. 929: ádou (ᴀᴀου)

• Translation: Hades (or underworld)

In Greek mythology, Hades was the fiery section of the underworld, which was adopted by Christians, Buddhists, and some Jews in the pre-Christian era. Hades and Tartarus were two places within the Abyss, which was itself sometimes referred to as a separate third location within the underworld.

Greek Apocalypse of Ezra: Chapter 5

The prophet begged, "Have mercy, Lord, on the Christian people."

I saw a woman hanging, and four wild beasts sucking her breasts. The messengers said to me, "She begrudged giving her milk, and even threw her infants into the rivers."

I saw a dreadful darkness, and a night that had no stars or moon, neither there neither young or old, brother with brother, mother with child, or wife with husband. I wept, and said, "My god Lord, have mercy on the sinners," And as I said this, there came a cloud and pulled me up, and carried me away again into the skies. I saw many judgments there, and I wept bitterly, and said, "It is better for a man to have never come out of his mother's womb."

Those who were in torment cried out, saying, "Since you have come here, holy one of God, we have found a little rest."

The prophet said, "Blessed are those who cry for their sins."

God stated, "Hear, beloved Ezra. Like a farmer throws the seed of grain to the ground, so also the man throws his seed into the parts of the woman. In the first month, it is all together, in the second it increases in size, in the third it gets hair, in the fourth it gets nails, in the fifth it is turned into milk, and in the sixth, it is made ready and receives life, the seventh it is completely finished, and in the ninth, the barriers of the gate of the woman are opened, and it is born safe and sound into the Earth."

The prophet replied, "Lord, it is better for man to have not been born. Woe to the human people then, when you will come to judgment!"

I asked the Lord, "Lord, why have you created man, and delivered him up to judgment?"

God answered, "With a lofty proclamation. And I will not by any means have mercy on those who transgress my covenant."

The prophet asked, "Lord, where is your goodness?"

God answered, "I have prepared all things for man's sake, and man does not keep my commandments."

The prophet asked, "Lord, reveal to me the judgments and paradise," and the messengers took me away towards the east, and I saw the tree of life. There I saw Enoch, Elijah, Moses, Peter, Paul, Luke, Matthew, and all the righteous, and the patriarchs. There I saw the air kept within barriers, the blowing winds, and the storehouses of the ice, and the eternal judgments. There I saw a man hanging by the skull. They said to me, "This man removed landmarks." I saw great judgments there.

I asked the Lord, "My god Lord, what man, then, who has been born has not sinned?"

They took me down into Tartarus, and I saw all the sinners lamenting and crying and mourning bitterly. I also cried, seeing the humans being tortured.

Greek Apocalypse of Ezra: Chapter 6

Then God said to me, "Ezra, know the names of the messengers at the end of the world: Michael, Gabriel, Uriel, Raphael, Gabuthelon, Aker, Arphugitonos, Beburos, and Zebulon."

Then a voice came to me saying, "Come here and die, Ezra, my beloved. Give that which has been entrusted to you."

The prophet asked, "From where can you bring out my mind?"

The messengers answered, "We can pull it out through the mouth."

The prophet replied, "Mouth to mouth I have spoken with God, and it does not come out of there."

The messengers stated, "Let us bring it out through your nostrils."

The prophet replied, "My nostrils have smelled the sweet savor of the glory of God."

The messengers said, "We can bring it out through your eyes."

The prophet replied, "My eyes have seen the back of God."

The messengers stated, "We can bring it out through the top of your head."

The prophet replied, "I walked around with Moses on the mountain, and it does not come out from there."

The messengers said, "We can pull it out through the points of your nails."

The prophet replied, "My feet also have walked around on the altar."

The messengers went away without having done anything, saying, "Lord, we cannot get his mind."

Then he said to his only begotten son, "Go down, my beloved son, with a great army of messengers, and take the mind of my beloved Ezra."

The Lord, having taken a great army of messengers, said to the prophet, "Give me that which I entrusted to you, the crown has been prepared for you."

The prophet answered, "Lord, if you take my mind from me, who will be left to plead with you for the humans?"

God answered, "As you are mortal, and from the Earth, do not plead with me."

The prophet replied, "I will not stop pleading."

God ordered, "Give up that which was entrusted to you, the crown has been prepared for you. Come and die, so you may gain it."

Then the prophet said with tears, "Lord, what good have I done pleading with you, when I am going to fall down into the earth? Woe for me, woe for me, that I am going to be eaten up by worms! Cry, all you saints and you righteous, for me, who has pleaded a great deal, and who is still delivered up to death. Cry for me, all you saints and you righteous, because I have gone to the pit of Hades."

Greek Apocalypse of Ezra: Chapter 7

God said to him, "Listen, Ezra, my beloved. I, who am immortal, endured a cross, I tasted vinegar and gall, I was laid in a tomb, and I raised up my chosen ones, I called Adam up out of Hades, that I might save the humans. Therefore do not be afraid of death, for that which is from me, that is to say, the mind, goes to the sky, and that which is from the earth, that is to say, the body, goes to the Earth, from which it was taken."

The prophet replied, "Woe for me! Woe for me! What will I set about? What will I do? I don't know."

Then the blessed Ezra said, "Eternal God, maker of the whole creation, who has measured the sky with a span, and who holds the Earth as a handful, who rides on the cherubs, who took the prophet Elijah to the heavens in a chariot of fire, who gives food to all flesh, who all things dread and tremble at from in the face of your power, listen to me, who has pleaded much, and give to all who transcribe this book, and have it, and remember my name, and honor my memory, give them a blessing from the sky, and bless him in all things, as you blessed Joseph in the end, and did not remember his former wickedness in the day of his judgment. Many who have not believed this book will be burnt up like Sodom and Gomorrah."

A voice came to him, saying, "Ezra, my beloved, all things whatever you have asked will I give to each one."

Immediately he gave up his precious mind honorably, in the month of October, on the twenty-eighth. They prepared him for burial with incense and psalms, and his precious and sacred body dispenses strength of mind and body perpetually to those who have recourse to him from a longing desire. To whom is due glory, strength, honor, and adoration of the Father, the Son, and the holy spirit, now and forever, and from ages to ages.

Amen.

Forward to the Vision of Ezra

The Vision of Ezra is a similar work to the Greek Apocalypse of Ezra, however, only survives in Latin manuscripts dating to the 11th through 13th centuries. The Vision is unique among the surviving Apocalypses of Ezra due to its significant Egyptian influence. The Vision may have started as a Christian reworking of an old Egyptian description of the underworld, as it references a lot of old Egyptian underworld iconography.

In the Vision, Ezra is taken on a tour of the underworld by messengers of the underworld (Tartarus) and then is taken to heaven where he begs for mercy for those in the underworld. This is similar to the Greek Apocalypse, except in the Apocalypse, Ezra is first taken to the Sky, where he meets God, and then God sends him to the underworld with the messengers from the sky to guide and protect him. The Greek Apocalypse appears to be an attempt to 'correct' the text, as 'messengers of Tartarus' could be read as either 'messengers from the underworld,' or 'messengers from the god of the underworld.'

In the 8th century BC, the ancient Greek poet Hesiod wrote in his Theogony, that Tartarus was the third oldest god, coming into existence after Chaos (creation) and Ge (Earth). He further described Tartarus as being as far beneath Hades, as the Earth was beneath the sky. He described the distance from the Sky to the Earth, the Earth to Hades, and Hades to Tartarus as being the distance it would take for an anvil to fall for one week. Therefore, in the Greek mindset of the early Christian era, the Vision would have been read as having messengers sent from either the deepest part of the underworld, or the leader of that place, which would have been the devil. As this is contrary to Orthodox teachings, in which the messengers work for God, and the demons work for the devil, it would have needed to be theologically corrected if it was to circulate in the Byzantine Empire.

The Vision itself appears to have been written by a Coptic Christian or Gnostic, as the underworld is largely inspired by the ancient Egyptian underworld. There are several unique underworld elements in the Vision that support a Coptic origin, including dogs attacking the dead, two great lions, and an immense worm, all at the western horizon. While dogs devouring corpses is not unique to Egypt, it was a significant concern in Egypt. Dogs were so closely associated with the dead that the embalming god Anubis was pictured with a jackal's head. The original point of embalming the dead was to stop dogs and jackals from eating the dead.

In the ancient Egyptian religion, two great lions protected the sun as it traveled through the underworld each night. Depictions of the sun on the horizon, guarded by the two lions are common, although different Egyptian cults believed that the lions were different specific lion deities. The oldest version was likely the Heliopolitan theology, which taught they were Shu and Tefnut, the first created by Atum, the creator. In the Heliopolitan theology, Shu and Tefnut, which means 'dryness' and 'moisture,' were the two primordial elements that the universe was made from, which in turn created Geb (Earth) and Nut (the sky). They were also viewed as being the first male and female, something akin to Adam and Eve. They were often depicted as either a set of humans, lions, or a hybrid of humans and lions. Later in Egyptian history, alternative lion deities were said to guard the sun in the underworld, including Sekhmet and Maahes, who were also depicted as human-lion hybrids. It is unlikely that a non-Egyptian Christian would have conceptualized the underworld with two lions guarding it.

The Vision's immortal 'worm' whose size could not be reckoned, is no doubt the origin of the 'worm that does not sleep' in the Greek Apocalypse. This is either a unique element in Christian texts or a mistranslation from a language in which the same word is used for 'worm' and 'serpent.' The Latin vermis, which means 'worm,' is most likely a mistranslation of the Coptic word fnt (ϥⲛⲧ), which means both 'worm' and 'snake.' While the terms for snake and worm are the same in many languages, they were not the same in Greek or Latin, supporting the text originating in another language, such as Coptic. The giant serpent in the underworld was Ôåpp ([illegible]) in ancient Egyptian beliefs, which lived in the far western region of the underworld, near the place the sun set each evening. During the early Iron Age, he became known as Åpåp ([illegible]), a demonic serpent of the underworld in Egyptian beliefs. The Greeks interpreted him as Apophis (Αποφις), an underworld serpent god. In the early Christian era, he was interpreted as Aphoph (ⲁⲫⲱⲫ) by Coptic Christians, the worm/serpent (ϥⲛⲧ) from the Garden of Eden who was sent to live eternally in the underworld. It is unlikely someone other than an early Coptic Christian would have written a vision of the underworld that included this giant worm/serpent.

While the Vision is supposed to originate with Ezra, the Ezra in question is not clarified. His genealogy is not listed, and no year is given that could identify this as either the exilarch Shealtiel or Ezra the scribe. Nevertheless, it is very similar in concept to the Greek Apocalypse, and as such, it would be the exilarch Shealtiel who supposedly had this vision. However, other than the name Ezra, there is nothing to tie the text to the ancient Judahites. Furthermore, the fact that having sex on the sabbath was identified as a major sin, on par with infanticide and giving people bad directions, it is unlikely that the author was Jewish. There is no prohibition on married couples having sexual relations on the sabbath, and it is encouraged by some schools of thought, as it fulfills both the commandment to enjoy the sabbath and the commandment to be fruitful and multiply.

Unlike in the Greek Apocalypse, God answers Ezra's questions, however, does not relent from punishing people for their sins before death. The motif of Ezra demanding answers from God was common in the various Apocalypses of Ezra, which were likely the reason the Byzantine Church ultimately did not include the prophet Ezra in the Byzantine Orthodox Bible. The leaders of the Byzantine Church were too wrapped up in important issues like Adoptionism versus the Trinity, and the debate over Mary's perpetual virginity to be bothered by their members demanding answers to minor questions like 'Why does God permit bad things to happen to good people?'

This debate seems to have filtered into the Vision, where church doctors who confused 'baptism and the law,' would spend eternity having molten lead poured over them. This verse indicates the Vision likely originated sometime after the schism between the Coptic church and the Byzantine Orthodox church, in 325 BC.

The Coptic Church refused to accept the proto-Orthodox interpretation of the origin of the son of God and claimed that God fathered his son, while the Orthodox view is that both had existed eternally. The Coptic argument was based on scriptural interpretation, while the orthodox view was supported by Emperor Constantine's mother, therefore, the 'baptism versus law' reference was likely in relation to this. It is unlikely that the ancient Egyptian elements in the Vision would have been found in Coptic works after 340 AD, when both the Orthodox and Coptic churches purged the texts they believed to have originated among the Gnostics. Caches of ancient texts have been found in Egypt dating to the purge, which sometimes includes ancient Egyptian iconography similar to the Vision of Ezra.

Vision of Ezra

Ezra prayed to the Lord, "Grant me courage, Lord, that I might not fear when I see the judgments of the sinners."

Seven angels of Tartarus[1] were sent, who carried him beyond the seventieth level in the infernal regions, and he saw the fiery gates. At these gates, he saw two lions[2] lying there, and from their mouths, nostrils, and eyes came the most powerful flames. The most powerful men were entering and passing through the fire, and it did not touch them.

Ezra asked, "Who are they, who walk safely?"

The angels answered him, "They are the just whose reputation has ascended to heaven, who gave to charity generously, clothed the naked, and desired to be good."

Others were entering, those who might pass through the gates, and dogs[3] were ripping them apart and fire was consuming them. Ezra asked, "Who are they?"

The messengers answered, "They denied the Lord, and sinned with women on the Lord's day."[4]

Ezra replied, "Lord, have mercy on the sinners!"

They led him lower, beyond the fiftieth level, and he saw in that place men standing in torment. Some were throwing fire in their faces, others, however, were whipping them with fiery scourges. The earth cried aloud, "Whip them and refuse to have mercy on them because they worked impiety upon me."

Ezra asked, "Who are they, who are tormented like this daily?"

The messengers answered, "They became aroused by married women. The married women are those who adorned themselves not for their husbands, but that they might please others, desiring an evil desire."

Ezra said. "Lord, have mercy on the sinners!"

Again they brought him to the south, and he saw a fire, and poor ones and also women hanging, and messengers were beating them with fiery clubs. Ezra said, "Lord have mercy on the sinners! Who are they?"

The messengers said, "They lived with their mothers, and had an evil desire."

Ezra said, "Lord, have mercy on the sinners!"

They led him downward in the infernal regions, and he saw a caldron in which were sulfur and bitumen, and it was in commotion just like the waves of the sea. Yet they just were entering, and in the midst of it, they were walking over the fiery waves, praising greatly the name of the Lord, just like those who walk over ice of cold water. Ezra asked, "Who are they?"

The messengers said, "They are the ones who were making better confessions before God and the holy priests every day, freely bringing alms and resisting sins."

The sinners came, wishing to pass over, and the messengers of Tartarus came and submerged them in the fiery stream. From the fire they cried out, saying, "Lord, have pity on us!" But he did not have pity.

A voice was heard, but a body was not seen because of the fire and the anguish, and Ezra asked, "Who are they?"

The messengers answered, "They were consumed with lust all their days. They did not receive strangers, and they did not give alms. They took unjustly the things of others for themselves, and they had evil desires. Therefore, they are in anguish."

Ezra said, "Lord, have mercy on the sinners!"

He walked as before and he saw in an obscure place and an immortal serpent,[5] its size he was not able to reckon. In front of its mouth stood many sinners, and when it drew a breath, they were sucked into its mouth like flies, and then when it exhaled, they all exited a different color. Ezra asked, "Who are they?"

They answered, "They were full of every bad thing and they went about without confession or penitence."

He saw a person sitting on a fiery throne, and his counselors stood around him in the fire, and they served him from the fire and out of every side. Ezra asked, "Who is that?"

The messengers replied, "That man, whose name is Herod, was king for a long time, who, in Bethlehem of Judea, slew the infant males on account of the Lord."

Ezra said, "The Lord's judgement is correct!"

He walked and saw men who were bound and the messengers of Tartarus were pricking their eyes with thorns. Ezra asked, "Who are they?"

The messengers answered, "They showed the wrong paths to those who were lost."

Ezra said, "Lord, have mercy on the sinners!"

He saw virgins with five-hundred-pound neck irons on them, near death and going to the west. Ezra asked, "Who are they?"

The messengers said, "They violated their virginity before marriage."

There was a multitude of old men, lying prostrate, and molten iron and lead were being poured onto them. He asked, "Who are they?"

The messengers answered, "They are the doctors of the law who confuse baptism and the law of the Lord, because they were teaching with words, but they did not spur on the work. For this, they are judged."[6]

Ezra said, "Lord have mercy on the sinners!"

He saw visions of a furnace, against the setting sun, burning with great fire, into which were sent many kings and princes of this world, and many thousands of poor people were accusing them and saying, "They, through their power, hurt us and dragged free men into slavery."

He saw another furnace, burning with pitch and sulfur, into which sons were thrown who acted wretchedly at the hands of their parents and caused injury by means of their mouths. He saw in a most obscure place another furnace burning, into which many women were thrown. He asked, "Who are they?"

The messengers answered, "They had sons in adultery and killed them, and those little ones themselves accused them, saying, 'Lord, the souls which you gave to us these women took away.'"

He asked, "Who are they?"

The messengers answered, "They killed their sons."

Ezra said, "Lord, have mercy on the sinners!"

Then Michael and Gabriel came and said to him, "Come into heaven!"

Ezra answered, "As my Lord lives, I may not come until I see every judgment of sinners."

They led him downward into the infernal regions beyond the fourteenth level, and he saw lions and little dogs lying around fiery flames. The just traveled through them and crossed over into Paradise, and he saw many thousands of the just and their habitations were the most splendid of any time.

After he saw this, he was lifted up into heaven, and he came to a multitude of messengers, and they said to him, "Pray to the Lord for the sinners," and they put him down within the sight of the Lord.

He said, "Lord, have mercy on the sinners!"

The Lord replied, "Ezra, let them receive according to their works."

Ezra said, "Lord, you have shown more clemency to the animals which eat the grass and have not returned your praise, than to us. They die and have no sin, however, you torture us, living and dead."

The Lord replied, "In my image I have formed man and I have commanded that they not sin, yet they sinned. Therefore they are in torment. The elect are those who go into eternal rest on account of confession, penitence, and their generosity in charity."

Ezra asked, "Lord, what must the just do in order that they may not enter into judgment?"

The Lord answered him, "Just as the slave who performed well for his master will receive freedom, so too will the just in the kingdom of heaven."

Vision of Ezra Notes

1 Manuscript AI/6: Tartarus

Tartaros (Τάρτἄρος) was the ancient Greek underworld, which like the older Egyptian underworld was entered somewhere in the far west. The ancient Greek historian Strabo believed this word had been invented by Homer, based on the city of Tartêssos (Ταρτησσός) in mind, it being west of the Pillars of Heracles, where the sun sank into Oceanus. Tartêssos was an ancient city-state in southwest Spain, recorded in the Neo-Assyrian records of Esarhaddon as Tarsisi (⁌⹔⹔), where it was used as a metaphor for the most distant known land. It was also recorded as Tršš (ʷʷ٩⊦), on the Phoenician language Nora Stone discovered in Sardinia, which is also believed to date to the same era. It was later known as Tartêssos (Ταρτησσος) in Greek myths, however, was no longer viewed as being a known land that people sailed to. In the 4th century BC, Aristotle identified Tartêssos as being on the Atlantic coast of Iberia. Around the same time, the Greek geographer and explorer Pytheas reported that the civilization once existed on the Baetis River, the modern Guadalquivir River in southwest Spain.

While the location of the civilization has been debated for thousands of years, it is commonly accepted as being the 'Tartessian' culture of southwest Iberia. During the 1900s, extensive remains of a bronze age civilization were discovered by archaeologists working in southwest Spain and southern Portugal. This civilization existed between approximately 1900 and 700 BC. It controlled extensive mines in southwest Iberia, which produced both metals and gemstones, and it also appears to have traded extensively with both the Phoenicians and Celts.

Tartarus was also the name of the god of Tartarus, whom the Greek poet Hesiod viewed as one of the primordial gods, who had fathered the monster Typhon. The classical era Greek philosophers believed Typhon and the Egyptian Apophis were the same god, supporting the interpretation of the giant worm/serpent in the Vision, as being Apophis. As there is no god of the underworld present, it is likely that the word was being used in regards to the place, and not the god, meaning these messengers of Tartarus were working for God.

2 In the ancient Egyptian religion, two great lions protected the sun as it traveled through the underworld each night. Depictions of the sun on the horizon, guarded by the two lions are common, although different Egyptian cults believed that the lions were different specific lions deities. The oldest version was likely the Heliopolitan theology, which taught they were Shu and Tefnut, the first created by Atum, the creator. In the Heliopolitan theology, Shu and Tefnut, which means 'dryness' and 'moisture,' were the two primordial elements that the universe was made from, which in turn created Geb (Earth) and Nut (the sky).

They were also viewed as being the first male and female, something akin to Adam and Eve. They were often depicted as either a set of humans, lions, or a hybrid of humans and lions. Later in Egyptian history, alternative lion deities were said to guard the sun in the underworld, including Sekhmet and Maahes, who were also depicted as human-lion hybrids. It is unlikely that a non-Egyptian Christian would have conceptualized the underworld with two lions guarding it.

3 The reference to dogs ripping up the bodies of the dead is a common motif in ancient Egyptian religion, where elaborate burial rituals were conducted to avoid the bodies being eaten by jackals. The god of embalming was the jackal-headed god Anubis. While this is not conclusive evidence of an Egyptian origin for the text, it does support it, as few cultures envisioned dogs defiling human corpses in the underworld.

4 There is no prohibition regarding sex on the Sabbath in Judaism. In point of fact, some Jewish schools of thought promote sex between married couples as a double-mitzvah, as it fulfills the duty of enjoying the Sabbath and the commandment to be fruitful and multiply. This line clearly indicates that the Vision was not written by an ancient Judahite, whether interpreted as Shealtiel or Ezra.

5 Manuscript AI/6: vermis

• Translation: worm

This appears to be a mistranslation of the Coptic word fnt (ϥⲛⲧ), which means both 'worm' and 'snake.' While the terms for snake and worm are the same in many languages, they were not in Greek or Latin, indicating the text originated in another language. The giant serpent in the underworld was Ôåpp (𒐍𒐍𒐍) in ancient Egyptian beliefs, who lived in the far western region of the underworld, near the place the sun set each evening. During the early Iron Age, he became known as Åpåp (𐤊𐤉𐤊𐤆), a demonic serpent of the underworld in Egyptian beliefs. The Greeks interpreted him as Apophis (Αποφις), an underworld serpent god.

In the early Christian era, he was interpreted as Aphoph (ⲁ̀ⲫⲱⲫ) by Coptic Christians, the worm/serpent (ϥⲛⲧ) from the Garden of Eden who was sent to live eternally in the underworld. It is unlikely someone other than an early Coptic Christian would have written a vision of the underworld that included this giant worm/serpent. As the original version of the Apocalypse would have been about a snake, not a worm, the word 'serpent' is used in this translation.

6 This line, regarding Church doctors being judged for confusing 'baptism and the law,' indicates the text likely originated sometime after the schism between the Coptic church and the Byzantine Orthodox church, in 325 BC. The Coptic Church refused to accept the proto-Orthodox interpretation of the origin of the son of God and claimed that God fathered his son, while the Orthodox view is that both had existed eternally. The Coptic argument was based on scriptural interpretation, while the orthodox view was supported by Emperor Constantine's mother, therefore, the 'baptism versus law' reference was likely in relation to this.

The churches never reunified, and so the text may originate at any point after the schism began.

Forward to the Syriac Apocalypse of Ezra and the Arabic Apocalypse of Daniel

The Syriac Apocalypse of Ezra is a separate apocalypse from the Judahite, Latin, or Greek Apocalypses, and is sometimes called the Revelation of Ezra. Like the Catholic Apocalypse of Ezra, it appears to have been reworked in the High Middle Ages. Another version of the apocalypse has survived in Arabic but is attributed to Daniel not Ezra, commonly known as the Arabic Apocalypse of Daniel.

The Arabic version is shorter and appears to be older, likely dating to earlier than the time of Muhammad, while the Syriac version has been reworked into an anti-Islamic apocalypse, likely between 1229 and 1244. The apocalypse includes a reference from the High Middle Ages to Muslims as Ishmaelites, and Mongols as Gog and Magog, forming an alliance and conquering Jerusalem. This idea would not have been conceivable until the Mongols defeated the Khwarazmian Empire, an Islamic Turko-Persian empire in Iran and Central Asia. Before that, the idea that the Mongols could reach Jerusalem was not a consideration.

The Apocalypse indicates that the city of Jerusalem was occupied by Christians at the time, which would place the anti-Islamic redaction sometime between 1229 and 1244. The Latin crusaders had been driven out of

FORWARD TO THE SYRIAC APOCALYPSE OF EZRA AND THE ARABIC APOCALYPSE OF DANIEL

Jerusalem in 1187, however, the kingdom of Jerusalem continued to exist, first from its capital in Tyre, and later Acre, however, in 1229 Jerusalem was recaptured, and held until 1244. As the Principality of Antioch was another crusader state to the north, and the name 'Antioch' appears to have been added earlier in the Apocalypse, the redactor may have meant it as a piece of propaganda intended to garner support from Byzantine Christians, who had not generally participated in the crusades and had better relations with the Muslims than the Catholics.

The older Arabic version of the apocalypse likewise appears to have been used for propaganda, however, was anti-Jewish instead of anti-Islamic, and appears to have been translated into Arabic before the time of Muhammad. Based on the dialect of Arabic, it most likely originated in Palestine among early Christians. The Arabic version is much shorter and is mostly paraphrased from the Gospels and other early Christian works, however, the content of the apocalypse is clearly something that was incorporated into the longer Syriac Apocalypse. While the content of the Arabic apocalypse is repeated in the Syriac apocalypse, it is not a direct translation, but a series of paraphrases that are reinterpreted in an anti-Islamic way. Nevertheless, while the longer

Syriac apocalypse must originate much later than the pre-Islamic Arabic apocalypse, it has much more content, most of which appears to have been composed in Neo-Babylonian sometime between 597 and 592 BC.

The Syriac apocalypse has many Greek loanwords, confirming it was written in Greek, as well as an Arabic word the Syriac translator chose over a Syriac word, suggesting the Syriac translation was done long after Northern Iraq became Arabic speaking. All known copies of the Syriac Apocalypse can be traced to Iraqi Kurdistan, or the old Christian churches of Mosul, just south of Kurdistan. All of the surviving manuscripts are also in the Eastern Syriac script, and ten of the known 15 manuscripts can be linked to the Rabban Hormizd Monastery, of the Chaldean Catholic church, suggesting that all known copies are derived from the texts maintained at that monastery.

The oldest known manuscript is from 1702 and is known as Ms. Mingana Syriac 11, or simplified to Mingana 11. It was copied on January 16, 1702, by a Hoshabo, son of Daniel, son of Joseph the priest, son of Hoshabo, and bought by Alphonse Mingana in the 1920s. Minanga was a British orientalist who had been born in Ottoman Kurdistan, and in the 1920s made multiple trips to northern Iraq to acquire ancient manuscripts, which later became the Mingana Collection at the University of Birmingham, in England. The Syriac apocalypse was commented on by European theologians in the early 1700s. Giuseppe Simone Assemani noted in the Bibliotheca Orientalis Clementino-Vaticana that the Apocalypse could not date back to Ezra's time, as it mentioned Constantine. This view still dominates academic analysis of the text, and almost all scholars who have bothered to publish their views of the Apocalypse interpret it as a medieval Christian anti-Islamic text.

In 1887, Ludwig Iselin broke with this tradition, by claiming it was a reworking of a pre-Christian apocalypse, written in Aramaic. His argument was based on the parallel between the four kings bound on the Euphrates in the Syriac Apocalypse and the four messengers bound in the Euphrates in John's Apocalypse. The words mlkyå ($N^{\wedge}\mathcal{I}L\mathcal{I}$), meaning 'kings,' and mlåkyå ($N^{\wedge}\mathcal{I}NL\mathcal{I}$), meaning 'messengers,' are spelled very similar in Aramaic, and Iselin's argument was that the author of John's apocalypse had misunderstood a reference in an older Apocalypse.

This was rejected by Christian theologians, who argued that John was seeing an original apocalypse from God, and therefore the error must have been made in the Syriac translation of John's Greek language apocalypse. However, the Apocalypse of John has never been accepted as canon by the Syriac churches, and it is unlikely that someone would have mistranslated the Greek word angelos (ἄγγελος), meaning 'messengers,' with archontes (ἄρχοντες), meaning 'kings.'

Later in 1887, the first Western translation of the Arabic Apocalypse of Daniel was published, in Hebraica. The manuscript was labelled as Paris Ms. 107 in Hebraica, however, is labelled as BnF Ms. Arabe 150 today. The manuscript originated in Egypt in 1606, which is a century earlier than any of the surviving Syriac manuscripts. The parallels with the Syriac apocalypse were noted and cautiously discussed, without any question of which came first, as the Arabic apocalypse did not include any mention of the four kings or messengers at the Euphrates.

In 1894, Jean-Baptiste Chabot produced a translation of manuscript BnF 326, and dismissed Iselin's claims that both the Apocalypses of Ezra and John were based on old Jewish Aramaic apocalypses. Iselin and Chabot's views had both been shaped by their religious preconceptions, as Iselin believed both apocalypses originated among Jews, and Chabot believed both apocalypses originated among Christians. Chabot's analysis assumed the apocalypse originated in Syriac, not Greek, and the Syriac author had a faulty translation of the Apocalypse of John, which included four kings bound on the Euphrates, instead of four messengers bound on the Euphrates.

Most later analysis builds on Chabot's conclusions while ignoring his assumptions. The Syriac version is now generally accepted as being a translation of a Greek apocalypse, and it is generally believed that the Apocalypse of John was not available until more recently in Eastern Syriac. Both the Apocalypse and Gospel of John were initially rejected by the Church of the East, and the Apocalypse of John is still rejected by many churches that descend from the Church of the East. The specific churches that have maintained the Apocalypse of John converted to the Eastern Catholic Church after the schism in the Church of the East of 1552 and would have had access to the Apocalypse of John after that. However, all scholars agree that the anti-Islamic version must have already existed before that time, with the latest possible date being before the fall of Constantinople in 1493.

In 1896, Wilhelm Bousset provided an analysis of the figures in the Apocalypse, based on the setting of the early Islamic era, ignoring the older version of the Apocalypse attributed to Daniel. He proposed that the horned serpent represented the Umayyads, the eagle represented the Abbasids, the viper represented the Fatimids, the four kings on the Euphrates and ravens represented the Turks, and the lion's cub represented one of the first Christian crusaders. This original form of the Apocalypse would have then been reworked in the 12th century based on the war between the Fatimids and Mamluk Turks, which is why it does not actually reflect either time period accurately.

In 1997, Robert G. Hoyland interpreted the Bull as Khusrau II, the Sasanian king who laid siege to Constantinople in 626, and the Lion's cub as Emperor Heraclius who allied with the Turks from Central Asia to repulse the siege and invade Persia. Hoyland's analysis places the later redaction into the final form in the 11th century, based on the conflict between the Fatimids and the Seljuk Turks.

However, all these explanations fail to note why Muhammed would be called a good man from the south in an anti-Islamic work, which has been noted by some of the scholars in their interpretations. Each interpretation has detractors, as there is no way to resolve all of the 'beasts' in the text. One common way to deal with this is to assume that the Panther (ܩܕܪܐ) of the North and Leopard (ܢܡܪܐ) of the South are the same character, regardless of the spelling of the word and opposing directions in the apocalypse.

FORWARD TO THE SYRIAC APOCALYPSE OF EZRA AND THE ARABIC APOCALYPSE OF DANIEL

One of the chief assumptions of analysts is that the extra content of the Syriac apocalypse was all added when the longer anti-Islamic version of the apocalypse was created, however, that does not address the curious names of the central character in the apocalypses. In the Arabic apocalypse, the prophet was called Daniel, and his student was called Ôzrh (عزره), which Western translations generally render as Ezra, however, the Arabic spelling of Ezra is Ôzrā (عزرا). Ôzrh (عزره) is an Arabic transliteration of the Hebrew word ôzrh (עזרה), meaning 'help.' In the Syriac apocalypse, the prophet is Ezra, however, his student has the Greek name Carpos. In both cases, it is the student, and author, with the odd name, however, both of these names could easily be explained as descending from the name Azariah (עֲזַרְיָה), if the apocalypse was originally written in Neo-Babylonian, and later two separate translations, one in Greek, and one in Aramaic, were made directly from the Neo-Babylonian text.

Azariah, meaning 'Help of Yahw,' is one of the three youths associated with Daniel, who was thrown into a furnace when Judah rebelled from Babylonian rule under the rule of King Zedekiah. The phonetic spelling of Azariah in Neo-Babylonian cuneiform would have been Eziraia (𒂊𒍣𒊑𒅀), however, this would include the name of the god Ia (𒂗), the name of the 'terrible god' of floods, whose name was not generally mentioned. All three youths were given alternative names in the Book of Daniel, none of which appear to be Babylonian. Azariah's alternate name was Aved Nego (עֲבֵד נְגוֹ) in Masoretic Daniel, which is a transliteration of the Aramaic Ôbd Ngh (עֲבֵד נְגֹה), meaning 'servant of (the planet) Venus.' The logical substitute for Ia (𒂗) would have been Ilu (𒀭), meaning 'god,' rendering the Neo-Babylonian spelling as Ezirailu (𒉒𒂍𒀭).

If the original Greek translation was made directly from the cuneiform version, the name could have been read logographically as 'grain strike god,' and as Carpos was the Greek god of harvesting grain, whose name was derived from the word for 'cutting,' Carpos (Καρπός) would have been the obvious translation. This indicates the original Ezra in the apocalypse was probably the youth Azariah, whose name was simplified to 'helper' in an Aramaic translation, which the Arabic apocalypse is based on. The simplification of the name in Aramaic is likely because the scribe recognized it could not have originally been Ôzryål (עֹזְרִיאֵל), commonly anglicized as Azrael, the name of the Classical Judahite psychopomp.

If the apocalypse originated in a Neo-Babylonian conversation between Daniel and his student Azariah, then it dates to between 597 BC, when they were taken prisoner by the Babylonians, and 587 BC, when Azariah was thrown into the furnace by Nebuchadnezzar. The political landscape of the region was entirely different, and the world of Daniel was divided between the four allied kings who defeated the Assyrians on the Euphrates, and the Assyrians' former allies: Egypt and Lydia. The apocalypse refers to the four kings bound on the Euphrates, which would be a reference to Cyaxares I of Media, Nebuchadnezzar II of Babylon, and Cyrus I of Persia, along with the king of Scythia. The four kings had been at war against the Assyrians for twenty years when they finally defeated the remnants of the Neo-Assyrian forces and their Egyptian allies in 905 BC, at the Battle of Cerchemish on the Euphrates River.

After the battle, the last of the Assyrian forces had been defeated, and the Egyptians withdrew permanently from the region, ceding their historic claims to Syria. It was the end of a twenty-year-long war, and the kings wanted to make sure the peace was permanent, so they agreed to bind their empires through marriage. There is no evidence that the Scythians married into the union, however they were one of the victors. This may have been because the Scythian tribes did not have hereditary leadership. The evidence that survives of their leadership at the time suggests a steppes confederacy, meaning the king was only the king until another Scythian killed him.

The three kings who united their families were Cyaxares I, Nebuchadnezzar II, and Cyrus I. Nebuchadnezzar married Amyris, Cyaxares daughter, and the sister of Cyaxares' heir Astyages. Cyrus, although quite old, later married Astyges' much younger daughter, also named Amytis, while his son and heir Cambyses I married Astyges' other daughter Mandane. The union of the four kings collapsed shortly after Nebuchadnezzar's reign when the kingship of the Babylonian empire was usurped by Neriglissar in 560 BC. The Persians and Medes maintained their union which later formed the basis of the Persian Empire. Cyrus II, the Persian king who conquered Babylon in 539 BC was the great-grandson of both King Cyaxares of the Medes and King Cyrus I of Persia, both of whom are believed to have fought at the Battle of Cerchemish.

Nebuchadnezzar and Cyaxares' daughter Amytis were the parents of the future King Amel-Marduk. Therefore, when Neriglissar led the coup against Amel-Marduk, he was also breaking the union of the four kingdoms. When Neriglissar usurped the throne, Daniel left Babylon and was later reported to be in Media and

285

Persia, indicating that he had supported Amel-Marduk, and had maintained his allegiance to the Medo-Persian royal family. Amel-Marduk had a complicated relationship with his father and appears to have been imprisoned for years for being part of a conspiracy against Nebuchadnezzar. The nature of the conspiracy is not understood, however, it seems to have happened a couple of decades after the era of the apocalypse.

According to the Leviticus Rabbah, a Byzantine-era Jewish text, Amel-Marduk was imprisoned by his father, because some Babylonian officials had proclaimed him king while Nebuchadnezzar was away. There is a very damaged surviving tablet from Nebuchadnezzar's reign which may support this. In the tablet, Amel-Marduk publically accused Nebuchadnezzar of defiling the temples of the gods in their home cities and taking their wealth to the Esagila, the great temple of Marduk in Babylon. This parallels what Nebuchadnezzar was reported as doing to Jerusalem in the Masoretic Book of Kings (Septuagint's 4th Kingdoms), and suggests he did it in many conquered cities. The Leviticus Rabbah goes on to claim that while Amel-Marduk was imprisoned, he met the Judahite exilarch Jeconiah, whose son was the future exilarch Shealtiel, also known as Ezra in the Judahite Apocalypse of Ezra.

Late in his reign, Nebuchadnezzar appears to have made peace with Amel-Marduk, and appointed him as his heir again by 566 BC, resulting in a smooth transition of authority in 562 BC when Nebuchadnezzar died. This appointment was likely more as a result of the fact that Amel-Marduk was the grandson of Cyaxares, and not declaring him the crowned prince would be a declaration of war on Media, Persia, and Scythia, as well as Lydia, which had married into the union of kingdoms. When he took the throne, Amel-Marduk is recorded as freeing both Jeconiah, the exilarch of Judah, and Baalezer, the exilarch of Tyre. It is unclear if he also freed other exilarchs, however, Judah and Tyre had previously been part of the anti-Babylonian alliance in southern Canaan, indicating that Amel-Marduk was likely concerned about the Egyptian frontier. Egypt was still outside the union of kingdoms, and a major threat to Babylon.

In the case of Tyre, Amel-Marduk went so far as to recognize Baalezar as king, meaning Tyre was independent again. According to the Septuagint's 4th Kingdoms, Amel-Marduk was also planning on freeing the Judahite captives in Babylon, which suggests that Amel-Marduk wanted to restore a buffer state between Babylon and Egypt. Unfortunately, Neriglissar's coup prevented this

from happening, and it may have been the reason for the
coup. Neriglissar was recorded as being a wealthy businessman during the reign of Nebuchadnezzar, and it is
theorized that much of his wealth originated in the
plunder of Jerusalem. This theory is based on the report
in the book of Jeremiah, who was present at the destruction of Jerusalem, that a government official named Nrgl
Shr-tzr (נרגל שר־אצר) was present when the temple and
palace were destroyed. If this was the same Neriglissar,
then he would have had a large number of Judahite
slaves, which Amel-Marduk reportedly wanted to
release.

Neriglissar was reported to be married to one of
Nebuchadnezzar's daughters, which he apparently
thought would be enough to maintain the union of kingdoms, however, Media and Persia appear to have embargoed the Babylonians. This was likely because
Neriglissar's power was based on his wealth, and
Babylon was left trading with Egypt, its biggest threat,
and the Arabs, Carians, Lydians, and Greeks. As the
Babylonians had a weak navy, they were at a major
disadvantage in the Mediterranean, and the Greeks and
Carians were closely allied to the Egyptians. In the south,
the over land trade with the Arabs was dominated by
the Qedarites, who had been attacking Babylonian trade

routes since they'd overthrown the Neo-Assyrian Empire.

In 599 BC, Nebuchadnezzar II moved his residence to Damascus, making it the de facto capital of the Neo-Babylonian Empire. He moved to Damascus so he could personally lead the war to stop the organized bands of raiders operating in Syria at the time. Within a year he learned that the raiders were actually Qedarites, and marched his army south to the Dumat Oasis, the Qedarite capital, where he seized the statues of their gods. This was a traditional Mesopotamian strategy to conquer nations, as the gods of those nations would become hostages in the capital city. In 598 BC, after capturing the gods of Dumat, Nebuchadnezzar returned to Babylon, however, the Qedarites had more gods in the ancient holy city of Tayma, and so they continued to raid the Babylonian trade routes until Nabonidus, the last Babylonian king, occupied Tayma in 552 BC. Nabonidus personally maintained a constant occupation of Tayma for a decade, making it the de facto capital of the Neo-Babylonian empire.

Tayma is mentioned repeatedly in the Syrian Apocalypse, however, as the name can also be translated in Syriac as the directions 'right' or 'south,' those directions are more often used by translators, as Tayma was not significant in the High Middle Ages. Tayma is significant in the apocalypse as the home to the nmrå (ܢܡܪܐ), which is routinely translated as 'leopard,' but is also the Syriac word for 'Asherahs.' This results in the translation of 'Leopard of the South,' for what could also be translated as 'Asherahs of Tayma.' Again, the translation of Asherahs makes no sense after the rise of Islam, and so 'Leopard of the South' is generally preferred by most translators. Nevertheless, on the Tayma Stele, which dates to the 6th century BC, Åshyrå (𐡀𐡔𐡉𐡓𐡀) was one of the four deities worshipped in Tayma, indicating that the original apocalypse was referring to the priestesses of Asherah at Tayma.

The Asherahs of Tayma (or Leopard of the South) were introduced when someone identified as the Lion's cub (ܓܘܪܝܐ ܕܐܪܝܐ) sent a messenger to them (or it) requesting they (or it) intervene to protect the Viper's Younger Chick from the Ravens, who were trying to kill him. The term Lion's cub is used interchangeably with Lioness' cub in some manuscripts, indicating that this was a reference to King Zedekiah of Judah, who was referred to as the Lioness' cub in the writing of Ezekiel, who lived at the time when the events took place. Asherah was one of the deities previously worshipped in Judah before Zedekiah's father King Josiah banned her worship a couple of decades earlier.

Zedekiah would have had a practical reason to contact the priestesses of Asherah in Tayma, as the Ravens (ܩܢܘܡܐ), which can also be translated as Crows or Vultures, appears to be a reference to the Qedarites, whose name translates as 'dark' or 'black.' During the era of the four kings, the Qedar (𐎒𐎄𐎗) tribe ruled north central Arabia, based out of their capital of Dumat (𐎄𐎅𐎚𐎗). The Akkadian cuneiform records from earlier than the 10th century BC referred to Dumat as being in the land of Edom (𒆳𒂀𒈠), suggesting that, like Edom, Dumat and Tayma were part of the kingdom of Judah before Edom rebelled in the 9th century BC. An inscription in Egyptian hieroglyphs dating to the rule of Ramesses III of the New Kingdom era has also been found, indicating the settlement was probably part of the Egyptian Empire, which included Edom.

The longer name of the oasis is Dumat al-Jandal (دُومَة الْجَنْدَل), which translates as 'Palms of the Stone.' The stone in question likely started as a reference to the 35-meter-long triangular megalith at the oasis, which is believed to have been constructed in the 6th millennium BC. If this is the origin of the name, it indicates the site had been continuously occupied since the megalith was exposed to the surface, however, it has been buried throughout recorded history and was not rediscovered until 2020. The megalith is believed to have originally been used for some ceremonial purposes, however, it is not clear what that was, or if it was associated with the deities worshipped there in the historic era.

Most of the deities worshipped at Dumat in the era before Muhammad were fertility deities, and both animal and human sacrifices are reported to have happened. In the 3rd century AD, the Neoplatonic philosopher Porphyry of Tyre reported that each year a boy was sacrificed and was buried under an altar in Dumat. This is similar to the human sacrifice practiced by other fertility cults in the Middle East and Mediterranean, and is similar to the human sacrifice which was banned in Judah circa 625 BC. In Judah, the human sacrifice took place at an altar in a graveyard (גֵּיא בֶן־הִנֹּם) near Jerusalem, described as looking like a grove, suggesting an Asherim, a sacred grave site where oak trees were planted.

The Qedarites were one of the north Arabian tribes who were labeled as Ishmaelites by the Israelites in the era. The Ishmaelites are the theoretical descendants of Abraham's abandoned son Ishmael. According to the Torah, Ishmael's mother took him to Arabia after

Abraham abandoned them to die in the desert, where he later married an Egyptian woman and had twelve sons. Several of the North Arabian tribes and oases had names associated with Ishmael's sons at the time, including the Qedarites, Tayma, and Dumah. This idea continued for a long time and is accepted within Islam, where, depending on the source, Muhammad is either descended from Nebaioth (نابت) or Kedar (قيدر), Ishmael's two eldest sons, and thereby ultimately from Abraham.

During the Neo-Assyrian era, Dumat was described as the capital of the Qedarites in Assyrian records, although Qedarites are also described as migrating to Edom in large numbers and marrying the Edomites during the era. This is likely the origin of the concept within the apocalypse of the people becoming 'sooty' under the Mountain of the South, as Kedar (קֵדָר) translates as 'dark' or 'black.' The Mountain of the South was likely a reference to the Mountain of the Altar, identified in pre-Byzantine times as Mount Sinai.

When the Neo-Assyrian Empire fell in 605 BC, the Qedarites joined the anti-Babylonian alliance, with Ammon, Edom, Egypt, Moab, Sidon, and Tyre. These kingdoms had been occupied or attacked by the Assyrians and did not want to fall under Babylonian control. Judah rejected the alliance and allied with Babylon. King

Nebuchadnezzar II attempted to invade Egypt in 601 BC, but his army was defeated, emboldening the anti-Babylonian faction, and Judah switched sides, joining the alliance. The Qedarites were particularly active around the edges of the Syrian desert and disrupted trade between Babylon and its Syrian territories, which resulted in Nebuchadnezzar moving his imperial residence, the de facto capital of the empire, to Damascus in 599 BC. After Nebuchadnezzar seized the gods of Dumat in 598 BC, the Ammonites and Moabites switched sides, and allied with the Babylonians. In the aftermath, the gods of Tayma became dominant among the Qedarites.

In 597 BC, Nebuchadnezzar, along with his Ammonite and Moabite allies, laid siege to Jerusalem and captured King Jeconiah, who was taken captive to Babylon. A revolt in Babylonia in 594 BC took Nebuchadnezzar back to Babylon and allowed a new anti-Babylonian alliance to form, which included Ammon, Edom, Egypt, Judah, Moab, Sidon, Tyre, and the Qedarites. After suppressing the revolt in Babylon, Nebuchadnezzar returned to Southern Canaan in 587 BC and destroyed the kingdom of Judah.

Sometime in the era, Nebuchadnezzar began the 13-year-long siege of Tyre, which ended when King Ithobaal III of Tyre died, and his son Baal II negotiated a surrender. As Tyre was on an island off the coast of Lebanon, they were able to trade with their colonies across the Mediterranean Sea, and so unlike most of Babylon's sieges, this one was a military failure and an embarrassment to the Babylonian military. The exact years of the siege are debated but generally dated to between 586 and 573 BC. Some historians believe it began in 598 BC, while others believe it was even earlier in 603 BC, however, all sources agree it lasted 13 years.

At the time, there were two cities of Tyre, the emporium on the island in the harbor, and the larger town on the mainland. King Ithobaal III and his court withdrew from the mainland to the island, which the Babylonians could not capture, and survived through long-distance trade with their colonies, as well as the Egyptians, Carians, Lydians, and Greeks. The majority of the indicators in this apocalypse suggest it was authored after 602 BC when Nabu-shum-lishir was involved in some kind of plot against Nebuchadnezzar, but before 592 BC, when Psamtik II destroyed the Kushite army. This supports either earlier date for the beginning of the siege of Tyre, either 602 or 598 BC. The middle option of 598 to 585 BC seems the most probable if this Apocalypse was about a planned war, as Tyre would have rebelled before the

Kushite army was destroyed, and surrendered in the aftermath of Jerusalem being destroyed.

Shortly after the siege of Jerusalem, Nebuchadnezzar's army also destroyed the kingdoms of Ammon and Moab, in 582 BC. To the south, the Edomites and Qedarites continued to be allies of Egypt. The situation changed in 553 BC, when King Nabonidus, the last king of the Neo-Babylonian empire conquered Edom and the Qedarites. He established his defacto capital in Tayma, reportedly because of some prophecy. As Daniel had left Babylonia for Media when Neriglissar seized the throne, he could not have been referring to the later king Nabonidus as the good man coming from Tayma, which suggests that Nabonidus had occupied Tayma because of Daniel's prophecy. If this is the case, Daniel's prophecy helped defeat the Babylonians, as Nabonidus' long absence from Babylon, between 553 and 543 BC, allowed his heir Belshazzar to become the de facto king, and reduced the strength of the empire to the point that Cyrus II could conquer it in 539 BC.

The original apocalypse appears to be the description of a conspiracy to destabilize the union of the four kings, and cause all the empires to destroy each other. It begins with a horned serpent from the east, or in some manuscripts from the desert, consuming everything it sees. This is a fairly clear reference to King Nebuchadnezzar, who was named after the god Nabo, who rode a horned dragon. The horned serpent (Nebuchadnezzar) is attacked by the Eagle (or Vulture) from Tayma, although it is later revealed that the Ravens (or Vultures) from Tayma are working for the Bull, who is likely the one that hired the Eagle. As the Ravens appear to have later stalked the Viper's Younger Chick for years, this appears to be a reference to a Qedarite assassin being hired from Tayma by the Bull to kill Nebuchadnezzar.

The Eagle failed and was in turn attacked by the Viper, and as the Eagle disappears from the apocalypse, it seems likely that the Viper killed him. The word generally translated as 'viper,' is åkdnå (ܐܟܸܕܢܵܐ), which is a Syriac word adopted from the Greek word echidna (ἔχιδνα), which meant both 'viper,' and 'traitor.' Based on the context, the original meaning was probably 'traitor.' This person appears to be Nabu-shum-lishir, Nebuchadnezzar's younger brother, who may or may not have led a coup in 602 BC.

Based on the surviving records of the event, the government in Babylon did not seem to understand what had happened, and this confusion is mirrored in the apocalypse. Nabu-shum-lishir and his family disappeared after that, and they were not recorded as being executed as traitors generally were, supporting the idea that they escaped to somewhere. It isn't clear how many children he had, but the apocalypse refers to him having two chicks, an elder and a younger, that appear to be his heirs.

The traitor took his heirs and fled to the Egyptian border, but appears to have been turned away, and fled to the south. It isn't clear exactly where he traveled to, but he was later reported to be in Kush, suggesting they traveled down the Red Sea to Dômt (𐩴𐩱𐩣𐩩), the kingdom that ruled the territory of northern Eritrea and the adjacent Ethiopian highlands. Dômt was a Semitic civilization that was highly interconnected with the South Arabian Sabean culture across the Red Sea, sharing everything from architecture to a script. The capital of the kingdom is believed to have been at Ḥu (𐩹𐩥), today called Yiḥa (ይሐ), which is in northern Ethiopia, near the later imperial capital of Axum. Yiḥa is situated between the Mareb and Tekezé rivers, meaning it had a direct trade route to the kingdom of Kush, and from there, a trade route to Egypt.

There is a gap of several years between the time that the traitor is turned away from the Egyptian border, and the time that the traitor was in Kush. In the intervening years, the Elder heir (chick) moved to Egypt, and the Younger heir (chick) moved to Judah. Zedekiah sent word to the Asherahs of Tayma to help the Younger heir and learned that the Ravens were working for the Bull.

The apocalypse seems to switch to prophecy at this point, predicting the Third Horn of the Bull attacking Jerusalem. This third horn can only be Nebuchadnezzar, as it is referred to as a man, and it disappears later when the Great Cities of Mesopotamia are destroyed, leaving the Bull with two horns. The Bull was initially described as having three horns, and during the period when Zedekiah sent the letter to the Asherahs of Tayma, the Bull was apparently making problems for the west. Based on these points, the Bull is undoubtedly Cyaxares, the patriarch of the royal families. Cyaxares was the father-in-law of Nebuchadnezzar and grandfather-in-law of King Cambyses I of Persia at the time. His own son Astyges was the head of the Median military and the heir to the throne.

After Assyria fell, the Medes fought for six years against Lydia, the former ally of the Assyrians, which ended during the Battle of the Eclipse. It isn't clear when exactly the Medes and Lydians started their war, or when exactly it ended, however, the final battle was

interrupted by a solar eclipse, as Herodotus reported in
The Histories:

> Afterward, on the refusal of Alyattes to give up his
> suppliants when Cyaxares sent to demand them of
> him, war broke out between the Lydians and the
> Medes, and continued for five years, with various suc-
> cesses. In the course of it, the Medes gained many vic-
> tories over the Lydians, and the Lydians also gained
> many victories over the Medes. Among their other
> battles, there was one nighttime engagement. As,
> however, the balance had not inclined in favor of ei-
> ther nation, the war continued in the sixth year, in
> the course of which, just as the battle was growing
> warm, the day was suddenly changed into night. This
> event had been foretold by Thales, the Milesian, who
> forewarned the Ionians of it, fixing for it the very year
> in which it actually took place. The Medes and Lydi-
> ans, when they observed the change, ceased fighting,
> and were alike anxious to have terms of peace agreed
> on.

The two kings decided to end the war, and kings
Nebuchadnezzar of Babylon and Syennesis of Cilicia acted
as mediators. King Alyattes' daughter Aryenis was
married to Astyages, making Lydia the fifth kingdom to
join the union of nations bound by marriage. Alyattes

died shortly after the battle, and there was a power struggle between his sons Pantaleon and Croesus, which Croesus ultimately won. Lydia had peaceful relations with the Medes, Neo-Babylonians, Greeks, and Egyptians throughout most of Croesus' reign, which ended when Cyrus II of Persia annexed Media.

The apocalypse refers to Jerusalem cryptically as the city of the temple built on seven hills, however, several other cities were also traditionally founded on seven hills, including Constantinople. The Syriac apocalypse specifically refers to the city of the temple as the city of the temple of Constantine, or the town of the temple of Constantinople in various manuscripts, however, it is also identified as the city of Zedekiah (the lioness' cub), confirming that it was originally Jerusalem. The apocalypse refers to Jerusalem as a fortress and claims that Nebuchadnezzar (the Bull's middle horn) would surround it in blood, indicating that the siege of Jerusalem was planned ahead of time by the Judahites. This would explain why the city had enough food within its walls to hold out for three years.

The apocalypse continued with the traitor's elder heir leading an army from Egypt, and attacking the Babylonians, which would have been a good strategy. Until the time of Julius Caesar hundreds of years later, attacking an army that was laying siege to a city almost always resulted in a victory. This is almost certainly what the people in Jerusalem were hoping for during the siege in 597 BC, which may have been when the scheme was first planned out. Daniel, Azariah, and Shealtiel had all been among the captives from that siege who were taken to Babylon as hostages, so the scheme could have originated with them.

Whoever developed the plan apparently didn't like the Egyptians any more than the Babylonians, as the traitor was sent to raise an army in Kush, which would invade Egypt from the south while the Egyptian army was engaged with the Babylonians in Judah. The Egyptians found out about the planned Kushite invasion and sent their army south on a pre-emptive strike in 592 BC. This attack on Kush was devastating, not only destroying the army that was amassing in the north, but also the capital city of Napata, and all the cities to the fifth cataract of the Nile.

This would have been the route that the traitor took to Kush, down either the Mareb-Atbarah River or the Tekezé-Atbarah River, from Dômt to Kush. Although the Mareb River no longer flows all the way to where it once connected to the Atbarah River, except after intense rain storms, it was once known as the Red Nile due to the red sand it flowed through in the desert of eastern Sudan. The river had been drying for thousands of years and was probably already a wadi by the early Iron Age.

On the other hand, the Tekezé (ተከዘ) river was so important in the early Iron Age, that the name is based on the Old Ge'ez word for 'river.' The Tekezé River flows into the Atbarah River, called the Black Nile by the ancient Egyptians as the water was muddy. The Black Nile enters the Nile at the fifth cataract of the Nile, where the city of Kerkis was located, which was mentioned in the records of Psamtik II's campaign into Kush in 592 BC. A well-documented graffito inscribed at Abu Simbel by the Greek mercenaries returning from the campaign reported:

> When King Psammetichus (Psamtik II) came to Elephantine, this was written by those who sailed with Psammetichus the son of Theocles, and they came beyond Kerkis as far as the river permits. Those who spoke foreign tongues were led by Potasimto, the Egyptians by Amasis (Apries).

Psamtik II's campaign into Kush, led by his heir and future king Apries, is believed to have been a preemptive strike when he learned that King Aspelta was amassing a Kushite and Nubian army in northern Kush. Kush had ruled Egypt for centuries before being driven out by the Neo-Assyrians, and as Egypt was the most likely target of the army, Psamtik decided to destroy the army, and all of northern Kush to prevent another attempt to invade Egypt. The Egyptian forces and their Greek and Carian mercenaries marauded through northern Kush, destroying the major settlements at the cataracts, including the capital city Napata at the fourth cataract.

After destroying Kerkis at the fifth cataract, they appear to have ventured up the Black Nile (Atbarah) 'as far as the river permits,' suggesting they were trying to destroy the trade route between Kush and Dômt, and perhaps Dômt itself. They do not appear to have found Hu, as there is no mention of any major engagements after Kerkis, suggesting they did not know exactly where Hu was, and followed the wider and faster flowing Atbarah River up into the mountains, possibly finding its source, but not any major settlements. As Prince Apries could not have been perceived as anything less than godlike, he would have declared that was his intent, turned the army around, and returned to Egypt.

The Classical Ethiopian book Kebra Nagast, which is generally considered fiction, tells the tale of King Solomon's son by the Queen of Sheba, who fled Jerusalem and traveled up the Nile into the Ethiopian highlands. His route followed the Blue Nile and ended up at Lake Tana, however, there is no evidence of Apries venturing as far south as the sixth cataract, and so he must have traveled up the Black Nile (Atbarah).

In the apocalypse, there was also a plan to break the union of the four kings while the Babylonians and Egyptians were fighting. It isn't clearly stated, but strongly implied that they planned to kill Nebuchadnezzar, and probably his wife and children. As Nebuchadnezzar's wife was Amytis, the daughter of King Cyaxares of Media, placing the traitor on the throne of Babylon would have effectively broken the bond, and probably initiated another great war to the north. It is unclear if the Medo-Persian bond would have broken, as the Persian prince and future king Cambyses I was married to Cyaxares granddaughter Mandane, however, Babylon would have been out of the union if the Median royals were killed in a coup that placed someone else on the throne.

This was the exact situation that occurred when Nebuchadnezzar and Amytis' heir Amel-Marduk and his

305

family were killed in 562 BC, and a Babylonian noble named Neriglissar assumed the throne. Neriglissar was married to one of Nebuchadnezzar's daughters, but Babylon was no longer part of the union. Instead of war, the Medes and Persians embargoed Babylon. This strategy was likely chosen because Neriglissar's power was based on his wealth. He died after only six years on the throne of an economically struggling Babylon, and his son was deposed almost immediately by General Nabonidus, who assumed the kingship and married another of Nebuchadnezzar's daughters to restore order. Babylon was still the outsider among the union of nations, which was comprised of Media, Persia, Lydia, and Parthia by that time.

The plan continued with the Egyptians returning to Egypt to fight the Kushites, and the Judahites defeating the Babylonians and subjugating the ancient cities of Mesopotamia to tribute. At this point, the Judahites would be attacked by the Bull Cyaxares' two remaining horns, Astyges of Media and Cyrus I of Persia. The Judahites would ally with the Panther from the north, and together they would defeat the Medes and Persians.

The Syriac word prdå (ܦܪܕܐ) can be translated as panther or leopard, and is often assumed to be another reference to the Leopard of the South. The apocalypse uses two different names for these entities, nmrå (ܢܡܪܐ) and prdå (ܦܪܕܐ), meaning the translator recognized the 'leopard' and the 'panther' were two different things. The Syriac word prdå (ܦܪܕܐ) is adopted from the Greek word párdos (πάρδος), meaning panther or leopard.

This Panther coming from the north cannot be the Leopard of Tayma (the south), and therefore, it is possible that this is a reference to the Parthians, whom Cyaxares had conquered, as the Parthians were northwest of the Medes, and would have probably rebelled if the union of the four kings was disrupted. The earliest surviving spelling of Parthia dates to the early Persian era, as Parithiva (𐎱𐎼𐎰𐎺), however, if the same word was spelled phonetically in Neo-Babylonian cuneiform, it would have been spelled as Pariṭiå (𒉺𒅈𒋾𒅀), as the Babylonians did not have the 'thi' sound in their language. The logogram ṭi (𒋾) can also be read as 'di', which could result in 'Parthians' being transliterated into Greek as parda (παρδα). The Parthians attacking the Medes and Persians from the rear while they were engaging the Judahites in Mesopotamia is essentially the same strategy planned against the Egyptians, who were attacked from the rear by the Kushites while fighting the Babylonians.

FORWARD TO THE SYRIAC APOCALYPSE OF EZRA AND THE ARABIC APOCALYPSE OF DANIEL

In the aftermath of the war, the union of the four kingdoms would be broken. Babylonia would be subject to Judah, and Egypt would be subject to Kush. Tyre would be rebuilt as an ally, and then the Judahites would go out to the desert and destroy the Ishmaelites. It is likely that the original apocalypse was referring to the Qedarites, not all Ishmaelites, however, at least Dumat and Tayma would have been destroyed. It isn't clear exactly where the hatred of the Qedarites stemmed from, however, it is mirrored in other Judahite writings from the time. According to this apocalypse, the Qedarites (the Eagle and Ravens), were working for Cyaxares (the Bull), to covertly attack Nebuchadnezzar, the Middle Horn.

It is unknown if this happened, however, it is possible that Cyaraxes wanted Nebuchadnezzar dead so Amytis could assume a regency on behalf of their young son Amel-Marduk. Amytis was recorded as being respected by the Babylonians, likely more than any of the kings to rule the Neo-Babylonian Empire. She was the architect of the rebuilding after the Assyrians were defeated, and is said to have personally overseen the building of the Hanging Gardens of Babylon. Cyaxares certainly would have had more direct control of Babylon if Nebuchadnezzar were dead.

Ultimately, very little of the plan transpired. The apocalypse appears to have originated sometime between 597 BC, when Daniel and Azariah were taken prisoner to Babylon, and 592 BC, when the Kushite army was destroyed by the Egyptians. Tyre and Jerusalem did rebel from Babylon, and Nebuchadnezzar did lay siege to them, but the Egyptians never took the bait, and Tyrians and Judahites ultimately surrendered to Nebuchadnezzar. Amel-Marduk may have learned of the plot at some point, as he did release the exilarchs of Judah and Tyre, but was killed himself by one of the leaders of those sieges before he could grant independence to Judah. Granting Judah and Tyre independence would have been economically valuable to Babylon, as Babylon had poor relations with the Mediterranean countries.

Tyre and Judah could have normalized trade with the Phonecian colonies in the Mediterranean and Egypt, opening indirect trade routes for Babylon. Additionally, Babylon and Egypt would have gained a buffer state. This is the exact policy that Cyrus II followed when he conquered the Babylonians decades later, granting independence to the southern Canaanite states to serve as buffer states between Persia and Egypt. Cyrus did not need to do this, as his army of Persians, Medes, Lydians, and Parthians, had conquered the Babylonians with ease.

It appears to be a plan that had been in the works for a long time to normalize relations with Egypt. When this didn't happen, his heir Cambyses II annexed southern Canaan and invaded Egypt.

Unfortunately, none of the plans in this apocalypse made sense after 592 BC, and therefore the apocalypse appears to have been generally misunderstood, and recycled for Christian propaganda, first against the Jews, and later against the Muslims. Assemani's original observations regarding the apocalypse in the early 1700s, that it cannot date back to the time of Ezra because it mentions Constantine, continues to shape modern analysis of the apocalypse, even after the pre-Islamic version of it attributed to Daniel was published in 1887. Iselin's analysis from 1887, that the Apocalypse appears to date back to before the Apocalypse of John misquoted it, is largely ignored.

This translation of both the Syriac Apocalypse of Ezra and the Arabic Apocalypse of Daniel is accompanied by a reconstructed Apocalypse of Azariah, which the two surviving apocalypses appear to be descended from. The analysis is focused on the older Judahite apocalypse, rather than the work of the anti-Jewish and anti-Islamic redactors. The anti-Jewish redacter was too generic to identify, reflecting similar sentiments to Christian theologians from Tertullian to Martin Luther. The language indicates it probably originated in Byzantine Palestine before the time of Muhammad. The anti-Islamic redactor was likely in Jerusalem between 1229 and 1244, however, did not do much more than merge the older Greek Apocalypse and the Arabic Apocalypse, along with adding the words 'Constantine' and 'Antioch.' If the original Apocalypse does date to between 597 and 592 BC, any analysis of the creatures fighting in it is not relevant to the early Islamic era.

Syriac Apocalypse of Ezra

[Again, through God, I write about the question that Ezra the scribe[1] asked when he was in the desert with his disciple (whose name was Carpos). He asked God to reveal to him the things that are going to happen in the end times. Then he said to Carpos his disciple:][2]

Listen, my son Carpos,[3] and I will tell you about the end times. It happened suddenly, in the manner of a dreadful vision. I asked God to explain (to me)[4] the end times of the Ishmaelites.[5] Then I saw a young man, one like I'd never seen, wearing white clothing, and he had the image of a scroll in his (right) hand.[6] He said to me, "Know that your prayer has been heard before God, and I have been sent to explain to you the end times of the children of Ishmael, that which has been concealed from many. Open this book of the scroll and read in it and see what is about to happen in the end times."

I opened the scroll and I read about the times and the terrors that are going to come. My tears flowed with groans and I said, "Have mercy on me, God, and have mercy on your creation," as a serpent of the desert had devoured them. I saw twelve horns on the serpent's head, and nine small and cruel horns on its tail. It came up from the desert,[7] contending against all creation (under the sky)[8] and oppressing the people of God. Then I saw a messenger, clothed in a flame (of fire),[9] who descended from the sky and tore the twelve great horns from the serpent's head.

[Then I said "I believe in you, Lord,[10] (because) today the prophecy of Moses is fulfilled."[11]

The messenger of the Lord[12] said to me, "Take heart, Ezra,[13] because it was also revealed to Daniel[14] about these nine small and cruel horns."][15]

Then I saw one great horn suddenly grow up on the tail of the serpent, and there were two small horns on its head. An eagle[16] came from the south[17] and broke the great horn and devoured the small ones. The world was filled with darkness and a whirlwind, and the whirlwind struck the eagle and tore out its two talons. Then there was a voice from the sky that said, "The eagle will be repaid according to its reward."

Then I saw a viper that came from the east. It poured poison on all flesh and ascended to the limits of the ancestors.[18] There was a great earthquake and rumblings and thunders in the sky, and a voice (from the sky)[19] was heard, "Let those four kings who are bound on the great river Euphrates,[20] those who are prepared to destroy one out of three people, be released." They were released, and there was a great uproar.

Out of the darkness came ravens[21] from the east, piercing the viper.[22] The viper escaped to the borders of

Egypt,[23] and there his mind became sad. He took the two chicks[24] and traveled to the south.[25] The younger chick went to the lion's cub[26] and took refuge with him. The lion's cub received him joyfully, and the younger chick persuaded the lion's cub to save him from the ravens that were seeking to destroy him. The lion's cub sent (an ambassador)[27] to the leopard[28] of the south[29] so that he would come out to his aid, because the bull[30] was troubling the land of the west with many evils. Since he was the king of the ravens, he gnashed his teeth against the lion's cub. There were three horns on his head.[31] He makes war with the right one, with the left one he destroys, and with the one in the middle he ravages.

He will begin to ravage the children of his house, and he will gather gold and a great deal of silver, and he will begin to afflict all who are under his power. He will become arrogant and he will not praise God.[32] One of his horns will go and make war against the lion's cub, and will ravage the rebellious fortress. They will contend against each other and ravage each other, and much blood will be shed between the two mighty men. Then the bull will devise an evil plot against the seven hills and the city of the house (of Constantine),[33] and he will fight against it, and a great deal of blood will be shed around the city.

Then the viper's chick will take a (great)[34] army from Thrace[35] with his invaders,[36] and he will enter in blood. The father of the younger chick will hear, and he will gather a great nation from the Kushites[37] and from the nations around them, and he will come to the aid of the chick and will ravage Egypt. Then the chick will come down from the land of the forefathers[38] and he will ravage the great cities. He will leave them devoid of their inhabitants because great iniquity was being perpetrated in them. He will throw the slain to the ground in heaps, and he will ravage Damascus[39] at that time.

Then the lion's cub will become inflamed with fierce anger, and he will go out after those ravens and ravage them and drive them out and destroy them from Antioch of Syria[40] as far as the borders of the east, the land that belongs to the ravens. The panther[41] will go out from the north,[42] (and with him) a nation numerous like the locusts that fly.[43] He will go up to the Euphrates River and he will rise up in aid of the lion's cub, and from there the two of them will go down to the land of Persia. The bull will go out to meet them with a great army, but the lion's cub will go between the bull's horns and break both of them.[44] He will ravage and plunder the land and burn it with fire.

The ravens will flee from his presence and go down to their land. The lioness'[45] cub will pursue them and will destroy them with the edge of the sword because God has turned his face from them on account of their great uncleanness. He will capture and plunder their land, and destroy it down to the foundations. It will never again be inhabited because they despised the Lord and mocked his commandments. There will be great commotion in the land, earthquakes, famines, and plagues, and fear and trembling will rule over the people until they fall dead, without diseases or illnesses, from the fear that rules over them.

The (lion's) cub[46] will go up with a great army to the land of the forefathers and will subject it to tribute, and there will be great tribulation in the land, the likes of which have never occurred. He will rebuild the fortifications of Phoenicia as an ally,[47] (and around the desolate places that are within it.)[48] He will destroy Damascus (which led the greatest derision), down to its foundations because of its great bitterness[49] against Jerusalem. From there he will return and go up to his regal city.

[50][After three and a half weeks a certain mighty man will come out of the south with a great nation, and his power will go forth over the land of the forefathers. He will make a great peace, and he will perform wonderous good deeds in the land for three years and seven months. Then the four winds of the sky will be stirred up, and the nations will rise up one against the other, and ravage

each other until the earth cries out because of the blood that is shed on her face.

Then I, Ezra, fell to the ground, and I was utterly filled with tears. And the messenger of the Lord said to me, "Do not be grieved, Ezra the scribe, because these things will not happen until uncleanness and wantonness and fornication defile the earth, when people have forsaken the marriage bed and defiled and polluted themselves and their bodies with the uncleanness of fornication, with drinking wine, and with sodomy, shameless about the disgrace they commit. Then the justice of God will be provoked so that the rebellious seed will be delivered into the hands of their enemies, because their end has come, and the end is coming quickly."

As my face was sweating in fear, the messenger of the Lord stretched out his hand and lifted me up, since I was trembling in fear. I asked, "Who will be able to live in that time?"

He answered me, "Those in whom God is pleased. A great rebellion will gain strength, and the faithful will be oppressed, but their cries and their groaning will ascend before the royal throne of God's majesty so that he will quickly send a fearsome messenger and take hold of the point of the destroying sword and destroy the rebellious seed without mercy. But woe to pregnant women and those who are nursing at that time, because a tribulation will happen the likes of which has not occurred since the worlds were created."

Suddenly the children of the north will be opened and will go out from the house of Gog and Magog and commit terrible atrocities on the earth. Two tribes from the seed of Ishmael and those who have become sooty at the base of the mountain of the south will come and take refuge with them. They will drink and go up until they reach Jerusalem, the city of the great king. There, God will send against them the fearsome messenger Michael, and he will ravage them without pity. If these days were not shortened, no flesh would live, because at that time a year is like a month, a month like a week, a week like a day, and a day like an hour.

Then one resembling the Messiah[51] will appear and will show his cruelty and the vehemence of his wickedness. He will go up to Enoch and Elijah[52] upon the altar and shed their blood upon the earth with great suffering. Then fearsome messengers will be sent out, and they will cast the Son of Perdition into the Gehenna of fire. This is the End. But preserve these words until their time."

Then I, since I had great fear, fell down to worship and gave thanks to God the Savior, who had deemed me worthy of this vision. And I said, "Blessed are you, God my Savior, and your holy name be glorified forever and ever, Amen."

Ended with the aid of our Lord is the vision that Ezra the scribe saw about the kingdom of the Ishmaelites. To God be glory.]

Syriac Apocalypse of Ezra Notes

1 Mingana 11: Ôzrå språ (ܠܕܪ ܣܦܪܐ). Translation: Ezra scribe (or writer, lawyer, clerk)

Ezra the Scribe was the Ezra from the Septuagint's books of Ezra, and the Masoretic book of Ezra-Nehemiah, not Shealtiel (who was also called Ezra), from the Judahite Apocalypse of Ezra, who was in Babylonia during the era of Daniel and the four kings.

The two were often conflated in the early Christian era, as evidenced by the Latin Apocalypse of Ezra. Jews had abandoned both the Exilarch Shealtiel and Daniel the astrologer as prophets during the Persian era. Neither the books attributed to Daniel nor Shealtial were translated and standardized in Hebrew under the Hasmonean Dynasty, although a partially translated Aramaic and Hebrew version of Daniel did later get adopted by the Masorites. References to 'Ezra the scribe' are missing from the Arabic Apocalypse, and therefore can have only originated with the Byzantine anti-Islamic redactor.

2 The introduction and conclusion of the Syriac Apocalypse of Ezra are the words of an unknown scribe, who appears to be quoting a lost source text. The introduction and conclusion are found in all copies, but are not always the same, and therefore the words only found in some sources are placed in parenthesis. If the scribe did not reatribute the apocalypse from the text from Daniel to Ezra, and change the student to Ezra to Carpos, then there must have been an earlier Apocalypse of Ezra that served as a source.

As the existing apocalypse contains many Greek words that were adopted into Syriac, and Carpos was a Greek name, it is likely the Syriac apocalypse was translated from Greek. As all surviving copies of the Apocalypse are in Eastern Syriac, it seems likely that the scribe who added the introduction and conclusion was the Eastern Syriac translator.

3 Mingana 11: Qrpws (ܩܪܦܘܣ). Generally anglicized as Carpos

- BnF Arabe 150: Dānyāl (دانيال). Translation: Daniel

Capros is unknown from other books attributed to Erza, Shealtiel, and Daniel. This name does not appear in the Masoretic book of Ezra-Nehemiah, the Septuagint's 1st and 2nd Ezra, the Vision of Ezra, or the Judahite, Latin, or Greek Apocalypses of Ezra. Its origin is debated, but is likely a transliteration of a name in the earlier Greek translation, as Carpos (Καρπός) was the name of a minor Greek god of fertility.

Variations of the name translate as 'melon' in many languages, including the Arabic ḵirbiz (خِرْبِز), Georgian xarbuzaki (ხარბუზაკი), Greek karpoúzi (καρπούζι), Hindi xarbūzā (ख़रबूज़ा), Latin karpus, Middle Armenian xarbzak (խարբզակ), and Turkish karpuz. These terms are all believed to be adopted from the Persian word for 'melon,' xarboz (خربز). Nevertheless, the word does not mean 'melon' in Aramaic or Canaanite dialects.

In the Arabic Apocalypse of Daniel, which is a shorter version of this apocalypse, the name of the master was Daniel, and the student was called Ôzrh (عزره) a transliteration of the Hebrew word ôzrh (עזרה), not the Hebrew name Ezra (עֶזְרָא), or the Arabic name Ôzrā (عزرا). Ôzrh (עזרה) is the Hebrew word for 'help,' suggesting that the original name in the Apocalypse was Azariah (עֲזַרְיָה), meaning 'Help of Yahw.' Azariah is one of the three youths associated with Daniel, who was thrown into a furnace when Judah rebelled from Babylonian rule under the rule of King Zedekiah.

The phonetic spelling of Azariah in Neo-Babylonian cuneiform would have been Eziraia (𒀸𒇎𒁹𒅀), however, this would include the name of the god Ia (𒅀), the name of the 'terrible god' of floods, whose name was not generally mentioned. All three youths were given alternative names in the Book of Daniel, none of which appear to be Babylonian. Azariah's alternate name was Aved Nego (עֲבֵד נְגוֹ) in Masoretic Daniel, which is a transliteration of the Aramaic Ôbd Ngh (עֹבֵד נְגֹה), meaning 'servant of (the planet) Venus.' The logical substitute for Ia (𒅀) would have been Ilu (𒀭), meaning 'god,' rendering the Neo-Babylonian spelling as Ezirailu (𒀸𒇎𒁹𒀭).

If the original Greek translation was made directly from the cuneiform version, the name could have been read logographically as 'grain strike god,' and as Carpos was the Greek god of harvesting grain, whose name was derived from the word for 'cutting,' Carpos would have been the obvious translation. This indicates the original Ezra in the apocalypse was probably the youth Azariah, whose name was simplified to 'helper' in an Aramaic translation, which the Arabic is based on. The simplification of the name in Aramaic is likely because the scribe recognized it could not have originally been Azrael (עֲזַרְאֵל) or Ôzryål (עזריאל), the name of the Classical Judahite psychopomp.

4 Most copies of the Apocalypse are missing these words, however, manuscript Sachau 131 includes 'to me,' and manuscripts BnF 326 and BL 28,875 include 'to you.'

5 Mingana 11: Åyšmôyly (ܐܝܫܡܥܠܝܐ). Translation: Ishmaelites

The Ishmaelites are the theoretical descendants of Abraham's abandoned son Ishmael. According to the Torah Ishmael's mother took him to Arabia after Abraham abandoned them to die in the desert, where he later married an Egyptian woman and had twelve sons. Several of the North Arabian tribes and oases had names associated with Ishmael at the time, including the Qedarites, Tayma, and Dumah. This idea continued for a long time and is accepted within Islam, where, depending on the source, Muhammad is either descended from Nebaioth (نابت) or Kedar (قيدر), Ishmael's two eldest sons, and thereby ultimately from Abraham.

During the era of the four kings, the Qedar (𐎖𐎅𐎗) tribe ruled north central Arabia, based out of their capital of Dumat (𐎄𐎅𐎎𐎚). The Akkadian cuneiform records from earlier than the 10th century BC referred to Dumat as being in the land of Edom (𒈬𒀭𒁀𒀀), suggesting that, like Edom, Dumat and Tayma were part of the kingdom of Judah before Edom rebelled in the 9th century. An inscription in Egyptian hieroglyphs dating to the rule of Ramesses III of the New Kingdom era has also been found, indicating the settlement was probably part of the Egyptian Empire, which included Edom.

The longer name of the Oasis is Dumat al-Jandal (دُومَـة الْجَنْدَل), which translates as 'Palms of the Stone.' The stone in question likely started as a reference to the 35-meter-long triangular megalithic at the oasis, which is believed to have been constructed in the 6th millennium BC. If this is the origin of the name, it indicates the site had been continuously since the megalith was exposed to the surface, however, it has been buried throughout recorded history and was not rediscovered until 2020.

The megalith is believed to have originally been used for some ceremonial purposes, however, it is not clear what that was, or if it was associated with the deities worshipped there in the historic era. Most of the deities worshipped at Dumat in the era before Mohamemed were fertility deities, and both animal and human sacrifices are reported to have happened. In the 3rd century AD, the Neoplatonic philosopher Porphyry of Tyre reported that each year a boy was sacrificed and was buried under an altar in Dumat. This is similar to the human sacrifice practiced by other fertility cults in the Middle East and Mediterranean, and is similar to the human sacrifice

SYRIAC APOCALYPSE OF EZRA NOTES

which was banned in Judah circa 625 BC. In Judah, the human sacrifice took place at an altar in a graveyard (גֵּיא בֶן־הִנֹּם) near Jerusalem, described as looking like a grove, suggesting an Asherim, a sacred grave site where oak trees were planted.

During the Neo-Assyrian era, Dumat was described as the capital of the Qedarites in Assyrian records, although Qedarites are also described as migrating to Edom in large numbers and marrying the Edomites during the era. This is likely the origin of the concept of the people becoming 'sooty' under the Mountain of the South, as Kedar (קֵדָר) translates as 'dark' or 'black.' The Mountain of the South was likely a reference to the Mountain of the Altar, identified in pre-Byzantine times as Mount Sinai.

The Qedarites were independent during the Neo-Assyrian era but then were ultimately conquered by the Neo-Babylonians under King Nabonidus. When the Neo-Assyrian Empire fell in 605 BC, the Qedarites joined the anti-Babylonian alliance, with Ammon, Edom, Egypt, Moab, Sidon, and Tyre. These kingdoms had been occupied or attacked by the Assyrians and did not want to fall under Babylonian control. Judah rejected the alliance and allied with Babylon. King Nebuchadnezzar II attempted to invade Egypt in 601 BC, but his army was defeated, emboldening the anti-Babylonian faction, and Judah switched sides, joining the alliance.

The Qedarites were particularly active around the edges of the Syrian desert and disrupted trade between Babylon and its Syrian territories, which resulted in Nebuchadnezzar moving his imperial residence, the de facto capital of the empire, to Damascus in 599 BC. In 598 BC, Nebuchadnezzar marched his army to Dumat al-Jandal, the capital of the Qedarites, and captured the statues of their gods. This caused the Ammonites and Moabites to switch sides, and ally with the Babylonians. In the aftermath, the god of Tayma became dominant among the Qedarites.

In 597 BC, Nebuchadnezzar, along with his Ammonite and Moabite allies, laid siege to Jerusalem and captured King Jeconiah, who was taken captive to Babylon. A revolt in Babylonia in 594 BC took Nebuchadnezzar back to Babylon and allowed a new anti-Babylonian alliance to form, which included Ammon, Edom, Egypt, Judah, Moab, Sidon, Tyre, and the Qedarites. After suppressing the revolt in Babylon, Nebuchadnezzar returned to Southern Canaan in 587 BC and destroyed the kingdom of Judah. A year later he began the 13-year-long siege of Tyre, which ended when King Ithobaal III of Tyre died, and his son Baal II negotiated a surrender. As Tyre was on an island off the coast of Lebanon, they were able to trade with their colonies across the Mediterranean Sea, and so unlike most of Babylon's sieges, this one was a military failure and an embarrassment to the Babylonian military.

During the siege, Nebuchadnezzar's army also destroyed the kingdoms of Ammon and Moab in 582 BC. To the south, the Edomites and Qedarites continued to be allies of Egypt. The situation changed in 553 BC, when King Nabonidus, the last king of the Neo-Babylonian empire conquered Edom and the

Qedarites. He established his defacto capital in Tayma (تيماء) in the Hejaz Mountains, reportedly because of some prophecy.

After Cyrus conquered the Babylonians he released Arabs and southern Canaanite kingdoms, which formed a buffer zone between the fledgling Persian Empire and the Egyptian Kingdom. Cyrus' heir Cambyses occupied the southern Canaanite nations and conquered Egypt and Cyrene. While he didn't conquer the Qedarites, they were limited to Arabia, and Edom was part of the Persian empire. The Qedarites built an extensive trade network with the Persians, but couldn't adapt to the Hellenistic world after Alexander conquered the Persians.

Their former kingdom, which had dominated trade in northern and central Arabia unraveled, and the Nabataeans occupied the region that had once been southern Edom and Midian. Within the genealogy of nations, the Nabataeans were descendants of Ishmael's eldest son Nebaioth (נְבָיוֹת). The first known Greek mention of the Nabataeans (Ναβαταῖος) as a unique political faction is dated to approximately 311 BC, however, there are older Neo-Babylonian records which treat the Nabâatu (𒀭𒈾𒁀𒀀𒌓) as the nobles of the Qedarites, indicating the reason why the genealogy of nations claims they are descended from the elder brother, even though they didn't form their own nation when the genealogy was written.

Therefore, if the Ishmalites are the original people the Apocalypse is about, and the reference to the people near the Mountain of the South becoming 'sooty' is a reference to the

Qedarites intermarrying with the Edomites living near the Mountain of the Altar, it can really only be dated to the late Neo-Assyrian or early Neo-Babylonian eras when Edom was briefly powerful before 553 BC. During this era, the Qedarites were a major irritant to the Neo-Babylonian empire, but Nebuchadnezzar could not risk a major campaign to suppress them as Babylonia could rebel again.

The Ishmalites are not mentioned in the shorter Arabic apocalypse, however, it is an anti-Jewish interpretation of the Apocalypse, which appears to pre-date the rise of Islam. This could be interpreted as something that was added, however, the longer Syriac Apocalypse appears to have survived independently, and therefore there is no reason to assume the Ishmalites were not present in the original apocalypse.

Once Islam arose, originally among the tribes associated with the Ishmaelites, the term Ishmaelite became a Christian and Jewish reference to Muslims in general, which allowed this prophecy to be reinterpreted in a new light, as an anti-Islamic apocalypse.

As Daniel had left Babylonia for Media when Neriglissar seized the throne, he could not have been referring to the later king Nabonidus as the good man from Tayma, which suggests that Nabonidus had occupied Tayma because of Daniel's prophecy. If this is the case, Daniel's prophecy helped defeat the Babylonians, as Nabonidus' long absence from Babylon, between 553 and 543 BC, allowed his heir Belshazzar to become the de facto king, and reduced the strength of the empire to the point that Cyrus II could conquer it in 539 BC.

6 Most copies of the Apocalypse do not specify the hand. Manuscripts BnF 326 and BL 28,875 specify it was his right hand. The Arabic Apocalypse of Daniel also specifies it was his right hand. It is unclear if this was added by a scribe influenced by Islamic thought, or removed as a rejection of perceived Islamic influence.

7 Mingana 11: maḏbrā (ܡܕܒܪܐ). Translation: desert (or wilderness)

• Manuscripts BnF 326 and BL 28,875: madnkhā (ܡܕܢܚܐ). Translation: east

8 The specification of 'under the sky' is only found in manuscripts BnF 326 and BL 28,875, and was likely a scribal note to clarify that the serpent did not threaten the abode of God.

9 The clarification of the flames being made of fire is clarified in most copies of the Apocalypse but is missing from manuscript BnF 326.

10 Mingana 11: mārā (ܡܪܐ). Translation: master (or owner, lord)

• BnF Arabe 150: ar-rabb (الرّب). Translation: the lord (or the master, the governor, the authority)

11 The clause of 'because' is only found in manuscripts BnF 326, BL 28,875, Sachau 131, and UTS 23. The prophecy of Moses is not clarified but assumed to be a reference to the Septuagint's Cosmic Genesis (Masoretic Bereshit) chapter 17, in which there is a prophecy that Ishmael would be the father of twelve princes.

12 Mingana 11: mlåkh dMryå (ܡܠܐܟܗ ܕܡܪܝܐ). Translation: messenger of the master

13 Mingana 11: Ôzrå (ܥܙܪܐ). Translation: Ezra

• BnF Arabe 150: Ôzrh (عزره). Translation: Ezrh

The spelling of the name in the Arabic Apocalypse of Daniel is not the standard Arabic spelling of Ezra, which is Ôzrā (عزرا), nor based on the Greek Esdras ('Εσδρας) or Hebrew Ezra (עֶזְרָא). The Arabic name is a transliteration of the Hebrew and Aramaic word ôzrh (עזרה), meaning helper. This itself indicates that the Arabic Apocalypse was translated from either Aramaic or Hebrew. It is not the same as the Syriac translation, which is based on a Greek translation, and no Canaanite (Judahite or Samaritan) or Hebrew translations are known to exist, so the source text is presumably lost. As the form of Arabic appears to be Palestinian, it was probably translated from an Aramaic source.

14 Mingana 11: Dniåil (ܕܢܝܐܝܠ). Translation: Daniel

15 No prophecies of Daniel have survived regarding a serpent with nine horns. There is a beast with ten horns in the Book of Daniel, but it is not a serpent. This suggests that a prophecy of Daniel was lost or destroyed at some point. Given that at least 14 significant variations of the book of Daniel have been documented, including two in various Septuagint manuscripts, it is not surprising something was lost. This section of text appears to be part of the later Greek redaction, as the author recognizes the similarity to an apocalypse of Daniel, yet does not recognize that Carpos is Ezra.

In this case, the horned serpent appears to be a not particularly cryptic reference to King Nabopolassar, who was named after the god Nabu. Nabu's mount was the horned serpent Mušḫuššu (𒀭𒈲𒁔). The twelve horns on its head and nine on its tail likely referred to those supporting Nabopolassar and those conspiring against him.

16 Mingana 11: nšrå ḥḏ qn tymnå (ܢܫܪܐ ܚܕ ܩܢ ܬܝܡܢܐ). Translation: eagle (or vulture, mythical plant, glue) one who nests (or works for, owns) right (or south, Tayma)

The word nšrå (ܢܫܪܐ) means 'eagle' or 'vulture' in Syriac and other Semitic languages, and is the synonym of the qrqså (ܩܪܩܣܐ) later in the text who attack the viper/traitor in the land of the forefathers, causing him to flee. In this case, the phrase could be interpreted as either coming from tymnå, working for tymnå, or owning tymnå. Tymnå (ܬܝܡܢܐ) is clearly a place in the verse and not a direction, and therefore the translation of Tayma makes the most sense. The indigenous spelling of the name was Tmô (𐎈𐎐𐎀) at the time, which is believed to have been pronounced similar to the modern Arabic name Taymā (تَيْمَاء). The Aramaic name of Temya, Tymnå (𐡕𐡉𐡌𐡀) was based on the ancient Canaanite name Tymn (𐤕𐤉𐤌𐤍), as preserved in the Masoretic book of Habakkuk as Teiman (תֵּימָן).

Based on Habakkuk's prophecy about the rising power of the Babylonians, and his appearance in some versions of the Book of Daniel, he is believed to have been active in Jerusalem sometime between 612 BC and 587 BC. Based on reference to the goddess (אֱלוֹהַ) coming from Tayma, it is clear that he viewed the Taymanitic goddess Åshyrå (𐎀𐎌𐎗𐎚) as the same goddess as the Canaanite goddess Asherah (אֲשֵׁרָה). As the Ravens are later identified as the 'children of the Bull,' it appears Cyaraxes (the Bull) was trying to destabilize the Neo-Babylonian Empire using Qedarite mercenaries (Ravens), and may have attempted to kill Nebuchadnezzar using a Qedarite assassin (the Eagle). This would have allowed Cyaraxes' daughter Amytis to assume the kingship paired with a more malleable Babylonian husband.

17 Mingana 11: tymnå (ܬܝܡܢܐ). Translation: right (or south, Tayma)

This word means 'right' in Syriac and other Semitic languages, however, it also means 'south,' in Hebrew and

Aramaic, and was the Aramaic and Syriac name for Tayma. In this case, the 'Right' or 'South' is a recurring location, and not simply a direction, suggesting that Tayma is being referenced. The indigenous spelling of the name was Tmô (ⵁⵏⵅ) at the time, which is believed to have been pronounced similar to the modern Arabic name Taymā (تيما). The Aramaic name of Temya, Tymnå (𐤍𐤌𐤉𐤕) was based on the ancient Canaanite name Tymn (𐤍𐤌𐤉𐤕), as preserved in the Masoretic book of Habakkuk as Teiman (תֵּימָן).

18 Mingana 11: wslqt lthwmå bmwldnå (ܘܣܠܩܬ ܠܬܚܘܡܐ ܕܡܘܠܕܢܐ). Translation: and ascended (?) the boundary (or end, limits) of the forefathers (or procreators)

The phrase is obscure, and the word sltq (ܣܠܩܬ) is probably a loan of the Arabic word salaqa (سَلَقَ), meaning to 'ignite,' 'insult,' or 'boil.' The Syriac equivalent is šāliq (ܫܠܩ), however, that only means 'to boil,' suggesting the Syriac translator trying to translate a Greek that meant 'ignite,' or 'insult.'

The term mwldnå (ܡܘܠܕܢܐ) is generally interpreted as the 'promised (land)', however, the viper/traitor (Nabu-shum-lishir) was not from Canaan, but Mesopotamia. The phrase probably originated in a Judahite using the Neo-Babylonian term qudmu (𒆠𒁴𒈬), as a translation of the Judahite qdm (𐤒𐤃𐤌), meaning 'easterners' or 'ancients.' The term was used in this context to refer to Mesopotamians as bənê-qedem (בְּנֵי־קֶדֶם) in Masoretic Judges. However, the Aramaic term qdm (קדם) and Neo-Babylonian qudmu (𒆥𒁺𒈫) do not mean 'Easterners,' but 'came before,' resulting in the Greek and Aramaic translations rendering 'forefathers.' Based on this reading, the original phrase would have been 'insulted to the limits of the ancestors.'

19 The specification of 'from the sky' is only found in manuscripts BnF 326, BL 28,875, Sachau 131, and UTS 23.

20 This verse is paralleled in the Apocalypse of John, chapter 13, except the four kings bound on the Euphrates were four messengers (ἀγγέλους). In 1887, Ludwig Iselin proposed that the reference in John was based on a misinterpretation of the Apocalypse of Ezra's four kings, based on the similarity of the Aramaic word mlkyå (ܡܠܟܝܐ), meaning 'kings,' and mlåkyå (ܡܠܐܟܝܐ), meaning 'messengers.' This was rejected by Christian theologians, who argued that John's apocalypse was original, and therefore the error must have been made originated in the Syriac translation. However, the Apocalypse of John has never been accepted as canon by the Syriac churches, and it is unlikely that someone would have mistranslated the Greek word angelos (ἄγγελος), meaning 'messengers,' with archontes (ἄρχοντες), meaning 'kings.'

In the context of the era of the Astrologist Daniel and his student Azariah, the four kings bound on the Euphrates were King Cyaxares of Media, Nebuchadnezzar II of Babylon, Cyrus I of Persia, and the King of Scythia whose name has not survived. The Battle of Cerchemish in 605 BC, which took place at the Euphrates, was the final battle of the alliance against Assyria. The last of the Assyrian forces had been defeated, and the Egyptians withdrew permanently from the region, ceding their historic claims to Syria. It was the end of a twenty-year-long war, and the kings wanted to make sure the peace was permanent, so they agreed to bind their empires through marriage. There is no evidence that the Scythians married into the union, but they were one of the victors. This may have been because the Scythian tribes did not have hereditary leadership. What evidence that survives of their leadership at the time suggests a Steppes confederacy, meaning the king was only the king until another Scythian killed him.

The union of four empires collapsed shortly after Nebuchadnezzar's reign when the kingship of the Babylonian empire was usurped by Neriglissar in 560 BC. The Persians and Medes maintained their union which later formed the basis of the Persian Empire. Cyrus II, the Persian king who conquered Babylon in 539 BC was the grandson of both King Cyaxares of the Medes and King Cyrus I of Persia, both of whom are believed to have fought at the Battle of Cerchemish.

Nebuchadnezzar married Cyaxares' daughter Amytis, and they were the parents of the future King Amel-Marduk. Therefore, when Neriglissar led the coup against Amel-Marduk, he was also breaking the union of the four kingdoms. It's worth noting that Daniel left Babylon when

Neriglissar usurped the throne, and was later reported to be in the Media and Persia, which does support this interpretation of the four kings bound on the Euphrates.

This would also place a rough limit on when the Apocalypse could have originated between 605 and 560 BC. It also overlaps chronologically with the interpretation of Carpos being Azariah, who was taken to Babylon as a captive in 597 BC.

21 Mingana 11: qrqså (ܩܪܩܣܐ). Translation: ravens (or vultures, crows, magpies)

The word can be translated as several kinds of predatory birds but is generally accepted as 'ravens' based on the Greek word corax (κόραξ). The Syriac word can be either the singular or plural form, however, based on the context the word is used later in the apocalypse, it is intended to be the plural form. The Greek word corax can also be read as 'hook' or as the name of an engine that was used to grapple ships, however, based on the animal iconography in the rest of the Apocalypse, the translation of 'ravens,' was likely correct.

The ravens in the apocalypse were probably meant to represent the Qedarites, as they attacked the viper/traitor from the east when he was in the land of the forefathers, as the Qedarites controlled the Syrian desert at the time. Kedar (קֵדָר) also translates as 'dark' or 'dusky,' and the Qedarites were reported to live in black tents so they could be recognized from a distance, meaning the symbolism would have been obvious at the time.

22 Mingana 11: åkdnå (ܐܟܕܢܐ). Translation: viper (or asp)

The Syriac word åkdnå (ܐܟܕܢܐ) was borrowed from the Greek word echidna (ἔχιδνα), which meant both 'viper,' and 'traitor.' Based on the context, the original meaning was probably 'traitor.' This person appears to be Nabu-shum-lishir, Nebuchadnezzar's younger brother, who may or may not have led a coup in 602 BC. Whatever happened, the government in Babylon did not seem to understand, and there is confusion in the records from the time. He did disappear with his family after that, and they were not recorded as being executed as traitors generally were, supporting the idea that they escaped to somewhere.

23 Mingana 11: Mṣyrn (ܡܨܪܝܢ). Translation: Egypt

The Syriac name for Egypt is the same as the Imperial Aramaic Mṣyrn (𐡌𐡑𐡓𐡉𐡍), and virtually identical to the Ugaritic Canaanite Mṣrm (𐎎𐎕𐎗𐎎), and Hebrew Mitzrayim (מִצְרַיִם). At the time of the four kings, Egypt was the main enemy of the four empires. Egypt had sent its army to support the Assyrians, where they were defeated and withdrew across the Euphrates. Egypt was also supporting the southern Canaanite and Arab kingdoms in their anti-Babylonian alliance. Any Assyrian fleeing the armies of the four kings would have headed south into Tyre, Sidon, Judah, Ammon, Moab, Edom, or if they could afford it, Egypt.

Nabu-shum-lishir (the viper/traitor) was turned back at the border of Egypt, which seems like an odd choice for the

Egyptian government, who later accepted the Elder Chick, presumably Nabu-shum-lishir's elder son. It is possible that the border guards had been bribed or blackmailed into turning away Nabu-shum-lishir. As Nabu-shum-lishir would have been fleeing at the time, there probably wasn't enough time for the Egyptian government to even receive a message that he was at the border and issue a command to send him away.

24 Mingana 11: prwgyh (ܦܪ̈ܘܓܝܗ). Translation: chicks (or nestlings, fledglings)

The traitor (viper) appears to be Nabu-shum-lishir, who may have led a failed coup d'etate in 602 BC. The Babylonian records are unclear if he was involved in a coup or not, and it is likely he was implicated, whether he was involved or not. There are no records of him being arrested or executed, yet he and his family are not mentioned again in the Neo-Babylonian records, suggesting they fled to another country, which could not have been one of the four bonded empires.

Their options would have been few, and Egypt was the best bet. Egypt was the enemy of the four kings, as it had backed the Assyrians. After being turned away at the Egyptian border, he traveled south with his two chicks, presumably his sons. Later, one of his sons traveled to Judah to live with the Lion's cub. The other chick ends up in Thrace, which appears to be a redaction of Egypt.

25 Mingana 11: ymynå (ܝܡܝܢܐ). Translation: right (or pledge, ordination)

The term ymynå had cognates throughout Semitic languages, as well as Egyptian, all meaning 'right.' However, it also means 'south' in Semitic languages, which makes more sense in the context of the Viper's movements. Based on the traitor (viper) later organizing an army in Kush, it seems likely they initially fled south from the Egyptian border to Dômt, in the region of modern northern Eritrea and Ethiopia.

This would have given the traitor a direct route to Kush via the Black Nile. The two chicks appear to have left the traitor earlier, one taking refuge with Zedekiah (the Lion's cub), and the other in Egypt (or Thrace).

26 Mingana 11: gwynå wårynå (ܓܘܝܢܐ ܕܐܪܝܐ). Translation: cub of the lion

The title 'Lion's cub' is used interchangeably with the title 'Lioness's cub' in this apocalypse. The lioness's cub is a metaphor used in the Book of Ezekiel chapter 17 for kings Jeconiah and Zedekiah, the last two kings of Judah. Jeconiah was only the king of Judah for a few months in 598 and 597 BC when King Nebuchadnezzar II took him captive to Babylon, leaving his brother Zedekiah on the throne of Judah. Jeconiah outlived Zedekiah and became the first exilarch of the Judahites after their country was conquered by the Babylonians. Shealtiel, who was also called Ezra in the Judahite Apocalypse of Ezra, was Jeconiah's son and the second Exilarch of the Judahites after Jerusalem was destroyed.

As Jeconiah could not have been the Lion's cub in question unless the apocalypse dates to his three-month reign, the Lion's cub in question must have been Zedekiah, who reigned between 597 and 586 BC. After Apries became king of Egypt in 589 BC, Zedekiah rebelled from Babylon's rule and allied with the Egyptians. This resulted in the 30-month-long siege that led directly to the destruction of the city.

The limited records of the siege found in the writing of Jeremiah and the books of the Septuagint's 4th Kingdoms (Masoretic Kings), the Judahites were prepared for a long siege, but were expecting allies from Egypt to attack the Babylonians during the siege, at which point the Judahite forces would attack from Jerusalem, forcing the Babylonians to fight on two fronts. However, the Egyptians never came.

The apocalypse goes on to state that the Kushites would then attack Egypt while the Egyptian army was engaged at Jerusalem. This indicates that this prophecy happened before Zedekiah rebelled from the Babylonians. As Jerusalem would have been one of the first targets of an Egyptian invasion, and new kings often launched invasions in their early years, it is likely that Zedekiah was expecting the Egyptians to invade, and allied with them to prevent them from attacking. Instead, the Egyptians found out about the Kushite army being assembled and marched south to destroy it.

27 The reference to the ambassador is missing from manuscript BnF 326.

28 Mingana 11: nmrå (ܢܡܪܐ). Translation: leopard (or Asherahs)

More than one word meaning 'leopard' is used in the Apocalypse. This word is Semitic, cognate of the Akkadian nimrum (𒉌𒅎𒊒), Aramaic nmrå (נמרא), Hebrew namer (נָמֵר), and Arabic namir (نَمِر). The Syriac word is also the translation for the Hebrew Asherim (אֲשֵׁרִים), the sacred oak trees that once marked important graves. As the leopard or Asherahs were almost certainly located in Tamya, this was probably a reference to the prophetesses of Asherah in Tayma, as, based on the Tayma stele, which dates to the 6th century BC, Åshyrå (𐤀𐤔𐤉𐤓𐤀) was one of the four gods worshipped in Tayma at the time. King Zedekiah was recorded as a heretical king by the Yahwist scribes, who blamed him for the fall of Jerusalem.

29 Mingana 11: tymnå (ܬܡܢܐ). Translation: right (or south, Tayma)

The indigenous spelling of the name of the Tayma Oasis was Tmô (𐪌𐪃𐪉) at the time, which is believed to have been pronounced similar to the modern Arabic name Taymā (تيماء). The Syriac name of Temya is based on the ancient Canaanite name Tymn (𐪉𐪃𐪚𐪉), as preserved in the Masoretic book of Habakkuk as Teiman (תֵּימָן).

At the time, the Qedarites controlled northern Arabia, including the ancient settlement at the Tamya Oasis, where one of the four gods worshipped was Asherah, the plural form of which happens to be spelled the same as 'Leopard' in Syriac. While Zedekiah could have sent a message to any leopard in the south, the translation of 'Asherahs of Tayma' makes more sense.

30 Mingana 11: twrå (ܬܘܪܐ). Translation: bull (or Taurus, confusion, wonder)

The Bull is identified as first attacking the west, but later defending Persia, indicating that in the era of the four kings, this was a reference to the Medes, or specifically King Cyaxares of Media. After Babylonia fell, their former allies, Egypt and Lydia became the enemies of the four kings. The Scythians marched to the border of Egypt, but the Egyptians paid them a tribute to not attack, so they returned to Scythia, the lands north of the Caucasus Mountains and the Black Sea. Media and Lydia, in western Anatolia, fought a six-year-long war, which only ended because a major battle was interrupted by a solar eclipse. Herodotus reported the Battle in *The Histories* as:

> Afterward, on the refusal of Alyattes to give up his suppliants when Cyaxares sent to demand them of him, war broke out between the Lydians and the Medes, and continued for five years, with various success. In the course of it, the Medes gained many victories over the Lydians, and the Lydians also gained many victories over the Medes. Among

their other battles, there was one nighttime engagement. As, however, the balance had not inclined in favor of either nation, the war continued in the sixth year, in the course of which, just as the battle was growing warm, the day was suddenly changed into night. This event had been foretold by Thales, the Milesian, who forewarned the Ionians of it, fixing for it the very year in which it actually took place. The Medes and Lydians, when they observed the change, ceased fighting, and were alike anxious to have terms of peace agreed on.

The two kings decided to end the war, and kings Nebuchadnezzar of Babylon and Syennesis of Cilicia acted as mediators. King Alyattes' daughter Aryenis was married to Astyages, making Lydia the fifth empire to join the union of nations bound by marriage. Alyattes died shortly after the battle, and there was a power struggle between his sons Pantaleon and Croesus, which Croesus ultimately won. Lydia had peaceful relations with the Medes, Neo-Babylonians, Greeks, and Egyptians throughout most of Croesus' reign, which ended when Cyrus II of Persian annexed Media.

31 One of the three horns is later described as a man who would make war against the Lion's cub (Zedekiah of Judah), indicating all three horns were men. As the middle horn also disappeared after being defeated by the Lion's cub, who was described as destroying the cities in the land of the ancestors (Mesopotamia), this would have been Nebuchadnezzar, who did lay siege to Jerusalem twice. Nebuchadnezzar married

Cyaxares daughter Amytis, making him the stepson of Cyaxares (the Bull).

The positions of the left and right horns would have been based on the rising of the sun, making the right horn King Cyrus I, and the left horn Prince Astyges, the designated heir to Cyaxares. Cyrus I married Astyges' daughter, also called Amytis, although he was old at the time, and she was a newborn, so the marriage appears to have been ceremonial.

His son and heir Cambyses I married her older sister, but she was not old enough to go live with him until he had been king for more than a decade. Nevertheless, the kings who would rule the three kingdoms after Cyaxares' death were his son, son-in-law, and grandson-in-law, making him the most influential person in the region until his death in 585 BC.

32 Mingana 11: lålhå (ܠܐܠܗܐ). Translation: the god

L'Alha is the Aramaic and Syriac Christian form of the Hebrew le'Elah (לֶאֱלָהּ) and Greek tô Theô (τω Θεω), later adopted into Arabic as Allāh (الله). The religion of Cyaxares is not documented, however, based on the later Persian and Greek records, the main goddess worshipped in the Median capital of Ecbatana was Anahita, the goddess of wisdom and feminine chastity. The other two gods documented in Median Ecbatana were the Zoroastrian supreme God Ahura Mazda, and Mithra, the god who died and rose each winter during the three-day solstice.

Based on the writings of many prophets and the author of the Septuagint's 1st Ezra, it's clear the Judahites of the era believed that other nations' supreme gods were the same as their God. The author of 1st Ezra and 2nd Maccabees equated the god of Jerusalem with Ahura Mazda, suggesting this was the god the author of the Apocalypse was referring to. If it was, then it was accurate, as the Medes apparently preferred Anahita.

33 Mingana 11: mdyntå dbtå qustntinos (ܡܕܝܢܬܐ ܕܒܬܐ ܕܩܘܣܛܢܛܝܢܘܣ). Translation: town (or region) of house (or temple, chamber, stable, urn) of Constantine (transliterated from Greek Κωνσταντίνος)

• Manuscript BnF 326: mdyntå dbtå qustntin (ܡܕܝܢܬܐ ܕܒܬܐ ܕܩܘܣܛܢܛܝܢ). Translation: town (or region) of house (or temple, chamber, stable, urn) of Constantine

• Manuscripts BL 28,875, Sachau 131, and UTS 23: mdyntå dbtå Qustntinopolis (ܡܕܝܢܬܐ ܕܒܬܐ ܕܩܘܣܛܢܛܝܢܘܦܘܠܣ). Translation: town (or region) of house (or temple, chamber, stable, urn) of Constantinople (transliterated from Greek Κωνσταντινούπολις)

The earliest surviving commentary of the Syrian Apocalypse of Ezra, from the early 1700s, was by Giuseppe Simone Assemani, in the Bibliotheca Orientalis Clementino-Vaticana, where he dismissed the idea that the Apocalypse could date back to Ezra's time, as it mentioned Constantine. This view still dominates academic analysis of the text, and almost all scholars who have bothered to publish their views of the Apocalypse interpret it as a medieval Christian anti-Islamic text. Occasionally scholars have suggested it was a reworking of an older Aramaic apocalypse, which is usually tied to the relationship of the four kings bound on the Euphrates, and the Apocalypse of John's four messengers bound on the Euphrates.

Since the Arabic Apocalypse of Daniel was discovered, which parallels a section of the text in this apocalypse, but with Daniel being the teacher, and Ezra being the student, it has become clear that there were significant variations of the Apocalypse in ancient times. Clearly, if the Syriac apocalypse is a reworking of an older apocalypse, the name Constantine is a late addition. Nevertheless, most scholars who have accepted the idea that it is a reworked text, still view the reference to the blood spilled around the 'Town of the Temple of Constantine' as a reference to one of the Arab sieges of Constantinople, the earliest of which was in 674 through 678 AD.

Without the name Constantine in the phrase, it is a simple reference to Jerusalem, as Jerusalem was built on seven hills, and was the city of the temple for Judahites. However, with the name attached to the phrase it becomes confusing, as it could be translated as the City of the House of Constantine, or City of the Temple of Constantine, or even City of the Urn of Constantine. This is generally resolved by rendering it as 'Great City of Constantine,' however, that is not accurate. Constantine was not born in Constantinople, but Naissus, modern Niš in Serbia, however, it is unlikely the Greek redactor was referring to Niš as the 'City of the House of Constantine.' Emperor Constantine was not cremated but interred in the Church of the Holy Apostles in Constantinople, however, it seems strange that the Greek redactor would refer to Constantinople as the 'City of the Temple of Constantine.' The most likely origin of the strange phrase is that the Greek redactor simply added 'of Constantine' to the original reference to the 'City of the Temple.'

The city is referred to as the home of the Lioness's cub, which is a reference to King Zedekiah also found in the book of Ezekiel, indicating it was originally Jerusalem. It is unlikely it was originally named though, as the king was not, and therefore the name was probably an addition made when the Apocalypse was reinterpreted as an anti-Islamic work. The spelling of both Constantine and Constantinople in all manuscripts other than BnF 326, supports the addition being made in Greek. BnF 326 has a curious spelling for Constantine, which cannot be derived from Greek, and also is not Syriac. It was probably influenced by the Arabic pronouciation of Qusṭanṭīn (قُسْطَنْطِين).

34 Most manuscripts claim the army was great, as in large, however, manuscripts BnF 326, BL 28,875, Sachau 131, and UTS 23 do not include this word.

35 Mingana 11: thrqnå (ܬܪܩܢܐ)

This is generally accepted as a scribal error of Thrqyå (ܬܪܩܝܐ), meaning 'Thrace.' While the term may be Thrace, this is most likely a Greek mistranslation, likely in the original Greek translation from Neo-Babylonian. Thrace was not even mentioned in Greek records until the 4th century BC. When the Persians conquered the region in 513 BC, they called it Scythia (𒅖𒂊𒅖𒀫), as the Scythians controlled it at the time. While 'Thace' could have been a redaction of Scythia, based on context, it appears to have originally been Egypt. This Thrqyå was prophesied to invade Mesopotamia, and in turn, be invaded by Kush. In the era of King Zedekiah, this appeared highly probable as soon as Apries inherited the throne of Egypt, which happened in 595 BC.

The original version of the Apocalypse almost certainly would not have named the country, as the other names are all hidden, and therefore, it is possible this name started as a variation of Tåhårqå (𓇓𓏏𓈖𓏤), recorded in the Masoretic books of Kings and Isaiah as Tirhakah (תִּרְהָקָה). Tåhårqå was the King of Kush and Egypt circa 700 BC when Assyria was conquering most of Southern Canaan. Tåhårqå assisted the Judahites in maintaining their independence and also worked with Tyre and other Canaanite kingdoms. As such, it is possible that Tåhårqå was being used as a code word to indicate the plan was for Kush to reconquer Egypt.

In Neo-Babylonian cuneiform, his name was spelled Tarquú (𒋻𒆪𒌑), however, it is unlikely a Greek translator would have recognized the name as being different from the

Aramaic name Trqyå (𐡍^𐡐𐡘𐡍), meaning Thrace. If the reference to Thrace originated early in the translation, before the rise of Byzantine, which was another name for Thrace, it would have seemed to be prophesying something about the Byzantine Empire, which would have naturally led to the town of the temple on the seven hills being identified as Constantinople, which was also built on seven hills.

36 Mingana 11: wntktš gmh (ܘܢܬܟܬܫ ܓܡܗ). Translation: and invaders of his

• Manuscript UTS 23: wntkš gmh (ܘܢܬܟܫ ܓܡܗ). Translation: and ntksh of his

The term is ntktš (ܢܬܟܬܫ) debated somewhat, as it's not spelled consistently in all manuscripts. It's composed of the words for 'protrude' (ܢܬ) and 'fight' (ܟܬܫ). The original word probably meant 'foreign fighters' or 'mercenaries.'

37 Mingana 11: kwšyå (ܟܘܫܝܐ). Translation: Kushites

There is some evidence of the Kushites, or someone in Kush, coordinating the anti-Babylonian alliance in southern Canaan between 603 and 553 BC. The reference to the father of the younger chick, suggests a reference to the traitor (viper) himself, who had traveled to Kush. If he was not permitted to enter Egypt, which seems apparent, the route to Kush would have been to cross the Red Sea to Dômt (𐩵𐩫𐩵𐩢), the kingdom that ruled the territory of modern northern Eritrea and the adjacent Ethiopian highlands.

Dômt was a Semitic civilization that was highly interconnected with the South Arabian Sabean culture across the Red Sea, sharing everything from architecture to a script. The capital of the kingdom is believed to have been at Ḥu (Ꮈ℗), today called Yiḥa (ይሐ), which is in northern Ethiopia, near the later regional capital of Axum. Yiḥa is situated between the Mareb and Tekezé rivers, meaning it had a direct trade route to the kingdom of Kush, and from there, a trade route to Egypt.

Although the Mareb River no longer flows all the way where in once connected to the Atbarah River except after intense rain storms, it was once known as the Red Nile due to the red sand it flowed through in the desert of eastern Sudan. The river had been drying for thousands of years and was probably already a wadi by the early Iron Age. On the other hand, the Tekezé (ተከዘ) River was so important in the early Iron Age, that the name is based on the Old Geʿez word for 'river.' The Tekezé River flows into the Atbarah River, called the Black Nile by the ancient Egyptians as the water was muddy. The Black Nile enters the Nile at the fifth cataract of the Nile, where the city of Kerkis was located, which was mentioned in the records of Psamtik II's campaign into Kush in 592 BC. A well-documented graffito inscribed at Abu Simbel by the Greek mercenaries returning from the campaign reported:

> When King Psammetichus (Psamtik II) came to Elephan-
> tine, this was written by those who sailed with Psam-
> metichus the son of Theocles, and they came beyond Kerkis

as far as the river permits. Those who spoke foreign tongues were led by Potasimto, the Egyptians by Amasis (Apries).

Psamtik II's campaign into Kush, led by his heir and future king Apries, is believed to have been a preemptive strike when he learned that King Aspelta was amassing a Kushite and Nubian army in northern Kush. Kush had ruled Egypt for centuries, and as Egypt was the most likely target of the army, Psamtik decided to destroy the army, and all of northern Kush to prevent another attempt to invade Egypt.

The Egyptian forces and their Greek and Carian mercenaries marauded through northern Kush, destroying the major settlements at the cataracts, including the capital city Napata at the fourth cataract. After destroying Kerkis at the fifth cataract, they appear to have ventured up the Black Nile (Atbarah) 'as far as the river permits,' suggesting they were trying to destroy the trade route between Kush and Dômt, and perhaps Dômt itself.

They do not appear to have found Hu, as there is no mention of any major engagements after Kerkis, suggesting they did not know exactly where Hu was, and followed the wider and faster flowing Atbarah River up into the mountains, possibly finding its source, but not any major settlements. As Prince Apries could not have been perceived as anything less than godlike, he would have declared that was his intent, turned the army around, and returned to Egypt.

The Classical Ethiopian book Kebra Nagast, which is generally considered fiction, tells the tale of King Solomon's son by the Queen of Sheba, who fled Jerusalem and traveled up the Nile into the Ethiopian highlands. His route followed the Blue Nile and ended up at Lake Tana, however, there is no evidence of Apries venturing as far south as the sixth cataract, so he must have traveled up the Black Nile (Atbarah).

This is the route that the traitor (viper) would have taken from Dômt to Kush, and likely the army that the apocalypse was predicted, suggesting that there was a plan to use Jerusalem (the Great City) as a snare for the Babylonians and Egyptians. Zedekiah's rebellion would bring the Babylonians to lay siege to the city, as they had in 597 BC, allowing the Egyptians to attack them while they were camped around the city. Attacking an army laying siege to a city was generally viewed as highly advantageous to the mobile outer army until Julius Caesar invented a counter five centuries later. Meanwhile, Kush would launch a campaign into Egypt, possibly recapturing the kingdom, but certainly weakening it.

The plotters also believed they had a way to break the bounds of the four kings, suggesting they planned to kill Nebuchadnezzar, and probably his wife and children. As Nebuchadnezar's wife was Amytis, the daughter of King Astyages of Media, placing the traitor on the throne of Babylon would have effectively broken the bond, and perhaps initiated another great war to the north. It is unclear if the Medo-Persian bond would have broken, as the Persian prince and future king Cambyses I was married to Astyages' other daughter Mandane, however, Babylon would have been out of the union if the Median royals were killed in a coup that placed someone else on the throne.

This was the exact situation that occurred when Nebuchadnezzar and Amytis' heir Amel-Marduk and his family were killed in 562 BC, and a Babylonian noble named Neriglissar assumed the throne. Babylon was no longer part of the union, however, the Medes, and Persians embargoed Babylon instead of attacking it. This strategy was likely chosen because Neriglissar's power was based on his wealth. He died after only six years on the throne of an economically struggling Babylon, and his son was deposed almost immediately by General Nabonidus, who assumed the kingship and married one of Nebuchadnezzar's daughters to restore order.

38 Mingana 11: lårôå bmwldnå (ܠܐܪܥܐ ܕܡܘܠܕܢܐ). Translation: the land (or country) of the forefathers (or procreators)

This term is generally interpreted as the 'promised land', however, the chick (Nabu-shum-lishir) was not from Canaan, but Mesopotamia. The phrase probably originated in a Judahite using the Neo-Babylonian term qudmu (𒄱𒁾𒁾), as a translation of the Judahite qdm (𐤒𐤃𐤌), meaning 'easterners' or 'ancients.' The term was used in this context to refer to Mesopotamians as venei-kedem (בְּנֵי־קֶדֶם) in Masoretic Judges. However, the Aramaic term qdm (𐡒𐡃𐡌) and Neo-Babylonian qudmu (ⵌ⳥ⵜⵌ) do not mean Easterners, but 'came before,' resulting in the Greek and Aramaic translations rendering 'land of the forefathers.'

39 Mingana 11: Drmsoq (ܕܪܡܣܘܩ). Translation: Damascus

In 599 BC, Nebuchadnezzar II moved his residence to Damascus, making it the de facto capital of the Neo-Babylonian Empire. He moved to Damascus so he could personally lead the war to top the organized bands of raiders operating in Syria at the time. Within a year he learned that the raiders were actually Qedarites, and marched his army south to the Dumat Oasis, the Qedarite capital, where he seized the statues of their gods.

This was a traditional Mesopotamian strategy to conquer nations, as the gods of those nations would become hostages in the capital city. In 598 BC, after capturing the gods of Dumat, Nebuchadnezzar returned to Babylon, however, the Qedarites had more gods in the ancient holy city of Tayma.

40 Mingana 11: Ånṭikiå dSôriå (ܐܢܛܝܟܝܐ ܕܣܘܪܝܐ). Translation: Antioch of Syria

Antioch of Syria is presumably a reference to Antioch on the Orontes (Ἀντιόχεια ἡ ἐπὶ Ὀρόντου), which was in Syria. The name of the city was originally Meroe, however, Seleucus I Nicator, the first king of the Seleucid Empire, changed the name to Antioch on the Orontes in 300 BC. Like the reference to Constantine, this reference could be used to date the apocalypse to the much later than the life of Daniel and Azariah, however, the geography in the text does not make sense, as Antioch on the Orontes was northwest of Damascus, not to the east. This suggests the original apocalypse was simply referring to Syria, and Antioch was part of the anti-Islamic revision.

Based on several indicators in the text that appears to be part of the redaction, the anti-Islamic version was likely created in the crusader state of Jerusalem, sometime between 1229 and 1244. To the north, Antioch was another crusader state, but both were struggling to survive. After more than a century of crusades, the Latin Christians had lost interest in supporting the crusader states, and the crusaders had alienated the Greek, Coptic, Syriac, and Ethiopian Christians. The creation of the anti-Islamic apocalypse appears to have been to generate support among the Greek Christians.

41 Mingana 11: prdå (ܦܪܕܐ). Translation: panther

The Syriac word is assumed to be an adopted form of the Greek word párdos (πάρδος), a Greek word meaning panther or leopard. This is a different word for 'leopard' than used in most of the Syriac Apocalypse, nmrå (ܢܡܪܐ), which also translates as 'Asherahs.' This Panther coming from the north cannot be the Leopard of Tayma (the south), and therefore, it is possible that this is not a relic of the Greek translation, but a reference to the king of Scythia.

Conversely, it may have started as a reference to the Parthians, whom Cyaxares had conquered, as the Parthians were northwest of the Medes, and would have probably rebelled if the union of the four kings was disrupted. The earliest surviving spelling of Parthia dates to the early Persian era, as Parithiva (𐎱𐎼𐎰𐎺), however, if the same word was spelled phonetically in Neo-Babylonian cuneiform, it would have been spelled as Pariṭiå (𒉺𒅁𒋾𒅀𒀪), as the Babylonians did not have the 'thi' sound in their language. The logogram ṭi (𒅀) can also be read as 'di', which could result in 'Parthians' being transliterated into Greek as parda (παρδα).

In any event, the nmrå (leopard or Asherahs) of Tayma (the south), cannot be the prdå from the north, and so prdå is translated as 'Panther' in the translation, and 'Parthians' in the restoration.

42 Mingana 11: jrbya (ܓܪܒܝܐ). Translation: north (or north wind)

43 Mingana 11: ômq ômå sgiåå åyk qmså dperḥ (ܥܡܗ ܥܡܐ ܣܓܝܐܐ ܐܝܟ ܩܡܨܐ ܕܦܪܚ). Translation: with him a nation (or people, paternal uncle) numerous (or more than enough) like (or as it were, approximately) locusts (or parsnips) that fly

• Manuscript UTS 23: ômå sgiåå åyk qmså dperḥ (ܥܡܐ ܣܓܝܐܐ ܐܝܟ ܩܡܨܐ ܕܦܪܚ). Translation: nation (or people, paternal uncle) numerous (or more than enough) like (or as it were, approximately) locusts (or parsnips) that fly

44 Earlier in the apocalypse, the bull has three horns, supporting this as a plan to break the union of the four kings. Cyaxares appears to be the bull, and the three horns are the three kingdoms he controlled or influenced. His son Astyages was his appointed successor in Media, and his daughter Amytis was married to Nebuchadnezzar II of Babylon. Astyages' daughter Mandane, Cyaraxes' granddaughter, was married to King Cambyses I of Persia. If the Panther is the king of Scythia, then the two remaining horns after Nebuchadnezzar was killed would have been Astyages and Cambyses.

45 Mingana 11: gwynå wårytå (ܓܘܝܢܐ ܘܪܝܬܐ). Translation: cub (or whelp) of the lioness

• Manuscripts BnF 326, Sachau 131, and UTS 23: gwynå wåryå (ܓܘܝܢܐ ܘܪܝܐ). Translation: cub of the lion

Most manuscripts deviate here, claiming it was a lioness's cub, not a lion's cub, however, this appears to have been corrected in some manuscripts. In most references to the cub, it is masculine, and so this alteration would have made sense to an editor, however, it is difficult to see why the masculine word would have been feminized in the first place. The lioness's cub, is a metaphor used for King Zedakiah by Ezekiel, suggesting this is the original form throughout the Apocalypse, which was later masculinized by editors that did not understand who the lioness's cub was.

46 Mingana 11: gwynå (ܠܕܘܢ). Translation: cub (or whelp)

- Manuscripts BL 28,875, BnF 326, Sachau 131, and UTS 23: gwynå wårynå (ܠܕܘܢ ܕܐܪܝܢ). Translation: cub of the lion

Most manuscripts don't specify it was the Lion's cub, however, some editors must have interpreted it that way. The manuscripts that have 'lion's cub' are mostly the manuscripts that used 'lion's cub' where the other manuscripts use 'lioness's cub' suggesting that the missing term may be a relic of the masculinization of the lioness.

47 Mingana 11: nbnå šwrå dPhuniqia kd ḥdrå (ܒܢܝ ܥܘܪܐ ܕܦܘܢܝܩܝܐ ܟܕ ܚܕܪܐ). Translation: rebuild fortification (or rampart) of Phoenicia by (or as) Khdrå

This phrase is often assumed to be a paraphrase of 'build walls around Phoenicia,' from the Apocalypse of Peter, however, appears to be a corruption of 'rebuild Tyre in Phoenicia as an ally.' The final word of the phrase is treaty differently by each translator as it isn't Aramaic, and could be either a reference to a place called Khdrå, or the Arabic word ḵudra (خُضَرة), meaning 'green.' The word is probably a scribal era of the word ḥbrå (ܚܒܪܐ), meaning 'ally,' which is the translation followed here, as there is no known settlement of Khadra in the region.

The myth that there would be a wall built around Phoenicia was a common part of the medieval Christian end-of-the-world literature. The Greek version of the Apocalypse certainly would have included the concept of a wall,

SYRIAC APOCALYPSE OF EZRA NOTES

however, if a Judahite wrote the Apocalypse in Neo-Babylonian, the word used would have probably been Ṣurru (目止), meaning Tyre, and which was related to Judahite name Ṣr (٩٣). The Neo-Babylonian word could also be translated as cliff, or rockface, which the Greek translator interpreted as wall.

During the era of the four kings, Tyre was allied to the anti-Babylonian league, and besieged by Nebuchadnezzar for 13 years, generally dated to between 586 and 573 BC. There is debate on when exactly it began, and some historians believe it began in 598 BC, while others believe it was even earlier in 603 BC, however, all sources agree it lasted 13 years.

At the time, there were two cities of Tyre, the emporium on the island in the harbor, and the larger town on the mainland. King Ithobaal III and his court withdrew from the mainland to the island, which the Babylonians could not capture, and survived through long-distance trade with their colonies, as well as the Egyptians, Carians, Lydians, and Greeks.

The majority of the indicators in this apocalypse suggest it was authored after 602 BC, when Nabu-shum-lishir was involved in some kind of plot against Nebuchadnezzar, but before 592 BC, when Psamtik II destroyed the Kushite army. This supports either earlier date for the beginning of the siege of Tyre, either 602 or 598 BC. The middle option of 598 to 585 BC seems the most probable if this Apocalypse was about a planned war, as Tyre would have rebelled before the

Kushite army was destroyed, and surrendered in the aftermath of Jerusalem being destroyed.

48 This section of text is missing from manuscripts BnF 326, BL 28,875, Sachau 131, and UTS 23.

49 Mingana 11: qrqrt lmryqa (ܡܪܝܩܐ ܠܩܪܩܪܬ). Translation: ascended the bitterness

50 Other than its concluding statements, this appears to be the end of the original Apocalypse, which was about the end of the Ishmaelites. What follows is mostly a restatement of Daniel chapters 7 to 10, but without context. The events have already happened in the Apocalypse, the good man who led the nation from the south is the lioness's cub, who already conquered Mesopotamia.

The rest is drawn from later literature and paraphrases Christian era works, such as the Gospel of Luke and Apocalypse of John. The earlier section of text was occasionally similar to Christian era works, however, the Christian era works were paraphrasing older books, mostly Daniel and Ezekiel.

The latter section introduces a false messiah, who is defeated in battle before the imminent end of the world. This parallels many medieval Christian works about the Last Roman Emperor, the emperor who would be on the throne when God returned to rule the world. Most of these theories about the Last Roman Emperor originated in the 400s AD when the world was approaching the year 6000 according to the chronology of the Septuagint. It was believed by many that the year 6000 would complete God's day of rest, and when he awoke he would restore order in the world, making Constantinople the capital of his government on Earth. The Latin Christians substituted Rome, and the Aramaic Christians substituted Jerusalem.

When it did not happen, the Byzantine Church switched to using the older Greek calendar based on Alexander's conquest, and the church in Rome used astrology to determine the end of the world would happen in the year 2000 AD, from which they calculated Jesus was actually born in 1 AD, instead of when Herod was alive. When Muhammad arose in Arabia, he became a false messiah or anti-Christ to the Christians, and the foe the Last Roman Emperor needed to defeat to bring God back to the world. This appears to be the mindset of the Byzantine redactor, suggesting the final Greek version of the Apocalypse developed in sometime after the 8th century.

The reference to the armies of Gog and Magog descending from the north and combining with the Ishmaelites before approaching Jerusalem indicates that Jerusalem was not under Islamic control at the time, suggesting that the crusader state of Jerusalem was being referenced. The concept of Gog and Magog was fluid in early Christianity, referring to the Germanic tribes when they overran the western half of the Roman Empire in the 5th century. In the

6th century, the term was applied to the Göktürks who conquered Central Asia.

In the era of the Crusades, it was applied to the Mongols, who advanced quickly across Eurasia in the 13th century. The Latin Kingdom of Jerusalem existed in some form until 1291 AD, suggesting the Apocalypse dates to before that. The reference to the Ishmaelites and Gog and Mogog combining would date the final Greek redaction to sometime after 1221 when the Mongols conquered the Khwarazmian Empire, an Islamic Turko-Persian empire in Iran and Central Asia. Prior to that, the idea that the Mongols could reach Jerusalem was not a consideration.

The Apocalypse indicates that the city of Jerusalem was occupied by Christians at the time, which would place the anti-Islamic redaction to sometime between 1229 and 1244. The Latin crusaders had been driven out of Jerusalem in 1187, however, the kingdom of Jerusalem continued to exist, first from its capital in Tyre, and later Acre, however, in 1229 Jerusalem was recaptured, and held until 1244. As the Principality of Antioch was another crusader state to the north, and the name 'Antioch' appears to have been added earlier in the Apocalypse, the redactor may have meant it as a piece of propaganda intended to garner support from Byzantine Christians, who had not generally participated in the crusades and had better relations with the Muslims than the Latin Christians.

50 Mingana 11: mšiḥå (ܡܫܝܚܐ). Translation: Christ (or Messiah)

- BnF Arabe 150: ālmsyḥ (المسيح). Translation: the Messiah (or the anointed)

51 Mingana 11: lHnwk ulÅlyå (ܠܚܢܘܟ ܘܠܐܠܝܐ). Translation: the Enoch and the Elijah

- BnF Arabe 150: lAlyas ... wāHnwh (النّاس ... واحنوح). Translation: the Elijah ... and the Enoch

Arabic Apocalypse of Daniel

[In the name of the Father, the Son, and the Holy Spirit,[1] the one God, who is glorious, Amen!

With the aid of God, the exalted, and his beautiful guidance, we will commence the explanation of the story of the Prophet Daniel, which he told to Ezra, his pupil, in reference to that which was to happen in the history of the children of Ishmael, the son of Hagar, the Egyptian. With the peace of God!

Amen! Amen! Amen!]

Daniel,[2] the prophet, said to Ezra,[3] his student, "Listen to my story, my son, and marvel at the works of God, the faithful one, and at his justice, and at [...damaged text...] of his utterance, and the stability of his word with all living and existing beings."

"Know that I saw a messenger, dressed in white clothing, his face shining bright like lightning, his hands and forearms and his arms like copper, his eyes like the rays of the sun. He came from the sky praising and glorifying, and in his right hand[4] there was a scroll full of writing. Then he said to me ' God has already heard your prayers and has sent me to you to tell you what will happen at the end of time. This scroll is for you, therefore open it and read what is in it.'

"I took the scroll from his hand with fear and trembling, and I opened it and read it. In it were terrible plagues and evils which were to come, terrible in [...damaged text...] Then I praised God, who uplifts whom he wishes, and brings down whom he wishes. To him belongs the kingdom and the power."

"Then I said, 'Oh Lord! Preserve and keep your people from the bloody serpent, whose mouth is full of poison. There is no escape from it but in you. You are God, the strong, the mighty one. I looked into the scroll, and saw there was a serpent upon whose head were twelve horns and upon whose tail nine bones, which protruded, and I saw that it would make war upon all mankind, and nations. Its leader was cruel to all flesh, and it was fearful, spewing poison like water and spitting upon whoever was near it. Then I saw a messenger come down from the sky and kill it and break its horns."

"The Judeans[5] will celebrate and they will say he is the Messiah[6] for whom they have waited, and he will collect them, and most men will follow him, except some hard-hearted ones who will remain in contention. Then Elijah will return, and Enoch,[7] and the two will drive him to the utmost limits, but he will fight fiercely, and he will shed their blood with his hands. Then the Lord[8] will come down from the sky with his messengers who surround him and destroy the wicked one."

"Those in the grave will hear the mighty horn. Then they will stand up, and fall down before God, and they will see the holy sign which they had denied. Then they will be astonished at it, and the good will rejoice and the damned ones will be sad. The good will come into the presence of their God in the clouds, to the kingdom, and the wicked will go into trouble and frightful punishment."

"When I, Daniel, had seen this vision, I wrote it down and left it for those that come after me. Praise be to God, the everlasting, the eternal, the perpetual one. Amen! Amen! Amen!"

Arabic Apocalypse of Daniel Notes

1 BnF Arabe 150: bāsm ālīb wālābn wālrwḥ ālqds (باسم الأب
والابن والروح القدس). Translation: the name of the father the son
and the holy spirit

The phrase form of Arabic indicates a Palestinian Christian
origin.

2 BnF Arabe 150: Dānyāl (دانيال). Translation: Daniel

- Mingana 11: Ôzrå (ܥܙܪܐ). Translation: Ezra

3 BnF Arabe 150: Ôzrh (عزره). Translation: Ezrh

- Mingana 11: Qrpws (ܩܪܦܘܣ). Generally anglicized as Carpos

The spelling of the name in the Arabic Apocalpyse of Daniel
is not the standard Arabic spelling of Ezra, which is Ôzrā
(عزرا), nor based on the Greek Esdras ('Εσδρας) or Hebrew
Ezra (עֶזְרָא). The Arabic name is a transliteration of the
Hebrew and Aramaic word ôzrh (עזרה), meaning helper. This
itself indicates that the Arabic Apocalypse was translated from
either Aramaic or Hebrew. It is not the same as the Syriac
translation, which is based on a Greek translation, and no
Canaanite (Judahote or Samaritan) or Hebrew translations are
known to exist, so the source text is presumably lost. As the
form of Arabic appears to be Palestinian, it was probably
translated from an Aramaic source. The word ôzrh (עזרה) is
sometimes theorized to be the origin of the name Ezra (עֶזְרָא),
and virtually identical to the name Azariah (עֲזַרְיָה), the name
of one of the three youths who associated with Daniel in the

Book of Daniel. The three youths were thrown into a furnace by Nebuchadnezzar in the year that Zedekiah rebelled, suggesting they were considered part of a Judahite conspiracy.

The phonetic spelling of Azariah in Neo-Babylonian cuneiform would have been Eziraia (𒐚𒂍𒌷𒅎), however, this would include the name of the god Ia (𒅎), the name of the Mesopotamian 'terrible god' of floods, whose name was not generally mentioned. All three youths were given alternative names in the Book of Daniel, none of which appear to be Babylonian. Azariah's alternate name was Aved Nego (עֲבֵד נְגוֹ) in Masoretic Daniel, which is a transliteration of the Aramaic Ôbd Ngh (𐡕𐡏𐡁 𐡍𐡂𐡄), meaning 'servant of (the planet) Venus.' The logical substitute for Ia (𒅎) would have been Ilu (𒀭), meaning 'god,' rendering the Neo-Babylonian spelling as Ezirailu (𒐚𒂍𒌷𒀭).

If the original Greek translation was made directly from the cuneiform version, the name could have been read logographically as 'grain strike god,' and as Carpos was the Greek god of harvesting grain, whose name was derived from the word for 'cutting,' Carpos would have been the obvious translation. This indicates the original Ezra in the apocalypse was probably the youth Azariah, whose name was simplified to 'helper' in an Aramaic translation, which the Arabic is based on. The simplification of the name in Aramaic is likely because the scribe recognized it could not have originally been Azrael (עֲזַרְאֵל) or Ôzryål (עֻזְרִיאֵל), the name of the Classical Judahite psychopomp.

369

4 The Arabic Apocalypse of Daniel does refer to the hand as the 'right hand,' however, most copies of the Syriac Apocalypse of Ezra do not specify the hand. Syriac manuscripts BnF 326 and BL 28,875 specify it was his right hand. It is unclear if this was added by a scribe influenced by Islamic thought, or removed as a rejection of perceived Islamic influence.

5 BnF Arabe 150: Yhwd (يهود). Translation: Jews (or Judeans)

The typical Arabic name for Jews is Yhwdy (يَهُودِي). This form is derived from the Aramaic name Yhwd (יהוד) which supports the Arabic Apocalypse being translated from an Aramaic source.

6 BnF Arabe 150: ālmsyḥ (المسيح). Translation: the messiah (or the annointed)

• Mingana 11: mšiḥå (ܡܫܝܚܐ). Translation: Christ (or Messiah, annointed)

7 BnF Arabe 150: lAlyas ... wāHnwh (واحنوح ... النّاس). Translation: the Elijah ... and the Enoch

• Mingana 11: lHnwk ulÅlyå (ܘܐܠܝܐ ܠܚܢܘܟ). Translation: the Enoch and the Elijah

The Arabic spelling of Elijah is the Arabic version of the name based on the Greek Elias (Ἠλίας), not the Hebrew Eliyyahu (אֵלִיָּהוּ), which is rendered as Iylya (إِيلِيَا) in Arabic.

This supports the Arabic translation as having been made by a Christian. The spelling of Enoch is specifically not Islamic, where a prophet that may be the same prophet is named Idrys (إذريس). Ḥnwḥ (احنوح) is the Christian and Jewish Arabic spelling of the Classical Hebrew name Ḥnwk (חנוך) and Syriac Ḥnwk (ܚܢܘܟ). The ancient Greek form of the name was Anôchos (Ἀνωχος), suggesting the addition of Enoch and Elijah happened in an Aramaic or Syriac version of the Apocalypse, and was later imported to the Greek. The phrasing between the Arabic and Syriac apocalypses is quite different, indicating that while the concept was imported to the Greek translation (which the Syriac is based on), it was not a direct translation.

8 BnF Arabe 150: ar-rabb (الرّب). Translation: the lord (or the master, the governor, the authority)

Reconstructed Apocalypse of Azariah

Daniel[27] said to his student Azariah:[28]

Listen, my son Azariah, and I will tell you about the end times. It happened suddenly, in the manner of a dreadful vision. I asked God to explain the end times of the Qedarites.[29] Then I saw a young man, one like I'd never seen, wearing white clothing, his face shining bright like lightning, his hands and forearms and his arms like copper, his eyes like the rays of the sun, and he had the figure of a scroll in his right hand.[30] He said to me, "Know that your prayer has been heard before God, and I have been sent to explain to you the end times of the children of Ishmael, that which has been concealed from many. Open this scroll and read in it and see what is about to happen in the end times."

I opened the scroll and I read about the times and the terrors that are going to come. My tears flowed with groans and I said, "Have mercy on me, God, and have mercy on your creation," as a serpent of Mesopotamia had devoured them. I saw twelve horns on the serpent's head, and nine small and cruel bones protruding from its

---

27 See note 1 on page 321 and note 2 on page 383.

28 See note 3 on page 322 and note 3 on page 383.

29 See note 5 on page 324.

30 See note 6 on page 330 and note 4 on page 385.

tail. It came up from Mesopotamia,[A1] contending against all creation and oppressing the people of God. Then I saw a messenger, clothed in a flame who descended from the sky and tore the twelve great horns from the serpent's head.

Then I saw one great bone suddenly grow up on the tail of the serpent, and there were two small horns on its head. An eagle[31] came from Tayma[32] and broke the great bone and devoured the small ones. The world was filled with darkness and a whirlwind, and the whirlwind struck the eagle and tore out its two talons. Then there was a voice from the sky that said, "The eagle will be repaid according to its reward."

Then I saw a traitor that came from Mesopotamia. It poured poison on all flesh, and insulted to the limits the ancestors.[33] There was a great earthquake and rumblings and thunders in the sky, and a voice was heard saying, "Let those four kings who were united on the great river Euphrates,[34] those who are prepared to destroy one out of three people, be released." They were released, and there was a great uproar.

---

31 See note 16 on page 332.

32 See note 17 on page 333.

33 See note 18 on page 334.

34 See note 20 on page 335.

Out of the darkness came Qedarites[A2] from the east, piercing the traitor.[35] The traitor escaped to the borders of Egypt,[36] and there his mind became sad. He took the two heirs[37] and traveled to the south.[A3] The younger heir went to King Zedekiah[38] and took refuge with him. King Zedekiah received him joyfully, and the younger heir persuaded King Zedekiah to save him from the Qedarites who were seeking to destroy him. King Zedekiah sent an ambassador to the Asherahs[39] of Tayma[40] so that they would come to his aid, because Cyaxares[41] was troubling the land of the west with many evils. Since he was the ruler of the Qedarites, he gnashed his teeth against King Zedekiah. There were three horns on his head.[42] He makes war with the right one, with

---

35 See note 22 on page 338.

36 See note 23 on page 338.

37 See note 24 on page 339.

38 See note 26 on page 340.

39 See note 28 on page 342.

40 See note 29 on page 342.

41 See note 30 on page 343.

42 See note 31 on page 344.

the left one he destroys, and with the one in the middle he ravages.

He will begin to ravage the children of his house, and he will gather gold and a great deal of silver, and he will begin to afflict all who are under his power. He will become arrogant and he will not praise God.[43] Nebuchadnezzar will go and make war against King Zedekiah and will ravage the rebellious fortress. They will contend against each other and ravage each other, and much blood will be shed between the two mighty men. Then Cyaxares will devise an evil plot against the seven hills and the city of the temple,[44] and he will fight against it, and a great deal of blood will be shed around the city.

Then the traitor's heir will take an army from Egypt[45] and his mercenaries,[46] and he will enter in blood. The father of the younger heir will hear, and he will gather a great nation from the Kushites[47] and from the Nubians, and he will come to the aid of the heir and will ravage Egypt. Then the heir will go down to

---

43 See note 32 on page 345.

44 See note 33 on page 346.

45 See note 35 on page 349.

46 See note 36 on page 350.

47 See note 37 on page 350.

Mesopotamia[48] and he will ravage the great cities. He will leave them devoid of their inhabitants because great iniquity was being perpetrated in them. He will throw the slain to the ground in heaps, and he will ravage Damascus[49] at that time.

Then King Zedekiah will become inflamed with fierce anger, and he will go out after those Qedarites and ravage them and drive them out and destroy them from Syria[50] as far as the borders of the east, the land that belongs to the Qedarites. The Parthians[51] will come out from the north,[52] a nation numerous like the locusts that fly.[53] They will go up to the Euphrates River and they will rise up in aid of King Zedekiah, and from there the two of them will go down to the land of Persia. Cyaxares will go out to meet them with a great army, but King Zedekiah will go between Cyaxares' horns and break

---

48 See note 38 on page 354.

49 See note 39 on page 355.

50 See note 40 on page 355.

51 See note 41 on page 356.

52 See note 42 on page 357.

53 See note 43 on page 357.

both of them.[54] He will ravage and plunder the land and burn it with fire.

The Qedarites will flee from his presence and go down to their land. King Zedekiah[55] will pursue them and will destroy them with the edge of the sword because God has turned his face from them on account of their great uncleanness. He will capture and plunder their land, and destroy it down to the foundations. It will never be inhabited again because they despised the Lord and made light of his commandments. There will be great commotion in the land, earthquakes, famines, and plagues, and fear and trembling will rule over the people until they fall dead, without diseases or illnesses, from the fear that rules over them.

King Zedekiah[56] will go up with a great army to Mesopotamia and will subject it to tribute, and there will be great tribulation in the land, the likes of which have never occurred. He will rebuild the fortifications of Phoenicia as an ally.[57] He will destroy Damascus (which led the greatest derision), down to its foundations because

---

54 See note 44 on page 358.

55 See note 45 on page 358.

56 See note 46 on page 359.

57 See note 47 on page 359.

of its great bitterness[58] against Jerusalem. From there he will return and go up to his regal city.

Two tribes from the seed of Ishmael and those who have become sooty at the base of the mountain of the south will come and take refuge with them. They will drink and go up until they reach Jerusalem, the city of the great king.[A4]

When I, Daniel, had seen this vision, I had great fear, fell down to worship, and gave thanks to God, who had deemed me worthy of this vision. And I said, "Blessed are you, God my savior, and your holy name be glorified forever and ever, Amen."

This is the End. But preserve these words until their time. Praise be to God, the everlasting, the eternal, the perpetual one.

---

58 See note 49 on page 361.

Reconstructed Apocalypse of Azariah Notes

A1 Mingana 11: maḏbrā (ܡܕܒܪܐ). Translation: desert (or wilderness)

- Manuscripts BnF 326 and BL 28,875: madnkhā (ܡܕܢܚܐ). Translation: east

This appears to be the same place as the Syriac phrase lårôå bmwldnå (ܠܐܪܥ ܕܡܘܠܕܢܐ) used later in the apocalypse, which translates as 'the land (or country) of the forefathers (or procreators)' This term is generally interpreted as the 'promised land', however, the chick (Nabu-shum-lishir) was not from Canaan, but Mesopotamia. The phrase probably originated in a Judahite using the Neo-Babylonian term qudmu (𒄑𒁇𒁉), as a translation of the Judahite qdm (𐤒𐤃𐤌), meaning 'easterners' or 'ancients.' The term was used in this context to refer to Mesopotamians as bənê-qedem (בְּנֵי־קֶדֶם) in Masoretic Judges. However, the Aramaic term qdm (𐡒𐡃𐡌) and Neo-Babylonian qudmu (𒄑𒁇𒁉) do not mean Easteners, but 'came before,' resulting in the Greek and Aramaic translations rendering 'land of the forefathers.'

A2 Mingana 11: qrqså (ܩܪܩܣܐ). Translation: ravens (or vultures, crows, magpies)

The word can be translated as several kinds of predatory birds, but is generally accepted as 'ravens' based on the Greek word corax (κόραξ). The Syriac word can be either the singular or plural form, however, the context the word it used later in the apocalypse confirms it is intended to be the plural form. The Greek word corax can also be read as 'hook' or as the name of an engine that was used to grapple ships, however, based on the animal iconography in the rest of the Apocalypse, the translation of 'ravens,' was likely correct.

The Ravens in the apocalypse were probably meant to represent the Qedarites, as they attacked the Viper/Traitor from the east when he was in the land of the forefathers, and the Qedarites controlled the Syrian desert at the time. Kedar (קֵדָר) also translates as 'dark' or 'dusky,' and the Qedarites were reported to live in black tents so they could be recognized from a distance, meaning the symbolism would have been obvious at the time.

It is worth noting that qrqså (ܩܪܩܣܐ) is the synonym of nšrå (ܢܫܪܐ), used earlier, and generally translated as 'Eagle.' The Eagle was the one who started the chaos that led to the Viper/Traitor leaving the land that is presumably Babylonia. As the Ravens and the Eagle were both working for the Asherahs of Tayma, it suggests the priestesses of Tayma set the Eagle to kill Nabopolassar and some of his supporters as part of a conspiracy to replace him as king.

The Viper, which can also be interpreted as 'Traitor' via the Greek text the Syriac was translated from, fled to Canaan with his two chicks, presumably his children. After being attacked in Canaan by Ravens, who also turn out to be working for the priestesses of Tayma, the Viper/Traitor fled to Egypt, but was turned back at the border, and headed to Tayma. The two chicks each travelled to a different country, the Elder to Thrace, which appear to have originally been

Egypt in the text, and the Younger to live with the Lion's cub, which is a reference to King Zedekiah of Judah found in Ezekiel chapter 19.

Ultimately, a war is predicted, where Thace (Egypt) attacks the Great City of Constantine (Jerualem), and the traitor (Viper) raises an army from Kush that ravages Egypt. The last part did not happen, as the Egyptians found out about the army the Kushites were assembling and destroyed it, and all of Kush north of the fifth cataract in 592 BC.

The Traitor was probably Neuchadnezzar II's younger brother Nabu-shum-lishir, who is believed to have been involved in a plot to overthrough Nebuchadnezzar in 602 BC. Very little is recorded of the event, and it seems that even the Babylonian government didn't understand what was happening, mirroring the confusion in text. If the Apocalypse is to be believed, the point of the conspiracy was not to kill Nebuchadnezzar, but to cause so much confusion that the bond between the four kingdoms broke, and they stated a war against each other. This would have allowed the smaller southern states time to rebuild before a new empire emerged in the north.

A3 Mingana 11: ymynå (ܝܡܝܢܐ). Translation: right (or pledge, ordination)

The term ymynå had cognates throughout Semitic languages, as well as Egyptian, all meaning 'right.' However, it also meant 'south' in the era the original apocalypse was likely written, and makes more sense in the context of the traitor's (viper's) movements. Later in the text the traitor's younger chick sends a letter to the Asherahs (or leopard) of tymnå (ܬܝܡܢܐ), which also translates as 'right,' or 'south,' or in this case 'Tayma.' In this sentence, the word could be read as 'right' or 'south,' but not Tayma, suggesting it was somewhere else. As the traitor later organized the failed Kushite invasion of Egypt, it suggests he sailed south to Dômt, a major South Semitic kingdom located in the territory of northern modern Eritrea and Ethiopia, which had a direct trade route to Kush via the Black Nile (Atbarah-Tekezé River).

A4 This reference to the two tribes of Ishmaelites joining 'with them' is from the Syriac Apocalypse, where they had joined with Gog and Magog to attack Jerusalem, however, appears to be extracted from the older Apocalypse, as there is no great king for them to take refuge with in the Syriac Apocalypse. As both Tayma and Dedan were viewed by the Israelites in the time of Zedekiah as religious sites, as was the Mountain of the Altar (Mount Sinai), this appears to be a list of tribes that the Judaites would not destroy.

The two surviving tribes of Ishmaelites would be a mirror of the two surviving tribes of Israelites, the Judahites and Levites, while the Edomites were descended from Esau, and the Israelites were prohibited from attacking them.

Manuscripts

The following is a list of the manuscripts referenced in the notes for this book.

<u>JUDAHITE APOCALYPSES OF EZRA</u>

Codex Ambianensis is dated to the 9th century AD. It is currently located at the Bibliothèque Communale of Amiens (Number 10).

Codex Sangermanensis (Latin 11505, f. 11v) is dated to 822. It is currently located at the Bibliothèque nationale de France in Paris.

Old Testament Ms. Add. 1570 is dated to 1597. It is currently located at Cambridge University (Add. 1570) in Cambridge, and available online from the University Library (https://cudl.lib.-cam.ac.uk/collections/ethiopianmanuscripts/1).

Manuscript B.21 Inf. (fols. 267a-276b) is dated to the 6th or 7th century. It is currently located at the Biblioteca Ambrosiana in Milan.

<u>LATIN APOCALYPSES OF EZRA</u>

Codex Sangermanensis (Latin 11505, f. 11v) is dated to 822. It is currently located at the Bibliothèque nationale de France in Paris.

<u>GREEK APOCALYPSE OF EZRA</u>

BnF Gr. 929 is dated to the 15th century. It is currently located at the Bibliothèque nationale de France in Paris.

<u>VISION OF EZRA:</u>

AI/6 (Hs 1) is dated to the 11th century. It is currently located at the Bibliothek des Priestseminars in Linz.

MANUSCRIPTS

SYRIAC APOCALYPSE OF EZRA:

BL 28,875 (Ms. Wright 922) is dated to 1709. It is currently located at the British Library (Add. 25,875) in London.

BnF 326 is dated to the 19th century. It is currently located at the Bibliothèque nationale de France (Ms. 326) in Paris.

Mingana 11 is dated to 1702. It is currently located at the University of Birmingham (Mingana Syriac 11) in Birmingham, and available online from the Institute of Textual Scholarship and Electronic Editing (ITSEE).

Sachau 131 is dated to 1862. It is currently located at the Staatsbibliothek (Ms. 73) in Berlin.

UTS 23 (Ms. Clemons 307) is dated to 1884. It is currently located at the Union Theological Seminary (Syriac 23) in New York.

ARABIC APOCALYPSE OF DANIEL:

BnF Arabe 150 is dated to 1606. It is currently located at the Bibliothèque nationale de France (Ms. Arabe 150) in Paris.

Also Available

ALSO AVAILABLE

- Octateuch: The Original Orit

ENOCH AND METATRON SERIES:

- Books of Enoch Collection

- Books of Enoch and Metatron Collection

- Books of Metatron Collection

- Secrets of Enoch

OTHER TRANSLATIONS:

- Apocalypses of Ezra

- Arabic Maccabees

- Hebrew Maccabees

- Life of Adam and Eve

- Memories of the New Kingdom

- Septuagint's Esther and the Vetus Latina Esther

- Septuagint's Ezekiel and the Ba'al Cycle

- Septuagint's Job and the Testament of Job

- Septuagint's Proverbs and the Wisdom of Amenemope

- The Amarna Letters

- Testaments of the Patriarchs Collection

- Tobit and Ahikar

- Ugaritic Texts: Ba'al Cycle

- Wisdom of Ahikar